W9-CJY-413

THE CREATIVE PERSONALITY AND THE CREATIVE PROCESS

A Phenomenological Perspective

Linda Melrose, Ph.D.

AL HARRIS LIBRARY
SOUTHWESTERN OKLA. STATE UNIV.
WEATHERFORD, OK. 73096

UNIVERSITY
PRESS OF
AMERICA

Lanham • New York • London

Copyright © 1989 by

Linda Melrose

University Press of America,® Inc.

4720 Boston Way
Lanham, MD 20706

3 Henrietta Street
London WC2E 8LU England

All rights reserved

Printed in the United States of America

British Cataloging in Publication Information Available

Library of Congress Cataloging-in-Publication Data

Melrose, Linda.
The creative personality and the creative process: a
phenomenological perspective / Linda Melrose.
p. cm.
Bibliography: p.
1. Creative ability. 2. Personality. 3. Creative ability—Case
studies. Personality—Case studies. 5. Phenomenological
psychology. I. Title.
BF408.M376   1988
153.3'5—dc 19   88–27791 CIP
ISBN 0–8191–7227–8 (alk. paper)

All University Press of America books are produced on acid-free paper.
The paper used in this publication meets the minimum requirements of
American National Standard for Information Sciences—Permanence of Paper
for Printed Library Materials, ANSI Z39.48–1984.

Dedication

This book is dedicated with love to my husband, Clark Melrose, and my parents, Margarette and Glenn Williams.

265016

265016

Acknowledgments

I acknowledge and thank my family of friends who supported, loved, and administered aid to me for the duration of this project, especially Shirley Fetter, Dr. Warren Bonney, Dr. Judith Goetz, Dr. Elizabeth Strickler-Kirkpatrick, Dr. Jeri Carter, Dr. Eugene C. Schaffer, Dr. Jerold Bozarth, Dr. Elizabeth Sheerer, Dr. Catherine Bruch, and Betty Sowell.

Special thanks goes to those creative and generous friends who participated as respondents in the pilot study for this research. Thank you Joel Arkin, Jennifer Kincaid Caldwell, Dr. R. Scott Cole, Mary Jo O'Niel, Alan Robbins, John Rosemond, Beth Heywood, and Lori Thomas.

To Tom Robbins, Dr. E. Paul Torrance, Arthur M. Young, George Leonard, Patricia Sun, Wendy Palmer, Frank Hogan, Niels Diffrient, Norma McLain Stoop, Rowena Reed, and the late Dr. Carl Rogers, I offer my gratitude and respect.

Table of Contents

CHAPTER 1

INTRODUCTION

At once it struck me what quality went to form a man of achievement, especially in literature, and which Shakespeare possessed so enormously--I mean <u>negative capability</u>. That is when a man is capable of being in uncertainties, mysteries, doubts, without any irritable reaching after facts and reason.

John Keats

The ability to refresh, to revitalize, or to bring into existence something new is an aptitude that inspires awe. Our myths, folklore, and history books are comprised of accounts of the lives and works of individuals possessing the capacity to create. They are the artists, scientists, builders, and visionaries who, because of openness, courage, and their power to form mental images of something not already there, influenced the course of society.

Most of us have at sometime used the term creativity as an attribute describing someone we know or admire. The word itself is provocative, presuming almost magical connotations. Other spirited words, such as imagination, originality, flexibility, divergence, and artistry, are sometimes used jointly or synonymously with creativity.

Webster (1983) defines creation as:

1: the act of creating; esp: the act of bringing the world into ordered existence 2: the act of making, inventing, or producing: as a: the act of investing with new rank or office b: creatures singly or in aggregate c: an orginal work of art d: a new, unusual, striking article of clothing.

"The act of bringing the world into ordered existence" describes both divine creation and human creation. The First Book of Moses, Called Genesis, describes the creation of heaven and earth:

> In the beginning God created the heaven and the earth.
> 2 And the earth was without form, and void; and darkness was upon the face of the deep. And the Spirit of God moved upon the face of the waters.
> 3 And God said, Let there be light: and there was light.
> 4 And God saw the light, that it was good: and God divided the light from the darkness.

In ancient Hebrew, there are three components to the genesis of earth: Bara, Aassa, and Yetser, meaning creation, structure, and form. Psychologically, all three are necessary if manifestation is to occur. These concepts refer to the divine inspiration of creation, creation in the realm of thought, idea, or theory, and the creative product. They are correlated to spirit, mind, and body and function cyclically and wholistically. Creativity carries with it a relationship with God.

Rollo May (1980) discusses the courage needed by the creative individual, seeing courage as essential because during this process one is engaged in an active battle with the gods. He demonstrates this thesis as it is presented in the myths of Prometheus and of Adam and Eve.

The ancient Greeks believed their civilization began when Prometheus, with concern for humankind, stole fire from the gods and gave it to mortals. Zeus was enraged and punished Prometheus by binding him to Mount Caucasus. During the days Prometheus's liver was eaten away by a vulture, only to rejuvenate each night so the vulture could return again and again and devour it.   Prometheus could be liberated   only if a god would   sacrifice his immortality.   This   offering   was made   by the   god Chiron, a then   divine creature who was half horse and half man, renowned for his healing abilities.   The gift of fire for which Prometheus suffered symbolizes the spark that occurs when knowledge unites with divine inspiration, resulting in the igniting of the creative spirit.

In the myth of Adam and Eve, the first couple lives in bliss in the Garden of Eden until they eat from the tree of the knowledge of good and evil.   With this act, the bliss of innocence is no longer possible, and Adam and Eve fall from the grace of animal consciousness, or   unconsciousness, and are awakened.   Yahweh is angry, and Adam and Eve are driven from the garden and are punished.

In both myths, human beings are given something previously belonging only to the gods; in the Greek myth it is fire; in the Jewish myth, knowledge of the paradox of good and evil.   Prometheus brings light, in the form of fire to mortals. The serpent, Lucifer, tempts Eve to eat from the tree.   The name Lucifer means "the bearer of light." In both myths, God is angry. May (1980) associates the knowledge and the fire with creativity, which before the dawn or light of consciousness belonged only to immortals.   May also views each myth as ultimately dealing with death.   "The battle with the gods thus hinges on our own mortality!   Creativity is a yearning for immortality" (p. 27).

Elsewhere (1969) May discusses creativity as divine and as mundane.   Eros, as myth has it, is of both heaven and earth; he is daimonic.   The daimonic is any natural force with the power to take over a person completely.   It is potentially creative and destructive.   The daimonic continually presents us with dilemmas, allowing us the opportunity to   deepen   and widen   our   consciousness.   This   daimonic power   and   the battle with the gods is   expressed in the   close relationship

3

between creative genius and psychosis, in the burden of guilt that accompanies creative output, and in the high suicide rate among artists, poets, and visionaries (May, 1980).

Creativity is an attribute desired and feared by individuals and society alike. Both feelings may stem from the connection creativity has to the divine. Whatever the reason for this ambivalence, the potential to create that is native to most people is usually diminished by a society that pressures its children and adults to conform and adjust. The unfortunate paradox we are facing is we are destroying our creative potential at a time when creativity is essential if our planet is to survive and our species flourish.

Purpose of the Study

The present need is to investigate the nature of creative people. Other investigators have sought to understand the creative process. Several of these are discussed in Chapter 2. The results of previous research have provided concrete ways of observing creativity, of defining creativity functionally, and of guiding creative development; however, they are incomplete. Current theories often are based upon thoughts about creative people rather than on thoughts by them. Of particular interest in this study were the ways in which creative individuals remember and describe their creative processes and the development and nurturance of their creative potential.

The purpose of this study was to generate theory about the essence of creative thinking and the character of the creator. The primary areas investigated were:

1. Life occurrences affecting creativity

2. Attitudes about creativity

3. Affective style of creative individuals: judgements, feelings, beliefs, and values

4

5.   Subjective experiences of the creative process

6.   The roles of inspiration and intuition in the creative process

7.   Self-perceptions and identity

8. Interactions between creativity and God, sex, money, and relationships

9.   Similarities and uniqueness in creative individuals

Brief Description of the Study

The focus of this book is the creative process as it is experienced by individuals who are described by their peers as exhibiting exceptional creativity.   In addition to being outstanding in their professional field or fields, these people are people for whom creativity is a way of life   and an essential component to self-expression.   Face-to-face interviewing was the data collection method.   Because of the exploratory nature of this investigation, an a priori design was too limiting.   A phenomenological case study design was chosen because it fosters the generation of theory, allowing for openness and sensitivity on the part of the researcher in previously untried areas of investigation.

Assumptions

This qualitative study of creativity is based on the following assumptions:

1.   Individuals can articulate   their   creative experiences, perceptions, and processes.

2.   Creative thinking can be nurtured in oneself and others.

3.   Creativity can be identified and investigated.

4.   People who have exhibited excellence in their occupational fields are more likely to manifest high levels of creative thinking than those who have not.

Research Questions

The research questions evolved primarily from my own interest in creativity and creative individuals, coupled with the discoveries and theories about creative thinking with which I am familiar.   My own ability to think creatively and my need to do so, have pushed this area of human potential into the forefront of my thinking.   I see my personal involvement as both the major strength and major weakness of this research.   A more complete account of the process of developing the research questions can be found in Chapter 3.   The major questions addressed were:

1.   What is the creative person's concept of creativity?

2.   What   personality   characteristics   enable   creative people to persist with their creative endeavors?

3. In what ways have creative people been influenced by relationships?

4.   What do creative people report as aids and obstacles to their endeavors?

5.   How do these people experience the onset of the creative moment? Through an act of will?   Through external stimulation?   Through spontaneous impulse?

6.   How do creative people characterize themselves as human beings?   How do they see themselves as similar to and different from other highly creative people and people in general?   Do these people see themselves as risk takers, rebels, and nonconformists?

Limitations

Creativity is a term describing a human attribute that is difficult to define. There currently exists no generally accepted measure of creativity. The limited amount of time I had with the respondents prohibited the use of any existing measuring instrument, therefore I carried the burden of selecting the individuals who were interviewed.

The respondents were chosen because of their face validity as creative, i.e., the people selected fit into the categories of being well known in their fields, having made meaningful and important contributions to society, generally being thought of by those familiar with them personally or professionally as highly creative, and as capable of supporting themselves financially via their creative work. Supporting themselves by their creative work was included as a selection requirement because it offers proof that the culture values their productions enough to pay well for them, and that the respondents value their creativity enough to make it the primary thrust of their work lives. Not everyone will perceive of every respondent as highly creative, and some will be perceived of as being more creative than others. The respondent selection procedure limited the generalizability of the findings.

As with any research, the object of study was affected by the act of observation (Zukav, 1979). My personal involvement and enthusiasm may have biased the research questions. It is possible I unconsciously reinforced the coresearchers during the interviews, influencing their responses. As stated earlier, I judge my intense involvement in the subject matter and the interview process as this research's greatest strength and greatest limitation. The limitations inherent to the research method are discussed in more detail in Chapter 3.

Significance of the Study

Creativity is a valued aspect of human behavior. Some people believe it is the most noteworthy attribute distinguishing human beings from other animals. The primary significance of this book is the illumination of the creative process and the creative individual. The secondary significance is the identification of the events that facilitate the growth of creative potential, so it can be nurtured.

The resulting information can be applied to numerous areas, including education and psychotherapy. An understanding of how creative potential is nurtured allows for active encouragement of this process. Schools, universities, private organizations, and individuals can manage their resources so that originality, flexibility, and artistry are enhanced. Psychotherapists can apply the insights about creativity to help clients release energy blocks and artistic blocks, allowing for a wider range of emotional expression and life experiences.

The ultimate application of the resulting knowledge is the empowerment of individual human beings. The information gained can be employed to invoke additional freedom. The ability to think creatively provides psychological space for additional freedom of thought, feeling, action, and choice.

CHAPTER 2

REVIEW OF THE LITERATURE

Throughout the centuries philosophers, scientists, educators, and psychologists have made attempts to understand more clearly the creative personality and the creative process. They asked the question, "What is creativity?" The word creativity is used often, yet it remains esoteric. This chapter is a presentation of the ideas and discoveries of these investigators.

Having reviewed the literature, Irving A. Taylor (1975) listed approaches to the study of the origins of creativity:

(1) vitalism, in which creativity has a theistic or mystical source (Kunkel & Dickerson, 1947; Rothbart, 1972); (2) nativism, or the belief that the origins are rooted in genetics (Galton, 1870, 1911; Hirst, 1931; Kretschmer, 1931); (3) empiricism, the view that creativity is essentially learned, held by a number of investigators (Hutchinson, 1949; Osborn, 1953; Torrance, 1962); (4) energentism, the view that creativity emerges as a synthesis of the hereditary and environmental forces (Arnheim, 1954; Wertheimir, 1945); (5) cognition, creativity resulting from thought processes (Guilford, 1968; Hersch 1973; Mednick, 1968; Wallas, 1926); (6) serendipity, the notion that creative discoveries are accidental, although the person may be prepared for a sudden insight (Cannon, 1940; McLean, 1941); (7) romanticism, the belief that

creativity originates through unanalyzable inspirations and that examining the illusory rootsof creativity will destroy it (Agha, 1959); (8) physiology, the contention that creativity is rooted in the biology of the human organism (Eccles, 1958; Gutman, 1967; Mumford, 1970; Sinott, 1959); (9) culture, or the determination of creativity by the historic Zeitgeist (Durkmein, 1898; Stein, 1967); (10) interpersonal relations, or creativity resulting from being triggered by group interaction as in brainstorming or synectics (Anderson, 1959; Gordon, 1961; Parnes, 1962; Prince, 1970); and personality, or the contention that the sources of creativity are understandable by examining the development of personality either psychoanalytically (Freud,1908; Jung, 1928; Rank, 1945) or through self-actualization theory (Goldstein, 1930; Maslow, 1959; May, 1959; Rogers, 1954). This led subsequently to the concept of personality transaction (Taylor, 1972c, p.300).

As the above quote demonstrates, no clear definition of the origins of creativity exists. There has been similar confusion about the best way creativity research can be organized. Hallman (1963) presented a method of organizing the data available on the subject of creativity. His proposal was that the study of creativity can best be analyzed in the forms of an act, an object, a process, a person, and the environment. Of these, the person and the process have emerged as relevant to this research. The literature reviewed in this chapter will be presented in two categories: the creative personality and the creative process. For the sake of simplicity, the creative situation will be included in the section on the creative process.

The Creative Personality

The creative personality has been approached in this book from two perspectives, a theoretical, conceptual perspective which includes psychoanalysis and humanistic psychology, and an empirical perspective. This review is not exhaustive; however, it deals with ideas central to this investigation.

Conceptual Perspective

The conceptual, theoretical perspective of the creative personality includes psychoanalysis and humanistic psychology. The work of Freud, Jung, Rank, and Adler is addressed under the heading of psychoanalytic views, and the work of Maslow, Rogers, and Fromm under the heading of humanistic views.

Psychoanalytic Views

The psychoanalytic perspective of creativity began with Freud (1901, 1908, 1910, 1924, 1947) who was first to develop a dynamic theory of the creative personality. The concept of the unconscious was central to his theory. Freud believed that the creative person was more capable of retrieving and using unconscious material than was the less creative individual. His views on the relationship of creativity and mental health were somewhat contradictory. His concept of creativity was closely associated with neurosis, in that the creative individual is frustrated and channels sexual energy not expended properly--via sexual intercourse--into creative pursuits. Although the individual is neurotically displacing sexual energy, the result of this sublimation is viewed as beneficial to society. At the same time, Freud recognized that poor art is often the result of conflict and openly expresses neurosis, whereas excellent art somehow transcends the purely personal neurotic motivations of the individual.

As did Freud, Jung (1959) viewed the creative person as bringing unconscious material into consciousness, modifying it in such a way as to be timely and acceptable, and then communicating it to others. Jung's two major additions to Freud's thoughts were his ideas about the relationship between creativity and his concepts of individuation and the collective unconscious.

Jung viewed people as striving to develop, with individuation as the goal. Individuation entails differentiation of the personality as well as a blending of all one's characteristics and unconscious imagery and motivations. The more fully individuated one is, the more likely that one's creative potentials will be realized.

Jung also emphasized the collective unconscious, the part of the unconscious common to all human beings and holding our racial memories in the form of images. Handed down in the embodiment of archetypes, these images offer the most fertile material for creative thought. Jung, like Freud, viewed dreams as an excellent way of gaining access to our unconscious minds.

Rank (1932, 1945) addressed art and creativity, specifying the creative or artistic type as functioning at a higher level than the neurotic or the average person. Through creativity, a person is able to resolve guilt and integrate the different aspects of the personality. Art, according to Rank, is an externalization of the personality of the creative individual.

Adler (Ansbacher & Ansbacher, 1956) considered creativity as supreme usefulness, viewing creative individuals as more useful to society than those less creative. Creative power was described by Adler as the most important attribute one could possess, with creative achievement being how we compensate for our inferiority. Unlike Freud and Jung, Adler described creativity as a component of the conscious mind. Although psychoanalysts have disagreed on the origins and mechanisms of creativity, they have agreed that creativity is an important attribute of personality. In the preceding section, the major ideas about creativity held by influential psychoanalytic theorists were described. In the following section the thoughts about creativity that have been presented by leading humanists are outlined.

Humanistic Views

Although humanistic psychologists agree with psychoanalyists that mankind is in conflict with society, they generally hold a more positive view of human nature. Freud theorized that creativity is the result of psychopathology. Humanistic psychologists view creativity as stemming from a movement toward health and fulfillment. Everyone is seen as possessing a drive toward self-actualization, which provides the motivating force behind creativity (Taylor, 1975).

Maslow, the founder of the third force in psychology, now most often referred to as humanistic psychology, dedicated most of his career to the study of healthy people. He did not define mental health as the lack of mental illness, but rather he defined it as the individual being a fully functioning human being. He called this way of being self-actualizing.

In a chapter published in 1968, Maslow reflected on his work with self-actualizing people and defined three types of creativity. They are (a) special talent creativeness, (b) self-actualizing creativeness, and (c) integrated creativeness. The first type, special talent creativeness, includes people who are usually described as having been born with a particular talent, such as an ear for music or the ability to draw. This type is usually attributed to an inherited gift.

Maslow's work dealt primarily with the second kind of creativity. He viewed this kind as being a part of the personality and as having more to do with life-style than with products. He described the self-actualizing person as more spontaneous, more expressive, fresher, more innocent, freer from stereotypes, less frightened by the unknown, less concerned about other's opinions of them, and less dependent than other, less self-actualizing people.

Another interesting observation of Maslow's is that self-actualizing individuals have personalities that encompass dichotomies in a workable, dynamic manner. For example, he described them as both more and less selfish than average people. This dynamic resolution enables them to be more fully functioning.

The third, integrated creativeness, is the type that is central to this research. The person who is functioning with integrated creativity is the person who produces exceptional art, ideas, products, or services. This person is able to use both the primary and secondary thought processes well. The primary process refers to unconscious psychic functions, such as dreams and psychotic fantasy. The secondary process refers to conscious psychic functions, such as those thought processes healthy people experience during normal waking activities. Maslow did not concentrate on this type of creativity; therefore it is my hope that this work will bring the third type of creativity into focus. It is possible that the third type combines the attributes of the first two in some dynamic manner.

In an article published in 1972, Maslow compared Torrance's description of creative people with his own description of self-actualizing people, finding them to be extremely similar. This similarity brings strength to the concept that the tendency toward self-actualization is a motivational force behind creativity.

As did Maslow, Rogers (1959) defined the motivational force behind creativity as our inborn tendency to self-actualize, a tendency found in all forms of life. " The underlying theme stressed by Rogers--keynoting other humanists--is the desire of the individual to achieve fully his potential through interaction with a supportive environment" (Taylor, 1975, p.8).

Fromm (1959) saw the acceptance of human sensuality as necessary for creativity to occur. He also believed that only after a state of inner maturity is reached, when distortion and projection are decreased, can the individual be creative. Creative people were described by Fromm as neither rejecting of their evil components nor as judging some experiences as more important than others. Creativity requires flexibility between the objective and the subjective.

In the preceding section thoughts about creativity from a conceptual perspective were described. Although the preceding works were often based on research, and the following works sometimes offer conceptual explanations, the literature was divided into these categories for organizational reasons. The following section describes the major contributions of other researchers who have investigated creativity. These findings have been reported because they have been influential in the developing field of the study of creativity.

<u>Empirical Views</u>

The personality of the creative individual has been the subject of systematic research. One way creativity has been studied is by addressing the idea that creative people have distinguishable personality characteristics. Rossman investigated the idea of personality characteristics in his 1931 study by collecting self-descriptions from inventors. The characteristics most often mentioned were perseverance, imagination, knowledge, memory, business ability, common sense, analytic ability, and self-confidence. Also in 1931, Hirst listed the six personality traits he most often observed in geniuses. They are bashfulness, oversensitivity, sincerity, melancholia, a need for solitude, and an extreme importance placed on friendship.

In 1950 Guilford suggested that a sensitivity to problems is a prerequisite for creativity. Other factors he listed as important for creative thinking are fluency of thinking--which includes word fluency, associational fluency, expressive fluency, and ideational fluency-- flexibility, originality, redefinition, and elaboration.

Torrance (1962) described many aspects of the creative personality. Some of these are altruism, acceptance of disorder, energeticness, persistence, assertiveness, versatility, withdrawness, an attraction to the mysterious, unconventionality, independence, oddities of habit, fault finding, discontentedness, stubbornness, sensitivity, an ability to accept the making of mistakes, and temperamentalness. He described creative boys as more feminine and creative girls as more masculine than their less creative peers.

Also in 1962, Henle posed two conditions necessary for creative thinking. The first condition is receptivity to creative ideas. The second condition is immersion in one's subject matter. Also important are the abilities to have detached devotion, to see the right questions, and to use errors.

Barron described original individuals in his 1963 work as (a) preferring complexity and imbalance in phenomena, (b) being more complex and having greater personal scope, (c) being more independent in their judgments, (d) being more self-assertive, and (e) rejecting of suppression. His 12 basic characteristics of creative people were that they (a) are more observant, (b) express part truths, (c) see things both similarly to others and differently from others, (d) are independent thinkers, (e) are motivated by their values and talents, (f) can hold various ideas at once, (g) have greater sexual and physical vigor, (h) live more complexly in what they view as a more complex universe, (i) are more aware of unconscious motivations, (j) have enough ego strength to regress and return to normalcy, (k) can sometimes allow the distinction between subject and object to disappear, and (l) are creative as a function of freedom.

Taylor (1964) named intellectual, motivational, and personality factors that he viewed as important for creativity to occur. The personality factors named were independence, self-sufficiency and self-confidence, femininity, and tolerance for ambiguity. Drive, dedication, resourcefulness, principles, and a desire for order were named as motivational factors. Among the intellectual factors were memory, convergence, divergence, cognition, and evaluation.

Another thought often held about creative individuals is that they have insane temperaments. In his 1904 study of British geniuses, Ellis demonstrated that only 4.2 % of those cited as geniuses by the Dictionary of National Biography were psychotic. In a similar study, Jacobson (1926) showed that those creative individuals who are disturbed do their best work during the periods in their lives when they are their healthiest.

One of the most complete studies of the personality of the creative person was described in a chapter titled "IPAR's Contribution to the Conceptualization and Study of Creativity" in which Donald W. MacKinnon related the research beginning in 1949 done by the Institute of Personality Assessment and Research (IPAR). The objective was to develop and use assessment to study effectively functioning people (MacKinnon, 1975). It is important to be aware that the creative subjects studied in this research were students expecting to finish their Ph. D.s within one year. These people were judged by their faculties as suitable for the research. They were not highly prominent, nor had they proven their creativity as have the respondents in this book.

17

Originality was studied at IPAR, and it was found that the original person is more serious, organized, rational, civilized, reliable, quiet, and responsible whereas the unoriginal person is more emotional, restless, stubborn, and defensive. High originality correlated with intellectual competency and self-assurance, but not with intelligence test scores. Highly original people prefer complex and asymmetrical designs (MacKinnon, 1975). In one portion of the IPAR research, Barron (1957) studied original people after removing intelligence as a variable. He found these people to be responsive to impulse and emotion, to be self-assertive, to have high energy levels, to be involved, to be disposed toward an integration of diverse stimuli, and to express femininity of interests.

Gough (1957) conceptualized five dimensions as determinants of originality. They are (a) intellectual competence, (b) inquiringness as a habit of mind, (c) cognitive flexibility, (d) esthetic sensitivity, and (e) a sense of destiny.

In his work at IPAR with original people, Schimek (1954) found that highly creative people were verbally fluent, curious, self-disciplined, and self-reliant. They were not especially gregarious and were not overly concerned about the opinions of others, or at least wished they were not. They experienced a rich inner life, were willing to admit fears and unconventional taste. They were autonomous and valued intellectual independence.

In a comparison of original but unintelligent people, intelligent but unoriginal people, and people who were both original and intelligent, Barron (1957) speculated after in further research at IPAR that the person who is original but unintelligent uses only the primary process well. The intelligent but unoriginal person is ego-bound, rendering the primary process inaccessible. The person who is both intelligent and original has easy access to both the primary and secondary thought processes.

In speaking of this third type of personality, Barron (1957) said that in the effectively original person there may be "an ability to regress very far for the moment while being able, quite rapidly, to return to a high degree of rationality, bringing with him the fruits of his regression to primitive and fantastic modes of thought" (p.739). Both higher levels of psychopathology and higher levels of ego-strength were found in highly creative individuals. These people were judged to have the courage to be open to experience, especially of inner life (Barron,1953).

Subjects in the IPAR research (MacKinnon, 1975) were administered the Myers-Briggs Type Indicator (Myers, 1962). Highly creative people showed a preference for intuition over sensation, perception over judgment, and tended to be introverted. A preference for thinking or feeling was related to the type of materials or concepts in which the creative person would choose to deal. As would be expected by followers of Jung (1928), creative men displayed a high score on the femininity scale on the Minnesota Multiphasic Personality Inventory (MMPI) (Hathaway & McKinley, 1943), and the researchers hypothesized that creative people are more likely to show reconciliation of opposites.

In a study of interests, Mackinnon (1975) discovered the interests of creative people are similar to those of psychologists, author-journalists, lawyers, architects, artists, and musicians, and dissimilar to the interests of purchasing agents, office workers, bankers, farmers, carpenters, veterinarians, police officers, and morticians as these were assessed by the Strong Vocational Interest Blank (Strong, 1943).

In the biographies of IPAR subjects, it is exhibited that early interests in their inner experiences with an introversion of interests because of unhappiness or loneliness in childhood may have contributed to their creativity. In childhood they also enjoyed some special skill and were rewarded for possessing it, had freedom in decision making early in life,

19

and experienced distance in their relationships with their parents. There was usually an effective adult member of each sex present in the child's life, frequent moving, and freedom from establishing an early professional identity (MacKinnon, 1975).

The research done at IPAR provided a good deal of information about creativity and the creative individual. No other research has been as comprehensive. Several of the scientists involved have continued to work in the field. One example is Barron. In 1968 he published the findings that complex people, who tend to be more creative than simple people, abhor racial prejudice and speak up when others make racial remarks, even if it makes them unpopular in the group. His studies also showed creative writers as both mentally healthier and mentally sicker than people in general. In speaking of a sample of male writers, Barron noted, "When one turns to the question of psychological health in relation to creativity, the picture is by no means a simple one. All three groups of writers earned markedly deviant scores on the MMPI. Distinguished writers scored particularly high on scales measuring schizoid, depressive, hysterical, and psychopathic tendencies. They also were well above the general population norms in terms of femininity of interests patterns on the California Psychological Inventory" (p. 243). In addition, they scored high on the MMPI scale that predicts the success for recovery from neurosis, a good assessor of ego-strength. Barron continued to describe these individuals as "clearly effective people who handle themselves with pride and distinctiveness, but the face they turn to the world is sometimes one of pain, often of protest, sometimes of distance and withdrawal, and certainly they are emotional" (p. 244).

In later research Barron (1975) discovered that writers report that their childhoods were unhappy, and that they felt isolated and were extremely sensitive. Helson (1965) reported similar findings in her studies with creative women. Barron

(1975) suggested that children of high creative potential tend to amplify their experience of loneliness. Of creative people Barron commented, "In terms of psychodynamics, I believe that the common and indeed adaptive 'normal,' 'healthy minded' defense against the feeling of solitariness is repression. The creative response to this and other painful aspects of fate is not repression, however, but openness and depth of feeling" (p. 151).

Getzels and Csikszentmihalyi (1975) claimed that in order to understand creativity we must redefine human beings as not only problem-solving, but also as problem finding. Problem finding behavior is a form of stimulus-seeking. They think we need to shift our ideas of intelligence to encompass creative thinking, which includes problem finding.

Getzels and Jackson (1962) conducted a series of research studies focusing on intelligence, divergent thinking, and creative performance. Two groups of adolescents were studied. Group A consisted of 28 adolescents. These subjects scored in the top 20% in IQ. The mean IQ was 150 with IQ scores ranging from 139 to 179. They also scored below the top 20% in divergent thinking. The second group, Group B, had 26 subjects. All 26 of the members of Group B scored in the top 20% in divergent thinking but below the top 20% in IQ. The mean IQ score for Group B was 127 with scores ranging from 108 to 138.

These two groups performed similarly on a number of standardized tests. The most interesting information gained, that Group B performed much better on creativity scores, went unnoticed at the time (Getzels & Csikszentmihalyi, 1975).

Following are examples of the differences between the responses of the two groups. In the first example, the students were shown a picture of a man riding in an airplane and were given 4 minutes to write a story.

The high IQ subject: Mr. Smith is on his way home from a successful business trip. He is very happy and he is thinking about his wonderful family and how glad he will be to see them again. He can picture it, about an hour from now, his plane landing at the airport and Mrs. Smith and their three children all there welcoming him home again.

The high divergent-thinking subject: This man is flying back from Reno where he has won a divorce from his wife. He couldn't stand to live with her anymore, he told the judge, because she wore so much cold cream on her face at night that her head would skid across the pillow. He now is contemplating a new skid-proof face cream. (Getzels & Jackson, 1962, p. 39.)

Here is the second set of responses to a stimulus picture perceived most often as a man working late, or very early, in an office.

The high IQ subject: There's ambitious Bob down at the office at 6:30 in the morning. Every morning it's the same. He's trying to show his boss how energetic he is. Now, thinks Bob, maybe the boss will give me a raise for all my extra work. The trouble is that Bob has been doing this for the last three years, and the boss still hasn't given him a raise. He'll come in at 9:00, not even noticing that Bob has been there so long, and poor Bob won't get his raise.

The high divergent-thinking subject: This man has just broken into this office of a new cereal company. He is a private eye employed by a competitive firm to find out the formula that makes the cereal bend, sag, and sway. After a thorough search of the office he comes upon what he thinks is the current formula. It turns out that it is the wrong formula and the competitor's factory blows up. Poetic Justice! (Getzels & Jackson, 1962, p. 40).

The above are examples of the superior creativity exhibited by Group B in writing. Group B also demonstrated superior creativity in drawing. In his own studies of intelligence and creativity, Torrance (1960) replicated these findings. In additional work using these data, Getzels and Csikszentmihalyi (1975) theorized that the difference in the creative behavior of Group A and Group B could be explained in terms of problem finding. Group A solved the problem of writing a story to illustrate the picture. Group B solved the additional unstated problem of writing an interesting story.

Once the problem finding hypothesis had been developed, Getzels and Csikszentmihalyi (1974) began a study in which they hoped to discover support for it. They designed an experiment in which they observed the problem-finding behavior of artists. The results demonstrated a positive correlation between the amount of problem finding behavior and the value of the work produced--particularly, the more problem finding behavior, the more creative the artwork.

It is difficult to separate clearly the aspects of the creative personality and the creative process. Although any division is artificial, for the purposes of this project the literature is divided into these two categories. The theories and discoveries about the creative personality have been discussed under primary headings dealing with the psychoanalytic perspective, the humanistic perspective, and the perspective of research.

The Creative Process

The following segment of Chapter 2 addresses the creative process. One important way in which the creative process has been discussed is as a phenomenon that occurs in stages. The role of the unconscious and the necessary environmental conditions are presented as well as the individualized nature of the process of creative thought. The literature dealing with the creative process is discussed below under the headings of the stages of creativity, creativogenic factors, the role of the unconscious in creativity, and the individualized nature of the creative process.

The Stages of Creativity

Researchers and writers, in their attempts to understand the creative process, have returned again and again to the idea of creativity occurring in stages, perhaps because stages can be based on the analysis of observation. Having observed his own creative process, Helmholtz (1896), a psychologist, made such an attempt. He established three stages: (a) an initial stage of investigation; (b) a rest period; and (c) a sudden and unexpected solution.

In 1913, Poincare added a stage to those established by Helmholtz. This stage followed illumination. It consisted of additional conscious effort to validate the insight previously gained. Poincare also addressed the idea that good combinations are made unconsciously. Heretofore, illumination had been attributed to chance. Believing the subliminal self to be as influential as the conscious self, Poincare suggested that the work had been done by the subliminal self. In 1926, building on the work of Poincare, Wallas addressed the idea of the stages of creativity. The stages Wallas named are (a) preparation, (b) incubation, (c) illumination, and (d) verification. In 1931 Rossman expanded these into seven steps:

1. Observation of a need or difficulty

2. Analysis of the need

3. A survey of all objective information

4. A formulation of all objective solutions

5. A critical analysis of these solutions for their advantages and disadvantages

6. The birth of the new idea--the invention

7. Experimentation to test the most promising solution, and the selection and perfection of the final embodiment by some or all of the previous steps (p. 57).

Stein (1967, 1974) presented a theory of the stages of creativity. His three stages of (a) hypothesis formation, (b) hypothesis testing, and (c) communication of the findings were preceded by education and preparation. He saw no clear separation of these stages.

The idea that creativity occurs in stages has not been accepted by all. Vinacke (1952) was particularly critical of these theories, pointing to the recurrence of some stages during the production of one creative work and to the lack of true separation between the alleged stages.

Evidently, the process of creative thinking can be divided into artificial stages. Even though it cannot be done with precision, separating this process into stages simplifies our attempts to conceptualize the elusive human endeavor of creating.

Creativogenic Factors

Certain environmental factors may enhance the probability of creative expression occurring. In addition to describing the creative personality, Arieti (1976) addressed the idea that the culture in which people live provides them with contingencies for creativity. Certain factors he listed as creativogenic are:

1. Availability of cultural means.

2. Openness to cultural stimuli.

3. Stress on becoming and not just being.

4. Free access to cultural media for all citizens, without discrimination.

5. Freedom, or even the retention of moderate discrimination, after severe oppression or absolute exclusion.

6. Exposure to different and even contrasting cultural stimuli.

7. Tolerance for diverging views.

8. Interaction of significant persons.

9. Promotion of incentives and awards (p. 324).

Arieti recognized that several of these are unlikly to coexist, and that only the first is essential.

<u>The Role Of The Unconscious In Creativity</u>

Barron (1968) described the role of the unconscious in the creative process. From the studies with which he had been involved, he extrapolated the concept that the unconscious provides the raw material for works of art. The unconscious material was viewed as chaotic, as is often the case in dreams and psychosis. The conscious mind later elaborates upon this chaotic material.

In creative expression, the censorship usually prohibiting unconscious images from moving into awareness is suspended so that these images pass into the preconscious, bringing with them associated ideas, feelings, and symbols. These images are vague, and their connection may not be recognized until some later time. Ideas already in the preconscious blend with the new material before it enters consciousness.

Although these ideas sometimes arrive in the conscious mind formulated, usually they are fragmented and effort is required to transform them into art. "The real work, of course, comes in making out of this material a communication, i.e., giving it a social reality, which involves discrimination, selection, technique, purpose, and understanding both of the material itself and of an audience of at least one other person who can appreciate it" (p. 228).

Arieti expressed similar ideas in his 1976 publication. In describing the role the unconscious plays in the creative process, he introduced two expressions, tertiary process and endocept, and explained why these phenomena are important. To understand the concept of the tertiary process, one must first understand the primary and secondary processes, both of which are important in creative expression.

As was stated earler, the primary process refers to one kind of psychic functioning, usually unconscious, and the secondary process refers to another, usually conscious. The primary process is active in dreams and psychosis. The secondary process operates when we are awake. It is logical whereas the primary process is not.

The dreamer, schizophrenic, and creative person seem to have freer access to the primary process than the average person. The dreamer loses the availability of the primary process on awakening. The schizophrenic is unable to freely move away from the unconscious. In contrast, the creative person is able to coordinate these two processes. Arieti proposed the term tertiary process to describe this special occurrence. "The tertiary process, with specific mechanisms and forms, blends the two worlds of mind and matter, and in many cases, the rational with the irrational" (p.13).

It is the ego strength of creative people that allows them to enter the world of the primary process and return again. The primary process provides creative individuals with a wellspring of imagery for expression. The secondary process allows for criticism, rejection, and refinement of these images. "The tertiary process ultimately comes into being as a 'click,' or match, between the primary and secondary processes, which brings about an accepted, emerging representation. Eureka! The new unity is created!" (1976, p. 186). This eureka experience often follows the stage called incubation. Arieti believed that incubation, at least in part, consists of what he called endoceptual activity.

To understand the endocept, we must first understand the two categories that are prerequisites for creativity. The first category consists of contingencies, the second of imagination and amorphous cognition. Contingencies are all things outside the person. The second category has to do with the person's inner life. Imagination functions when the person is awake and able to produce or reproduce symbols. Amorphous cognition is an internal occurrence that cannot be expressed in the usual ways. Arieti used the Greek endo, meaning inside, because, unlike a concept, the endocept remains private. Arieti believed that in the rare moments of inspiration, the creative individual immediately converts an endocept into some kind of expression, for example, a painting. He described this occurrence the same as what Maslow termed a peak experience. The most important contribution made by Arieti to the study of creativity emerged from his clinically gained understanding of mental processes. His extensive work in the area of schizophrenia provided him with insight into the primary process.

The unconscious undoubtedly plays an important and necessary role in creative production. In the following discussion on the individualized nature of creative thinking, examples of two composers' creative processes are presented. In each, the unconscious processes are discussed. The second, a description of the work of Beethoven, exemplifies Barron's ideas dealing with the conscious work following illumination.

<u>The Individualized Nature Of The Creative Process</u>

In the book <u>The Creative Process</u> (1952), Ghiselin gathered together a number of articles, letters, and papers. All of these are interesting; however, two have been chosen for mention here. These two both deal with musical creativity and differ significantly in the description of the process of musical composition. The first is a letter by Mozart, quoted partially below.

> When I am, as it were, completely myself, entirely alone, and of good cheer--say, traveling in a carriage, or walking, or after a good meal, or during the night when I cannot sleep; it is on such occasions that my ideas flow best and most abundantly. Whence and how they come, I know not; nor can I force them.
>
> When I proceed to write down my ideas, I take out of the bag of my memory, if I may use that phrase, what has been previously collected into it in the way I have mentioned. For this reason the committing to paper is done quickly enough, for everything is, as I have said before, already finished.
>
> But why my productions take from my hand that particular form and style that makes them

Mozartish, and different from the works of other composers, is probably owing to the same cause which renders my nose so large or so aquiline, or, in short, makes it Mozart's and different from those other people. For I really do not study or aim at any originality (pp. 34-35).

Another paper in the collection is by Sessions. It deals with the work of Beethoven. Below are excerpts quoted from that paper.

I have in my possession photostatic copies of several pages of Beethoven's sketches for the last movement of his "Hammerklavui Sonata"; the sketches show him carefully modeling, then testing in systematic and apparently cold-blooded fashion, the theme of the fugue. Where, one might ask, is the inspiration here? Yet if the word has any meaning at all, it is certainly appropriate to this movement, with its irresible and titanic energy of expression, already present in the theme. The inspiration takes the form, however, not of a sudden flash of music, but a clearly envisaged impulse toward a certain goal for which the composer was obliged to strive. Inspiration, then is the impulse which sets creation in movement: it is also the energy which keeps it going (p. 38).

The significance of these two descriptions of the creative process lies in their differences. For Mozart, music came complete, finished. He had only to write it down. For Beethoven, on the other hand, notes came in small scraps and required conscious effort to grow into great music. The point here is that Beethoven and Mozart were not only two great composers, they also were two individuals.

As Barron (1969) stated, "There has been a marked tendency in psychological research on originality to focus attention upon the single original act itself, rather than upon the total personality of the originator. We tend to disembody the creative act and the creative process by limiting our inquiry to the creator's mental content at the moment of insight, forgetting that a highly organized system of responding lies behind the particular original response that, because of its validity, becomes an historic event" (p. 200).

Summary

In this chapter a number of theories about creativity were presented. The two primary headings under which creative expression was addressed were the creative personality, which included psychoanalytic views, humanistic views, and empirical views, and the creative process which included sections on the stages of creativity, creativogenic factors, the role of the unconscious, and the individualized nature of the creative process. Explorers in the area of creative thinking have made meaningful discoveries. Other discoveries are yet to come.

Creativity is complex. Too often researchers have attempted to explain this complex human behavior in simplistic terms. As was demonstrated by the quotes about the creative processes of Beethoven and Mozart, individuals, especially those who are creatively expressive, are unique. Therefore creativity may be experienced by these people differently. It is important to acknowledge the subjective aspects of creativity, and doing so was a goal of this study.

Different research projects and theoretical orientations have made conflicting discoveries and formulated disagreeing theories. One example can be found in two sections of the research at IPAR (MacKinnon, 1975). These studies showed the unoriginal person to be more emotional in one study and the creative person to be more responsive to emotion in another.

There exist areas of discrepancy in the study of creativity. This volume adds to the body of knowledge available in the field of creative thinking. It considers the complex, individualistic aspects of the creative personality and process.

It is an assumption of this research that in order for people to be judged creative, they must have produced a creative product. That product may be an idea, service, product, or work or art. In 1966, Gray published the criteria by which he would rate an individual's creative work. He believed that a creative work would be appreciated long after the death of the creator, would display humanistic qualities, surpass the limits of the era, influence others, show social consciousness, and be original, versatile, and beautiful. It is impossible for all of these criteria to be met in this study, however Gray's description of a creative product is eloquent.

Although not exhaustive, Chapter 2 contains a comprehensive overview of the discoveries made about creativity by educators, psychologists, and others. It is the purpose of this research to gain understanding of the individual who is creative. Because creative people are creative in different ways, a number of individuals have been interviewed. How the data were gathered and analysed is explained in the following chapter.

CHAPTER 3

RESEARCH METHODS AND PROCEDURES

Creativity is a potent quality, one about which we still know little. The goal of this study was to generate theory about the creative individual and the creative process. A deeper understanding of this process and the environmental factors and personality characteristics that facilitate creative behavior was developed by comparing the thoughts and histories obtained in interviews with 11 especially creative individuals. The information acquired lends itself to a description of what was influential in the lives and creative pursuits of these people.

Goetz and LeCompte (1984) commented, "The research questions that investigators formulate are influenced implicitly or explicitly by the personal experiences and philosophies that shape their interests and the way they think" (p.41). My interest in doing this research grew from my desire to understand the thinking of the creative person. It also grew from the pressing need I see for divergent thinkers. My belief is that the potential to think creatively is native to most individuals and that socialization suppresses originality and flexibility in many. This study describes occurrences in the lives of some people who remained creative, as well as characteristics that existed in their personalities that enabled them to persist in their creative activities.

My interest during this research was in the subjective. I searched for richness and color because I desired understanding of how creation feels to an individual, what thoughts about creativity the especially creative person has, and what factors contribute to the maintaining of spontaneity and flexibility. The insights gained in this investigation can help foster creative thinking, teaching us how to nurture this quality in ourselves and others.

Many past investigators of creativity have emphasized a need for further research. In Creativity, The Magic Synthesis, Arieti (1976) stressed this need several times. "All of the methods used to study creativity have been rewarding to various degrees, and some of them seem very promising. On the other hand, it is true that no major breakthrough has occurred" (p. 34). He viewed creativity research as potentially beneficial because, if we could "define the personality of the creative individual, or at least differentiate the individual characteristics that make a person creative we could reach some conclusions, we would be in a better position (1) to promote the special characteristics, and (2) to recognize people who already have such characteristics, so we could encourage them toward creative pursuits" (p. 339). He saw creativity research as still in its initial stages, viewing current studies as pioneer work.

Pioneers throughout history have reported their observations. In this research I have made a special kind of observation, reported the findings, and generated theory to explain what I observed. The key word here is generated as opposed to verified theory. To do so, I decided a qualitative, phenomenological approach was most desirable.

Rationale for Research Method

In choosing a method of research, one must first ask in what ways the questions of interest can best be answered. There exists a large number of quantitative and qualitative research strategies. Because it was my objective to approach the creative person with the aim of understanding the creative process as it is subjectively experienced, because I wanted to understand the meanings creative people attach to their experiences of themselves and the world, and because I desired comprehension of the multiple realities of creativity, I chose what I believed to be the most appropriate strategy, a multiple case study format (Bogdan & Biklen, 1982).

This section would be incomplete if I did not include a statement about my aspiration to increase the acceptance of qualitative research in the fields of psychology and counseling. The need to do so is well described in an unpublished paper by Carl Rogers (1985), "Toward a More Human Science of the Person." I agree with Rogers and many others, that a legitimate arena for research in humanistic and existential psychology needs to exist in our universities and that qualitative research methods are tools necessary to the investigation of human experience.

Respondent Selection Procedure

Once the question of study and the method of research had been determined, I faced the problem of locating respondents. It was important that the respondents for this research be selected because they met the conceptual category of the creative personality. After discussing this concern with fellow graduate students, faculty members, and others from several creative fields, I decided the coresearchers should be viewed by their peers as exhibiting exceptional creativity in their professional fields. Individuals from various professions were selected purposefully, in order to represent the diversity of creative thinkers and to avoid the biases choosing people from only one area might have induced. For example, had I interviewed all painters I may have made discoveries about people with particular visual skill, hand-eye coordination or aesthetic values rather that the ability to think creatively. All of the respondents were, at the time of the interviews, supporting themselves financially via their creative endeavors, which is relevant because it provides the information that the culture values their products enough to pay for them, and that these people are invested enough in their creative productions to make them the focal point of their professional lives. It would, of course, be impossible to include all creative individuals in any study; however, all the respondents share the attributes of interest with the subpopulation of creative individuals. Because of these commonalities, inferences about this subpopulation can be proposed (LeCompte & Goetz, 1982).

For this investigation, 11 individuals were interviewed. Because of the prominence of these people, more potential respondents were contacted than agreed to be interviewed. Interviews were conducted with those who agreed. Respondents were selected both before and during the process of analyzing the data. No additional individuals were contacted for interviews beyond the point of theoretical saturation (Glaser & Strauss, 1967). Because knowledge of respondent selection is crucial to design assessment and pertinent to other researchers, I shall describe it in some detail below.

The first step I took in this process was to solicit suggestions for suitable coresearchers from a variety of sources, including professionals in art, design, music, education, psychology, and business. This step was easy. Everyone with whom I spoke had several excellent candidates to recommend.

I expected the next step, contacting these prominent individuals, would present significant difficulty. My first list was comprised of the names, Carl Rogers, Liza Minnelli, Tom Robbins, May Sartin, George Leonard, Patricia Sun, Paul Torrance, and Shirley MacLaine. It was a surprisingly easier task than I had expected.

I was told by one of his former students, Elizabeth Sheerer, that Carl Rogers's telephone number was listed. It was. I called him at his home one Sunday morning in the summer of 1984. He graciously agreed to be interviewed. The first person I had contacted agreed to participate in my research, and this person was Carl Rogers! I felt my project was charmed.

Next, I made an appointment to see Paul Torrance, a member of the faculty of the University of Georgia from whom I had taken two courses. I explained my request, and he agreed as well. I felt overjoyed.

Following my meeting with Paul Torrance, I wrote Tom Robbins, May Sarton, George Leonard, Shirley MacLaine, Patricia Sun, and Liza Minnelli. About 2 weeks later I received a telephone call from Tom Robbins, accepting my proposal to be a respondent. At this point, I had no doubt that my project had somehow fallen into a state of grace. Soon I received positive replies from George Leonard and Patricia Sun and the first of many rejections, from May Sarton and Shirley MacLaine. It was some time later before I received a letter saying Liza Minnelli would be unable to participate. My overriding feeling at this point was one of amazement that so many of the people contacted were open to supporting this endeavor. I had commitments for interviews from Carl Rogers, Paul Torrance, Tom Robbins, George Leonard, and Patricia Sun.

I mailed letters to additional individuals, including Walter Cronkite, Joan Armatrading, Michael Graves, Louise Dalh-Wolfe, John Fowles, and Barbara MacClintoc. Of this group only Michael Graves accepted; however, he failed to respond to any of my following letters and was dropped from the study. At this point in the selection process the interviewing began. In August of 1984--the time that best fit his schedule--I conducted the first interview with Tom Robbins.

From then on, the solicitation of respondents occurred sporadically. I continued contacting creative individuals, attempting to obtain interviews with as many different kinds of people as possible. My goal here was diversification. I received many rejections. In a few months I received a positive reply from Paul Erdos; however, the interview was never arranged and he was dropped from the study.

I was glad I had so many positive reactions early in this process, because obtaining acceptances from potential respondents had become difficult. I received no reply from many of the people I contacted. In most cases I had no idea if my letters were received. I generally wrote in care of publishing, film, or record companies. The ways in which I made contact began to change. I began networking through the people I had already interviewed as well as through friends to help me contact potential respondents.

Tom Robbins had suggested I interview Arthur Young. Tom had met him at a "Mad Scientists Convention," and Arthur impressed him. A few months later a Rolfer in Atlanta, Les Kertey, also recommended Arthur. Les gave me Arthur's address. I wrote, and the interview was arranged.

In the fall of 1984 I interviewed Paul Torrance. Because Paul is an expert in the fields of creative education and creative thinking, I especially wanted to interview Paul early in the process so I could make any changes he might recommend in the interview guide. He liked the interview as it was.

During the winter of 1984-1985, I scheduled interviews with Carl Rogers, George Leonard, Arthur Young, and Patricia Sun. Those interviews took place in March 1985. At that time I was becoming aware of a problem in my selection procedure. Even though I had contacted the same number of women and men, I had interviewed 5 men and only 1 woman. I talked with Judith Goetz, and she suggested I use the respondent network I had built to locate additional appropriate women. I wrote George Leonard because when I was with him he had suggested I interview two of his friends, Wendy Palmer and Michael Murphy. I wrote, and both Wendy and Mike accepted.

Clark Melrose introduced me to Niels Diffrient and suggested he would make an excellent coresearcher. I wrote Niels and he accepted. In September 1985 I interviewed

Wendy. I went to Mike's Mill Valley home; however, he felt too distracted to participate in the interview and was dropped from the research. In October I interviewed Niels.

While in New York to interview Niels, I dined one evening with Bill Hogan, a friend. Bill suggested I interview his uncle, Frank Hogan. I explained I needed women coresearchers, and Bill spoke with Frank, who not only agreed to be interviewed, but also arranged interviews for me with Norma McLain Stoop and Leora Sies.

A few weeks after my New York trip, another friend, Johanna Burke, telephoned to recommend Rowena Reed. I wrote and arranged interviews with Rowena, Frank, Norma, and Leora for January, 1986. The interview with Leora was canceled because she was ill, and she was dropped from the study.

In February of 1986, the final transcripts were completed. After reading them and discovering that little new information was surfacing, I decided that no more interviews were necessary.

Limitations

Whenever sampling is not done randomly from the group being researched, there exists a question of reliability. In this case, there was no group until I created one. Unlike other groups, such as a church congregation or a freshman class, no group of creative thinkers existed. I defined the group and selected members.

Not only was the group atypical for the reason described above, a group of exceptionally creative thinkers is atypical by definition. Being atypical was a requirement for membership. From this atypical group, I interviewed even less typical members. The people I interviewed attracted my request and were open to being interviewed. They knew creative thinking was the topic, and probably would not have accepted if they did not consider themselves creative, have some ideas about creativity, and care about enhancing the available knowledge about creative thinking. These limitations are posed by the selection procedure, the design, and the study's purpose.

It is necessary for anyone judging this study to understand that the research strategy imposes a limitation on the reliability of the findings. Interviews, rather than purely objective tests, were used to gather data. These interviews were not conducted with randomly selected respondents. Because reliability is primarily concerned with replicability, the methods of this research are presented clearly with the intent that others can use it as an operating manual (LeCompte & Goetz, 1982). The inclusion of the interview guide as Appendix A, numerous direct quotations, and the description of the process should provide reasonable guidelines for future replication. It is my opinion that others conducting replication studies would collect both similar and different data because of the respondents idiosyncrasies. Describing the idiosyncrasies of these creative individuals was one my goals. My description of the selection process was intended to be clear enough for others to judge the reliability of this work in whatever way best suits their purposes.

Coresearchers

Below is a brief biographical description of each of the individuals interviewed. These descriptions deal primarily with the careers of these people. They are described in the sequence in which they were interviewed. The biographical information below was provided by the respondents.

Tom Robbins was born in North Carolina on July 22, 1937, and spent his youth in Virginia. He studied art and religion and still practices his personal version of both. Before beginning his career as a fiction writer, Tom worked as an art critic and journalist.

Tom is best known for his four novels, the underground classics, Another Roadside Attraction (1971) and Even Cowgirls Get the Blues (1976), and his best sellers, Still Life with Woodpecker (1980) and Jitterbug Perfume (1984). In addition to writing articles for such publications as Esquire, he also designs stamps and uses them in his own visual art, which is shown and sold in art galleries on the West Coast. He has a zest for life that is reflected in his work and play. He enjoys travel to exotic places and white water rafting. Once a critic wrote, "Tom Robbins writes like Dolly Parton looks." Tom felt flattered. He currently lives in Washington State. The interview was conducted in Tom's living room.

E. Paul Torrance was born in Milledgeville, Georgia, on October 8, 1915, on his parents' farm. He received an associate's degree from Georgia Military College, a bachelor's degree from Mercer University, a master's degree from the University of Minnesota, and his Ph.D. from the University of Michigan. He is an internationally recognized leader in education.

Paul has published 30 books and over 1,100 journal articles, chapters, monographs, research reports, and several tests of creative behavior and styles of learning and thinking. He is a fellow in the American Psychological Association, a trustee of the Creative Education Foundation, and a member of many other professional organizations, including Phi Delta Kappa. In 1974, Paul was listed in Who's Who in the World; in 1976, he was listed in International Who's Who and Personalities of the South; and in 1983, he was elected to Who's Who in the World and Who's Who in Frontier Science and Technology.

He continues to be an innovator in education, with special involvement in the area of creative thinking. Paul lives in Athens, Georgia. He is Alumni Foundation Distinguished Professor of Educational Psychology: Emeritus, at The University of Georgia. The interview was conducted in Paul's study.

Carl Rogers was born in Illinois, in 1902 and died in California in 1987. He received a bachelor's degree from the University of Wisconsin in 1924, a master's degree from Columbia University in 1928, and his Ph.D. from Columbia in 1931. He worked for 6 decades in the field of psychology and was the founder of Client-Centered Therapy. His theory is now applied to many different areas, including education, administration, and international affairs, and is referred to as the Person-Centered Approach.

Carl wrote innumerable books and articles. Two of his most widely read books are A Way of Being (1980) and Freedom to Learn for the 80's (1983). He was a past president of the Association of Applied Psychology, the American Psychological Association, and the American Academy of Psychotherapists. He was awarded eight honorary doctorates and the American Psychological Association's Distinguished Scientific Contribution Award. He was elected Humanist Of The Year by the American Humanist Association. Carl was a fellow at the Center for the Studies of the Person in La Jolla, California, and at the time of the interview was enjoying new adventures, such as hot air ballooning. The interview was conducted in Carl's living room.

George Leonard was born in Atlanta, Georgia. He holds a bachelor's degree from the University of North Carolina and Doctor of Humanities from Lewis and Clark College. His books include, among others, Education and Ecstasy (1968), The Transformation (1961), The Silent Pulse (1978), and The End of Sex (1984).

From 1953 to 1970, George served as senior editor for Look. From 1966 until 1969, he was vice-president of Esalen Institute. He is a past-president of the Association of Humanistic Psychology. He wrote the words and music for two Air Force musicals, one of which toured in Korea. His musical comedy Clothes was produced as the Mountain Play on Mt.

Tamalpais, in 1977. His articles have appeared in Esquire, Harper's, Atlantic, The Nation, Saturday Review and others.

George is generally considered one of the founders of the human potential movement, and it was he who gave it its name. He is chief instructor of aikido at the school Aikido of Tamalpais, and he is the founder of the Energy Training Institute. He plays jazz piano. His energy is reflected in his work and life-style. George is living in Marin County, California, and is a contributing editor for Esquire. The interview with George was conducted in his living room and his favorite restaurant.

Arthur M. Young was born to American parents in Paris, in 1905. Following his graduation from Princeton University, he decided to devote his life to the study of philosophy. Later he became fascinated with the concept of a helicopter, and, in 1929, he began working alone, building small models. In 1941, the Bell Aircraft Company hired Arthur to design and build a full-scale helicopter. On March 8, 1946, his helicopter, the Bell Model 47, received the first commercial helicopter license.

Because nuclear weapons were being developed and used, Arthur grew concerned about the meaning of human existence. He combined his backgrounds in philosophy and science and his thoughts about reality as we know it, conceptualizing a new theory of evolution and the cosmos. In 1952, he established the Foundation for the Study of Consciousness in Philadelphia, and in 1972, he established the Institute for the Study of Consciousness in Berkeley. Arthur's books include, amoung others, The Bell Notes: A Journey from Physics to Metaphysics (1958), Which Way Out? And Other Essays (1980) The Reflexive Universe (1984), and The Geometry of Meaning (1984).

In 1984 Arthur's highly successful helicopter, the Bell-47D1, was placed on permanent exhibition at the Museum of Modern Art in New York City. Arthur lives in Berkeley and Philadelphia. He continues to develop theory about the evolution of consciousness and the universe. I conducted the interview with Arthur in his den.

Patricia Sun was born on February 23, 1941, in New Jersey. She graduated from the University of California at Berkeley, Phi Beta Kappa, earning both a Bachelor of Arts and a Bachelor of Science in 3 and 1/2 years.

Since 1973, Patricia has lectured professionally worldwide. Her message is one of joy, creativity, communication, and our continuing evolution as a species and planet. Patricia has appeared on "The Phil Donahue Show" and "Hour Magazine," as well as local television and radio shows throughout the world. She has lectured at the University of Madrid, Hayward State University, San Jose State University, the University of Alberta, the University of Hawaii, San Francisco State University, the World Symposium on Humanity, the Findhorn Foundation, the Long Beach Naval Medical Facility, and the Center for the Studies of the Person.

Patricia is known to those who have experienced her workshops as an empowering human being. She lives in Berkeley where she sees clients in her private practice. The interview was conducted in her office.

Wendy Palmer attended the American School in Switzerland, in 1964 and 1965, and Sarah Lawrence College, in 1967 and 1968. She is best known for her work with aikido. She studied aikido with Robert Nadeau, Frank Doran, and Mitsugi Saotome. Wendy is an aikido instructor, teacher, and psychotherapist, and has worked as a singer with a rock band.

Wendy is the co-founder and director of the school Tamalpais Aikido where she teaches basic, beginning, and advanced courses. She is co-founder of the International Movement Arts Center in Stanford, California, Executive Director of the Lomi School in Mill Valley, California, and has been a faculty member at the Naropa Institute in Boulder, Colorado. She is a faculty member at the Center for Investigation and Training Institute in Berkeley, California. Wendy leads energy awareness, movement awareness, and aikido workshops at Esalen Institute, and across the United States. Her favorite activity is windsurfing. The interview was conducted in her bedroom and a restaurant.

Niels Diffrient was born on his parents' farm in Star, Mississippi, in 1928. He graduated from Cranbrook Academy of Art in 1953. While there, he won the First Medal in Design in 1950, 1951, and 1952. After graduation, Niels received a Fulbright grant and worked in Italy where he and Marco Zanuso designed the Borletti sewing machine. In 1975, he was awarded an Honorary Doctor of Human Letters.

For 25 years, Niels was a partner in Henry Dreyfuss Associates, a major industrial design firm. From 1961 until 1969, he served as Assistant Professor in Residence at the University of California at Los Angeles. In 1952, he placed first in the Packard Automobile Design Competition, and, in 1976, he received the Government Award for the Handicapped for Humanscale 1/2/3. He also received awards from ID Magazine's annual design review, the American Institute of Graphics Arts, the Institute of Business Design, and the Industrial Designer's Society of America. His projects have been published in Domus, Abitare, Ottogono, Mobilia, Business Week, House and Garden, New York Times, Interior Design, Interiors, Industrial Design, House Beautiful, Design and Environment, Contract, Aspen Magazine, and Quest.

Niels' designs are varied: partition systems, lighting, and seating for SunarHauserman; heavy duty highway trucks for Freightliner; graphics and furniture for United California Bank; lift trucks for Hyster; thermostats and computer equipment for Honeywell; high voltage towers for Edison; and aircraft interiors, seating and graphics for Hughes, Lockheed, and

American Airlines. Niels has authored and co-authored numerous books and articles. His activities include serving in high posts for such organizations as the Industrial Designer's Society of America, the National Endowment for the Arts, and Architectural League of New York. Niels is an important and highly visible leader in the design community. He is a warm, reserved person who operates within the "Humanscale." Niels now lives in Connecticut, where he works as an independent consultant. The interview was conducted in his studio.

Norma McLain Stoop was born on July 20, 1910, in the Panama Canal Zone. She is a multitalented woman, currently working as senior editor of Dance Magazine, writing film and dance reviews and feature articles, taking performance photographs, and editing. Norma has been with Dance Magazine since 1969. Since 1983, she has been chief film critic of Manhattan Arts. Recently, Norma was featured in the documentary film, Forever Young. She has appeared on "The David Susskind Show," "Midday Live," WOR's "Straight Talk," "The Joe Franklin Show," and "The Nick Vanni Show."

Norma is represented in Who's Who in the World, Who's Who of American Women, Who's Who in the East, The Concise Oxford Dictionary of Ballet, The World's Who's Who of Women, The International Authors and Writers Who's Who, and Contemporary Authors. Her photographs have been exhibited at Harvard University and Tufts College.

Norma's poems, essays, and fiction have been published in Atlantic Monthly, Chicago Review, Texas Quarterly, Roanoke Review, The New York Times, The New York Herald Tribune, McCalls, Ladies Home Journal, Gourmet, and others. She also is well known as an interviewer, having interviewed Ben Vereen, Alan Bates, John Houston, Federico Fellini, Frank Zappa, Alvin Ailey, and Agnes de Mille. Norma resides in New York City, and can frequently be see on the dance floors of the local discos. I interviewed Norma in her living room.

46

Frank Hogan was born in Somerville, Massachusetts, on June 6, 1916. He graduated from Vesper Geirge Art School in 1939. He wrote and staged the musical Bars and Strips as his graduation project. In 1945 he won a prize for a one-act play.

In 1946, Frank moved to New York City where he freelanced, selling scripts to CBS Network Radio, articles to Coronet Magazine, and jingles to Towle Silver. In 1947, he worked as a promotion writer for Mutual Broadcasting.

From 1949 until 1961, Frank was employed by McCall's. While there he set up the Award to Women in Radio and T.V.; interviewed the Duchess of Windsor and Eleanor Roosevelt; arranged and produced the Teacher of the Year Award; and in 1959, became senior editor of the magazine.

Frank freelanced from 1961 until 1962, when he was hired by WPAT. While there he wrote the play Moiri McCree Loves Me and interviewed a number of individuals, including Paul Newman, Tennessee Williams, and Rosemary Harris.

Frank began freelancing again in 1969. He wrote three one-act plays. In 1968, he wrote Finn McKool, which was produced at the O'Neil National Playwriter's Conference. Frank has written for Life, The Wall Street Journal, and House Beautiful. Frank is a responsive person who often demonstrates his caring in his political commentary. He is currently living in New York City, and is writing a biography. The interview with Frank was conducted in his living room.

Rowena Reed was born in Kansas City. She attended the University of Missouri from 1918 until 1921, Kansas City Art Institute from 1922 until 1925, and the Art Students League from 1925 until 1926. She was a student of Alexander Archipenko from 1929 until 1930, of Hans Hofmann from 1931 until 1932, and of Alexander Kostellow from 1936 until 1939.

Rowena's experience with education continued, but as a teacher rather than a student. She has been a professor in the Department of Industrial Design at Pratt Institute since 1938. From 1962 until 1966, she was chairperson of that department. Rowena founded the school of three dimensional design, and in addition to her work at Pratt, she teaches three dimensional design to private students in New York City. Some of the companies for which Rowena has worked as a design consultant are General Motors, United States Glass Company, George Kress Associates, Donald Deskey Associates, La Verne Associates, and Alexander Kostellow Associates.

Rowena has judged numerous art exhibits and has lectured extensively. She won the Founder's Day Award from Pratt in 1972, and was the first educator to receive the Industrial Design Society of America Award, also in 1972. She received the Golden Apple Award for outstanding contribution to the field of industrial design in 1978, and became a fellow for the Industrial Designers Society of America in 1981. She has been featured in several publications, including Industrial Design Magazine, in 1982, and Innovation, The Journal of the Industrial Designers Society of America, in 1983. Rowena currently teaches at Pratt and lives and works in her loft in the SoHo district of New York City. She continues to be an innovator in the fields of industrial design and education. Rowena was interviewed in her loft.

As the above individuals are coresearchers, I am a correspondent. I was a vital part of the interviews, and, for that reason, I shall include a brief biographical sketch of myself.

I was born in North Carolina in 1951. I graduated from Limestone College, in 1973, with a Bacholor of Arts in Theatre Arts. My specialty area was play production. I was captain of The Instant Theatre Team, a traveling improvisational acting troop, and President of the Tau Psi Chapter of Alpha Psi Omega,

48

and honorary dramatics fraternity. I did a small amount of professional acting during that time. I graduated from the University of North Carolina at Charlotte with a Master of Human Development and Learning degree in 1979. My specialty area was group counseling. In June of 1987, I was awarded a Ph.D. from the University of Georgia. My specialty areas were research methodologies, creative education, and expressive psychotherapies.

I studied dance most of my youth and now enjoy ballet from the audience. I paint and write poetry and short stories for pleasure. I enjoy reading, especially novels and non-fiction in the areas of psychology, philosophy, and metaphysics. I enjoy listening to music, especially rock and roll, and dancing. I live in Atlanta, Georgia. I am involved in business, teaching, and have a private practice as a psychotherapist. I see individuals, couples, and groups. I plan to begin a new book in the fall of 1988.

Data Collection Procedures

The interviews usually were conducted in the homes or offices of the respondents. Interviewing in surroundings familiar to these people supported their feelings of comfort and privacy. Because it was important for these individuals to express their experiences and perceptions of themselves, their environments, personal histories, and creative processes, a sense of comfort was important.

The interview guide incorporated questions designed to address a variety of the respondent's experiences. It dealt with history, perceptions, worldview, private and personal experiences, thoughts, feelings, and behaviors. The original interview guide was generated during a class taught by Judith Goetz. All the class members were, at the time of the class, involved in their own qualitative research projects. In addition to having knowledge of the field of qualitative research, most of the members of the class had studied creative thinking with Paul Torrance. These fellow researchers were actively involved in the development of the interview guide, and I am grateful to them for their assistance.

Pilot interviews were conducted with creative people during this process. The people interviewed during the pilot study were: Mary Jo O'Niell of Atlanta, Georgia, designer; R. Scott Cole of Charlotte, North Carolina, artist, musician, and psychotherapist; Beth Heywood, of Pawley's Island, South Carolina, writer and poet; Joel Arkin of Gastonia, North Carolina, clothing designer, musician, and businessperson; Jennifer Caldwell also of Gastonia, businessperson and artist; Alan Robbins of Atlanta, Georgia, designer and businessperson; Lori Thomas of Atlanta, Georgia, professional designer and project manager; and John Rosemond of Gastonia, North Carolina, musician, writer, and child psychologist. The pilot study afforded me the opportunity to experiment with a variety of questions in order to determine which ones would be most fruitful as well as an opportunity to develop a sense of comfort with the interview and the interviewing process. After each of the pilot interviews I discussed the interview with the respondent. I found their input valuable in the development of the interview, and I am grateful to these people for their help.

The interview guide is unstructured and open-ended. It changed slightly throughout the interview process as a result of the information gained in previous interviews. The guide is included as Appendix A.

After a brief introduction with each respondent, the interviews began. Before an interview began, each respondent was assured of receiving a copy of the transcript in order to edit it before any sections were quoted. In this way the respondents felt free to talk openly without concern that they might disclose information they wished held in confidence.

The amount of time spent building rapport before the interview varied from person to person, and ran anywhere from 5 to 30 minutes. The interviews lasted an average of about 3 hours and 30 minutes. The longest interviews were with Patricia Sun and Frank Hogan, lasting over 4 hours. The shortest was with Carl Rogers and ran 2 and 1/2 hours. The interview with Carl ended before it was completed because he was tired. All interviews were recorded on an audio tape machine and at a later time, were transcribed by one of 2 professional transcribers. These transcripts, along with relevant literature and later communication with the respondents, comprised the data.

Limitations

Data collection procedures can affect the validity of any study. "Although the problems of reliability threaten the credibility of much ethnographic [qualitative] work, validity may be its major strength" (LeCompte & Goetz, 1982, p. 43). One reason is "informant interviewing... necessarily is phrased more closely to the empirical categories of participants and is formed less abstractly than instruments used in other research designs" (p. 43). One way in which internal reliability was increased in this study was by the use of an audiotape recorder. In this way the raw data were preserved and precise transcripts were made possible.

Internal validity is sensitive to data collection procedures. The same areas that present problems in experimental design present problems in qualitative design, although they are dealt with differently. These are history and maturation, observer effects, selection and regression, and spurious conclusions (LeCompte & Goetz, 1982).

In this research, history and maturation might have a slight effect. The possibility does exist that some coresearchers might have had a change of mind about some of the ideas or thoughts they presented. My continuous contact with the respondents for some time after they received copies of their interviews offered some control of this factor. Because each individual was older than 38, some stability in their opinions and perceptions could be expected.

Observer effects may have had an influence. The maturity level and self-actualizing tendencies of the coresearchers make it unlikely they would have altered a response to influence my opinion of them.

Selection has been discussed in a previous section. It is unlikely regression would pose a threat in this design. There was only one group, and no treatments were administered. Spurious conclusions are possible; however, this limitation pertains to data analysis, and will be discussed in that section.

Data Analysis

The process of analyzing the data began with the verbatim transcription of all the interviews, each one after it was completed. After each interview was typed, it was read. Insights about the interview itself and the process of interviewing were applied to the following interviews. Once four interviews were transcribed, the process of inductive and logical analysis as described by Patton (1980) began. The coding and analysis of data were performed throughout the collection process. Quoting Glaser and Strauss (1967), "The generation of theory, coupled with the notion of theory as process, requires that all three operations be done together as much as possible" (p.43). During the process of analysis, it is important for the researcher to remain open to any categories that might exist, without committing to any one (Glaser & Strauss, 1967).

Once all the interviews were completed, the transcripts again were read, and then the data were sorted and resorted according to categories. Throughout this process old categories were eliminated and new ones created. Connections surfaced, and these were viewed logically and in relationship to currently existing theories. The "focus on the emergence of categories solves the problems of fit, relevance, forcing, and richness" (Glaser & Strauss, 1967 p. 37).

Limitations

Using logic, intuition, and analytical skills, my perceptions of the respondents' experiences of creativity were compared, contrasted, and synthesized. Themes and patterns that seemed to arise were identified, and I generated inductive statements about them. Spurious conclusions are possible, because I brought with me to the analysis knowledge, prejudices, experiences, and beliefs which colored my perceptions. I attempted to keep my prejudices from presenting themselves during the gathering and initial analysis of the data; however, I utilized my resources, including my prejudices, during the final stages of analysis, which could operate as both a strength and a weakness in this work.

Conclusions

In concluding this chapter, I wish to address the idea of theory. When doing research of this nature, it is important to be aware of the theories in existence, without allowing them to dramatically color one's thinking about the area under investigation. There are four theorists whose ideas about creativity have influenced my thinking. They are Jung, Maslow, Arieti, and Torrance. These theorists were discussed briefly in Chapter 2. The effect of this influence is reflected in the questions included in the interview guide as well as in the analysis of the data. Several questions were added to the guide to include issues discussed by these writers. These questions were worded in a manner that did not influence the respondent to agree with any particular idea about creativity. In Chapters 4 through 9, my statements of concept are sometimes resultant of my theoretical perspective.

Summary

An exploratory investigation into the nature of creativity was undertaken through a multiple case study format. Interviews were conducted with 11 especially creative individuals, and were analyzed qualitatively using inductive analysis. Categories of phenomena were developed from the data, themes and patterns were discussed, and finally, theory was generated to explain the findings.

Chapter 4 is the first chapter containing data. The data have been divided topically, with chapters 4 through 8 consisting of questions and responses from the transcripts, as well as comments about them. In each of the five chapters containing data, large portions of interviews are reported, and because of the conversational nature of the interviews, topics other than the ones directly addressed in a particular chapter may be briefly mentioned. Chapter 9 presents my conclusions, including the answers to the research questions first stated in Chapter 1.

The following chapter, Chapter 4, addresses the effects of relationships on creative development. It also contains the descriptions of the respondents childhoods. Chapter 4 is the first of five chapters primarily containing direct quotations from the interviews and discussions about these, followed by preliminary concepts and explanatory hyphotheses.

CHAPTER 4

CHILDHOOD HISTORIES
AND THE EFFECTS OF RELATIONSHIPS

This chapter presents the interview questions and responses about the coresearchers' childhoods. It addresses the question of a mentor. Large portions of the interviews are included because they provide the reader with additional insight into these creative peoples' personal experience of childhood and the influence of their childhood relationships with their friends and families on the growth of their creativity.

The research question presented in Chapter 1 that relates to the portions of the interviews recorded or discussed in this chapter is: In what ways have creative people been influenced by relationships? This question is considered as it relates to childhood relationships and experiences. It also includes the idea of a mentor, because a relationship with a mentor has been considered important in creative development (Torrance, 1984). The primary areas of investigation under which this question falls are (a) life occurrences affecting creativity, (b) self-perceptions and identity, and (c) similarities and uniqueness in creative individuals.

Childhood

The first respondent to be quoted is the industrial designer, Niels Diffrient. In the following segment, Niels describes his childhood in a small town in Mississippi and in Detroit. His exceptionality was noticed early in his life; however, he reported his perception that little was done to encourage its development. His father did provide him with materials with which to work, and his artistic pursuits were not discouraged. His parents were often surprised and pleased by his childhood artistic productions. Niels was the oldest child. His first sibling was born when he was 15; like George Leonard, he said it was as if his parents had two families.

LM: I'd like you to talk about your childhood. If you could, describe your family, siblings, where you lived, and in what kind of environment you were reared.

ND: Well, I was born in a little place called Star, Mississippi. There were about 200 people there. It was a little sawmill town and farm center. My father had lived there, and his parents were farmers, my mother's parents were farmers, all the relatives were farmers, but my father couldn't make much of a living. It was during the Depression. He had heard that you could get jobs in the north, in Detroit, working on the automobile assembly lines. He went there to get a job. While I was in Mississippi, and the first time I knew I could do something others couldn't do was, I drew a picture out of a book. I looked at the picture in the book and I drew it. It didn't occur to me that this was anything unusual. I wasn't pleased with myself or anything. It was just for amusement. I was 3 or 4 years old. And everybody else--I still can remember--was amazed. A neighbor came over and argued with my father, telling him there was no way I could have drawn that picture. And he was saying, "No, I saw it with my own eyes." It was a picture of a bird. And not just any bird sitting on a limb, but a bird flying. We had two books on the place: one was the Bible and the other was a Sears and Roebuck catalogue. My bible was the catalogue. I would spend hours looking at that catalogue. I think I got something of a rudimentary education from looking at that catalogue.

Although he did not have a great many books available to him as a child, Niels was sensitive to what was available. His father provided him with different types of paper, and he used these resources to develop his skills. His father's providing these materials, combined with his parents showing his construction to neighbors, may have served as subtle reinforcement to continue his experimentation and growth.

ND: I can't remember the actual age when we moved to Detroit because I still spent summers in Mississippi on the farm. Another thing that happened that was unusual--the place we lived, in the dining room there was a big round oak table, and at one point--well, my father would bring home odds and ends for me to work with because I was always drawing and building models. Once he was able to bring home a lot of sheets of cardboard, the kind you put shirts in, and rolls of water-wetted tape, sticky tape I call it--you know, you put water on it and it sticks. I started fooling around with this stuff. One thing led to another, and I ended up covering the entire top of the dining table with this factory, starting out with this truck. I built all the buildings, little conveyors and ramps. To me this was just sheer amusement. But my father and mother would bring in the neighbors to see the construction. I remember that they ultimately gave me $5 to get rid of it because it kept them from eating off the dining table for months.

Another time, my father brought in some rolls of wallpaper because the back side was plain, and I could draw on it. By this time, I had fallen in love with airplanes, and I was acquiring various magazines and the like showing airplanes of the time. I was absorbing the way they were made and built. After I had drawn a little while on the back of this wallpaper, it occurred to me that since it was a roll and quite wide, I could tape it up on the wall and draw a full-size airplane. It wasn't really full-sized, but to my small scale--I was probably about six or so. I wanted it full size, at least to my scale. So I drew it, and it was apparently pretty accurate. Again, my parents were overwhelmed. It had a fully detailed engine on it, more or less copied out of the magazine, but it was pretty realistic as I have it in my mind. It wasn't long after that that I was introduced to the availability of model airplane building. The first thing I did, in my ignorance of the situation, was to buy some blocks of wood, from which I carved out an airplane. It was reasonably good, but it was crude because I wasn't used to it. Then I found out there were kits you could buy. Well, that launched me into a career of model airplane building that lasted until I started high school. I built every manner of airplane you could name. I was enthralled with it. Every penny I could get, every present I got, had something to do with a model airplane. That led to eventually buying little gasoline engines and entering contests and winning awards. I did that for many years. In my spare time, I would draw airplanes. By that time, I was meeting other little boys that could draw, and we had drawing contests.

Living in a simple family and still spending quite a bit of my spare time down on the farm, my ignorance of the world was pretty complete. I knew nothing about what I was headed for, and my parents were unable to tell me anything about the future. But a sort of determining event occurred when I was in junior high school, seventh grade through ninth grade. At the end, I remember being called into the principal's office. He congratulated me that I had won a scholarship. I didn't know what that meant. I sat and listened, and he said, "The Ford Motor Company has presented you with a scholarship because you have the best overall grades and manual skills." I still didn't know what that meant. I took the piece of paper home, and my father saw it and went through the roof. He thought it was the most wonderful thing that could happen to a young boy. He didn't explain to me what it meant, except to say, that, well, he'd been working on the assembly line for so many years and he was still just working his way up, but he said if I went to this trade school, I would automatically be a foreman when I graduated in the Ford plant. And a foreman, to him, was a sort of a god, the man who had control of a large number of others, so that was something to aspire to.

Well, sure enough I went and reported to the Ford Motor Company on the day I was supposed to go. I had just finished junior high school. I have to confess, I was so ignorant about how things were, with no aid from my parents, and their friends were all working-class people, so they didn't know anything about all this. It never occurred to me that there was another choice, high school or some other direction to go in. I just followed whatever occurred. So this occurred, and I went, and the first thing that happened when we arrived was that we walked through a factory building and passed row upon row of young boys, my age or older, at machines. It was acres of these young boys at all these machines, standing there at a lathe or a drill press. This impressed me and I guess in a deep way oppressed me at the same time. We passed all that and went up these steps into another area of this factory building and got to the medical center. The nurse came in and asked a lot of questions about our family and medical history and what-have-you. When she finished that she said, "Okay, boys, strip." We stood there dumbfounded, and she said, "Take your clothes off. You're going to get a medical examination." So I stood there a little while, and the other boys began taking their clothes off. I got up and walked out, down the steps, out past all the boys, out of the factory, got on the streetcar and went home. I don't know what drove me to do it. At the time, I thought I was afraid to take my clothes off. When I got home--of course I broke down in tears and was really chagrined at myself, thought I was a coward, afraid to face it and all. But something inside of me knew that I didn't want to be there. Of course, my father blew up and wouldn't talk to me for a long time. But the result was I had to go on to high school and...

LM: Did you, as a child, as an adolescent or a young adult, have a dream or vision about your future?

ND: No. I had fantasies, but they were nothing like what I'm doing. I was the kind of child that looked forward to going to bed, only for one reason: to fantasize, to dream. Fantasizing carried me into worlds beyond.

Educator and writer Paul Torrance, also grew up on a farm in the South, and, like Niels, he demonstrated creativity at an early age. Also like Niels, Paul did not perceive of himself as receiving any special guidance because of this attribute. Whereas Niels's creativity was expressed in art and spatial relationships, Paul's was expressed in school and practical problem solving.

Like Niels, Paul began an output of creativity early in life. Both men received an education because they did not follow in their family's path. Niels, to his father's dismay at the time, did not use the trade school scholarship offered to him by the Ford Motor Company. Paul, because of his learning disability, could not farm and instead sought an education.

Paul was the oldest child in his family, with one sister 4 years younger. Paul mentioned competition several times during the interview.

> PT: I think I probably am creative, and I think that probably throughout my whole life that one of my personal strengths has been my creativity. When I was in school and tested for intelligence, I always came out fairly well, but not as well as suggested by my grades and some other things. As I look back over my education, when I was in courses where the grading was really difficult, it was my creativity that got me the grade. And in those courses where the competition was stiff and I didn't have a chance to use my creativity, then I made B's. So I think that was one of the early signals I got that my creativity was one of my strengths.

> LM: Were you aware of that then?

> PT: No, I don't think I was and I think it caused me some pain that I really didn't need to suffer. Because it was disappointing to work very hard on

a course and then be graded by a multiple choice or a true/false test and not have a chance to really show the depth that I had attained in the course. When I look back on it now I see that it was my creativity that made the difference and gave me the superiority over the people that I was competing with.

LM: Did you have brothers and sisters?

PT: I had one sister. Four years younger.

LM: Did you spend a lot of time together as children?

PT: A good bit. There were just the two of us, and we were on a farm so we were fairly isolated. There was nobody else to spend time with. My father was the oldest child in his family, so that made me the first grandchild in his family. My mother's family was somewhat different. She was about a middle child. Both of them had an eighth grade education. That was the most that you could get in those days in rural schools. I thought I would also farm. I guess very early I didn't know anything else. Then it became clear I was never going to make a living being a farmer, and so my father said I had better learn how to eat peas with a fork. And get an education. And so thereafter I pretty much...well, the decision had been made. It kind of was the blueprint for the rest of my life.

LM: How old were you then?

PT: I was about 12 or 13.

LM: When you were a child did your family think of you as being creative?

PT: No, I don't think so.

LM: Is there anyone else in your family that you would describe as artistic or creative?

PT: I always thought my mother was creative, but she never had the chance for any artistic or musical or any other kind of training beyond eighth grade. The way she did things and the way she decorated the house and designed things was creative.

LM: You were talking about being a "minority of one" as a child, and feeling very different than the other children. Was there some way that you felt similar to other children?

PT: Well, I was poor and they were poor. So in that way we were alike. I guess I was probably more aware of the differences. In many thousands of ways I was made aware of that.

LM: You said earlier that you had a lot of work around the farm milking cows and other things.

PT: Yes.

LM: So you had to do a lot of problem solving?

PT: Yes. It was tested all the time.

LM: In a way it was a hardship, and in a way it was very facilitating?

PT: Probably so.

LM: Some of the things that you said of your childhood have led me to think that perhaps you spent a great deal of time alone when you were a child?

PT: Yeah.

LM: Do you think that fact, that you spent a great deal of time alone, had an influence on your development?

PT: Yes, I think so.

LM: In what way?

PT: Well, for example when I was 10 years old, I had an appendectomy. I had a drainage for about 6 or 7 months afterwards and couldn't do much strong physical activity and missed about 4 or 5 months from school. I did a lot of writing in this time and read many books and criticized the books. I think the skills that I was practicing at that time helped me later on.

LM: How old were you when you first started writing?

PT: Well, I was about 10 years old at that particular time. I did a good bit of writing when I was in the 3rd grade because I had a teacher that imposed it.

Wendy Palmer, who now teaches aikido, practices counseling, and conducts trainings with psychotherapists, grew up in a more affluent environment in the Midwest; however, she also faced hardship. She attributes her creativity partly to this early hardship. Wendy was the younger of two sisters;

however, she accepted the role of caretaker of a terminally ill parent. Both Wendy Palmer and Patricia Sun mentioned the importance of using adversity as opportunity.

WP: I have a hard time working with success. As I see it, that is because in my early childhood it was set up that in order to work effectively, I had to be a good struggler. I had a difficult childhood--my mother had MS, so I helped to take care of her. Having an invalid mother seemed like a big problem. What it did was, in the end, I'm going to digress a little bit, was it gave me a gift. She had a hard time communicating. She couldn't talk after I was about 12, and I never saw her walk. So I had to learn how to communicate and pick up intuitively what was going on with her. What seemed to be the great problem of my early childhood turned out to be the gift and the thing that allows me to be a good teacher and communicator and I guess creative, in some sense.

I rode horses as a youngster. When dealing with something that's larger than you are, you have to have a lot of energetic finesse. You can't fight a horse--that's ridiculous. You need to be able to work with them. So I guess that was sort of special. I also grew up in a very wealthy midwestern town, so that material things were not an issue. We had all the best doctors for my mother. That was a great gift, because down the line I've lived many different ways and now, of course, I'm in the middle. At one point, I was a hippie on welfare. I have seen that it is not the material possessions that make it one way or another, because in the town where I grew up, people had lots of whatever they wanted and they weren't necessarily happy. In fact, not quite as happy as some of the people I've been around who have had less. There are always exceptions to that. So it was an interesting childhood. It had both a lot in the area of having everything I wanted on the material plane, and very little in the area of the emotional support, and a rich connection to animals. I was fortunate to be able to have horses and ride.

LM: Your sister was younger?

WP: She's 2 1/2 years older.

LM: Your father was present when you were growing up?

WP: Yes, he was around. He was a corporation lawyer. Worked very hard taking care of my mother. I felt, I mean he went to the city every day to do his job, but he would come back and get her out of bed and feed her and take care of her and was quite devoted actually. He drank a lot, had mistresses. But, you know, he also could have put her in an institution. He hung in for 20 years.

LM: And so your mother died when you were how old?

WP: Twenty. It gave me a very positive thing, which is that death can be wonderful. It was such a relief when she died. It was such a wonderful release. Also, I know it can be terrible, but I don't have this black negative attitude toward death because that experience was positive. I had communication with her the night after she died. She came and visited me, her spirit. My grandfather was this really wonderful physician, very highly respected, and his daughter had this incredible and difficult disease that he couldn't deal with. He was the town physician. His funeral was so--I mean the whole town came out for it. He was really a wonderful man.

LM: Where did you grow up?

WP: Lake Forest, Illinois.

LM: Did you feel alike or different as a child?

WP: One of my friends was very deeply into horses. I related quite strongly to her. We had a nice friendship. But mostly, I felt by myself a lot, in my own world. I guess I can remember being very young, 2 or 3, and thinking, looking up at all these big adults, and thinking they are not telling the truth. It was heavy to me. It was like I knew they were feeling one thing and saying another. So I always knew they could be manipulated. I sort of resented them for that. Sometimes they called me a little witch because I could always see the truth. Most adults were really easy to manipulate because they were split with themselves, so in that way I did feel isolated and different. I saw most people sort of going along with what looked like a game on the outside. I felt I could read through it. Also, I had an intense spiritual relationship, I guess you could say with God. I was very mad at Him doing that to my mother. That also felt very different from anybody I knew. There were people who either liked it or didn't, but I really liked it and at the same time, I was very angry so I would go to church and pray angrily. It was an interesting kind of set up. That made me feel different too.

LM: Did you feel, you said you had one friend involved in horses with whom you experienced some closeness--did you feel other similarities to other children as well? Or was it more a feeling of being different?

WP: Mostly I felt pretty different.

LM: When you were growing up, did your friends or family or anyone with whom you were close think of you as being creative?

WP: Yeah, a real go-getter. They always thought of me as being a go-getter, wanting to do something and going after it. That was always my style. I can spend years and not get discouraged.

LM: You've said already that your mother had multiple sclerosis, that it was a very different childhood.

WP: There are a couple of things outstanding about it. Between my sister and I, we behaved very differently in the situation. I didn't take on a surrogate-type mother. I remained very independent and anti authoritarian during it. It was sort of the good son my father always wanted. I felt like I was on the front lines taking care of my mother and sister. Where I put most of my emotional attachment, I think, was into the horses. I was a very devoted horseback rider.

LM: What is your sense of being alike and different from other adults?

WP: Mostly I've been friends with guys. This was my one good friend from my whole background that

I've stayed in touch with. She's in L. A. Most of my friends are guys, and I like to do a lot of guy stuff. I like to windsurf and aikido and do that kind of thing. That seemed to me more simple and straightforward and a little bit easier to relate to. I don't meet too many other people that I feel have the energy level that I do, that want to keep going and doing and exploring all these new things. I like the feeling of being into something intensely and exploring and pushing the edge. That's a really great feeling, and so it seems like about every 3 or 4 years, I get a new obsession. Now it's windsurfing; I'm a total addict. I'm fortunate because here in the Bay, there are some of the best winds in the world under the Golden Gate. The wind really comes through there, and it's such a beautiful environment. The big towers and huge supertankers going through. It's really exciting. So I feel myself as being different in that way. I don't have a lot of close friends. I have very few close friends. When I get insecure or if I'm not feeling really good, I would never make a phone call and call someone and say I'm not feeling good. I would only call someone if I was feeling good.

One person who has influenced me is my godfather, who is the most creative man I know. He's a modern Michelangelo. He was DuPont's leading designer and still consults with them. He just had his 79th birthday. The most fascinating characteristic about him is his tremendous interest, fascination with the ongoing process of life. Now he is almost 80 and has tremendous energy. and it's not like he knows it all yet. He knows quite a bit, but he's fascinated still. He is still drawing and painting and carving. He has developed a floating house. He was the first man to do that, a prototype, years ago, when I was about 7. You could helicopter into lakes and let it go and it would float. All the furniture was styrofoam. Then he made these huge statues out of styrofoam, sprayed them with brass and fixed them in a fountain so that when the water hit them, they would turn. For me, just to be able to continue the fascination and the interest, that continued wealth of possibilities that come through him. So I would say interest, excitement, openness, and then on top of that, you really have to have whatever that thing is, you can go the distance with it. My joke and what I tell the students about--anyone who ever took LSD in the sixties has had a million insights. In a way, they are a dime a dozen if there isn't some kind of embodiment. You have to bring your fascination and interest and excitement through to manifestation.

LM: Are there others--he's your godfather--are there people in your family who are creative?

WP: Well, like I said--it's interesting. The only living member of my family is a politician. He's a senator in Washington. He's very controversial, but actually as I get older and older, I realize he is creative and he's very exceptional. He's a very energetic guy, very devoted, and I think that's an aspect of creativity. My grandmother. She did that screen; she did many beautiful rugs, chairs. She stood out as a creative person in that way. The rest of them--no.

As did Wendy Palmer and Paul Torrance, the writer and psychologist Carl Rogers had a strong sense of being different from other children. He also described his childhood as unusual, and he demonstrated intellectual superority at an early age.

CR: I was the fourth of six children, all boys except one older sister. By the time I was 5 or 6, we were living in a very nice home in a nice suburb. I don't remember much about those days, not nearly as much as I do when I was 13 and we moved to the farm about 30 miles from Chicago. They had both been, my mother especially, reared on a farm. My father was very close to the farm. Part of it was a hobby for him and to them, for him primarily; and part of it was to get the children away from what they regarded as the evils of suburban life. As I look back, it seemed pretty clean to me, the evils of suburban life compared to now. They were quite fundamentalist in their thinking. We belonged to the Congregational Church. There was heavy emphasis on family prayers and Bible reading and a long series of things we do not do in our family. We don't drink, we don't smoke, we don't go to the movies much, we don't even drink carbonated drinks. And as a boy, and this is important too, it wasn't until much later that I really rebelled against any of that, partly because we were a close family unit. My parents certainly cared well for their children. I don't remember much physical expression from either one of them, but as I look back, I realize that they showed a lot of interest in us, reading us stories and so on. We traveled a lot. Most of the discipline was from Mother. She was not so much strict as righteous; however, there were so many things that were not good. Father never revealed anything significant to Mother because he would be sure to be judged. It might possibly be judged as being right, but much more likely it would be judged as being wrong. So my life was very much an inner life. I was very absentminded, because I was always a daydreamer.

LM: You were talking about being an absentminded child. Would your peers in school have said that you were absentminded? Is that how they might have classified you, stereotyped you?

CR: They possibly would have. I think people would be more likely to say I was shy and didn't have many friends, which would have been true, partly because we should come right home from school because there were always chores to do. So we didn't stay around and play with kids, and because the morals of most others were suspect, we weren't encouraged to go to other friends' homes either. I remember being at friends' homes only a few times. One of my mother's family prayers was "Come out ye from among them and be ye separate." She felt that we had to be separate and different.

LM: It's good for you that you had some brothers and sisters.

CR: I was going to say, that's what made up for it. I greatly admired my oldest brother, and my two younger brothers who were a little younger, we gradually formed quite a trio. There were lots of family activities, so I wasn't without social activities or social interaction, but a lot of it was with family members.

LM: Did you have a sense of being different than the other children, or was that more influenced by your mother, that you would be separate from other children?

CR: Yes, I do have a sense of being different in the respect that being the fourth of six children it would be hard to imagine that I was adopted, but that is what I thought. They would have to be somewhat weird parents to do that, but I felt that I didn't quite belong, that I was in some way different. I didn't feel like I was loved as much as my older brother. So I had the theory that I was probably adopted.

LM: You felt different from children not only outside of your family, but different than the other children in your family as well. Were you a good student?

CR: Without exception, everybody in the family was a good student. I remember my oldest brother made the highest score on the Army Alpha Test at Camp Grant. I was proud of that. I never had trouble with studies. In fact, I have no idea how I learned to read. I just know that I was reading a big thick Bible storybook before school, so it's real strange. We weren't an intellectual family. My parents used to scorn book learning. And yet there were all these magazines, and I read. Now that my vision is not so good, it's just a treat--I have some large print that I can read--and it's such a treat to get really involved in a book again that I forget everything that is going on. As a boy, I would read two or three books a week.

LM: Reading is a very personal experience. Very private.

CR: Yeah, it is.

Rowena Reed, teacher and industrial designer, grew up in an affluent, creative environment. Unlike Carl Rogers, Paul

Torrance, or Wendy Palmer, she did not feel especially different from other children. Rowena had friends and a happy childhood. Like Niels Differient, who also is an industrial designer, she demonstrated an interest in and ability for art as a child. Rowena Reed attended church with her parents, and like Frank Hogan, Tom Robbins and Carl Rogers grew critical of their religion later in life, although Rowena, unlike Carl, rebelled against the people, not the beliefs. As was true for several respondents, Rowena's family cared for her, but were not demonstratively affectionate. She has always liked interesting people and prefers to avoid people who do not express unusual ideas. Rowena is the oldest of three children. Although she did not want a traditional education, her father insisted she go to college before art school. Like Niels's parents, Rowena's parents seemed to like the things she made, and as was true for Niels, the reinforcement she received from them was subtle.

LM: What is your fondest childhood memory?

RR: I don't know. I don't know whether it's the fondest or not, but it's kind of an interesting memory. One time I was sent to a girls' camp, and I was getting kind of bored. I started wandering around the campgrounds, and they had tents of all different kinds of activities. I wandered into one, and they were all making little pots, ceramics, out of clay. I thought, "Where has this been all my life? Why didn't somebody tell me about this?" That was my first introduction to three dimensional design.

LM: Were other members of your family artistic or creative?

RR: Well, there was an uncle, my mother's brother, who was a professional artist--painter. I considered my mother creative in a different way. She was very good with words. She didn't really write professionally. She wasn't strong minded enough to protest her life, but I think she might have. My father was creative as a scientist. He was very original. He was in <u>Who's Who</u>. I don't think it matters particularly what branch of creativity it is. I consider creativity originality, imagination, and intelligence, don't you? All those things. Imagination, first of all, but it has to be a personal, original kind of imagination, an original way of looking at life.

LM: Was art an interest for you as a child?

RR: Oh yes.

LM: Can you remember about how old you were when you first started showing interest?

RR: I guess I was somewhere in elementary school.

LM: Did your parents encourage your art?

RR: They thought it was alright, except they didn't take it seriously. They just thought it was nice and fun. I guess they liked the little things I did in school. But there was one thing I wanted to mention. When it came time for me to go to college, I didn't really want to go to college. I didn't go to a private school. There was only one in Kansas City, and it was too far away. I wanted to go directly to an art school. Then my father stepped in, not in a dominating way at all, but he said you will go to college.

LM: In what ways were you alike and different from other children?

75

RR: I find it hard to say. I was kind of smart. I don't think I was ever number one in my class, but I was consistently number two. I often wondered about that.

LM: So you didn't feel particularly different?

RR: No, I don't think so.

LM: Would you describe your childhood as happy?

RR: Yes. I guess I had my little disappointments. I never thought I was very pretty. Maybe I wasn't, but by today's standard I would be considered pretty. But that was not the standard at that time.

LM: Did you have a large group of social friends?

RR: Oh yes, we always belonged to...the kind of school I went to, we always belonged to clubs. I went to two elementary schools because we moved. I went to nice little clubs. In fact, the club that I belonged to when I was about 12 years old, I still am in touch with some of those people. Then there was a club in high school, and when I got to college, there was a sorority.

LM: When you were living at home, where did you live? Here in New York?

RR: No, I was born and brought up in Kansas City. If you dare say Kansas City is in Kansas, I'll never speak to you again! I think I had an ideal family life. My mother and father were both intelligent and very kind people.

LM: So you were the eldest of how many children?

RR: Three. One sister, one brother.

LM: You were born and how many years later was the next child born?

RR: Five years later. I was the eldest. That was a girl. My brother was born 3 years later.

LM: When you were growing up, did you get along with your brother and sister?

RR: Oh yes, I got along fine with them. They didn't get along with each other. They were too close together. They were competitive siblings. After they were grown up, they became very fond of each other, but they were not very happy together as children.

LM: So they fought, and you got along with both of them?

RR: Oh yeah. Here I was, the superior older. I suppose I did have my problems; I know I thought I did at the time, but I can't remember what they were. My father was a doctor. My mother would have loved to have a professional degree of some kind. She would have loved to have gone to college, but in her family at that time, they sent the two brothers to college, but it was just about 5 or 10 years too early, and they were not sending girls to college. They didn't think that would be a nice thing for her to do, to go to college.

LM: And your mother and father, were they close to the same age?

RR: I think my father was older. I'm trying to remember. I don't remember ages very well. I think he was 8 or 9 years older.

LM: Was your family religious?

RR: Yes, they were. They went to church regularly, and I went along with them. I thought it was alright, although I guess I got critical. I've always been critical, and that's been my fault. I don't keep quiet. I didn't mind the church services. I thought they were sometimes interesting, but I got bored with the people. I thought the kind of people who went to church were not the kind of people that I wanted to really have as my friends. They were not stimulating; they were too nice, too good, too quiet, or whatever. After I grew up and was married, I guess I fell away from it because I didn't find a group to be associated with in religion. I like to read religious books. My mother was genuinely religious. After my father died, he died when she was in middle life, it was quite a comfort to her.

LM: Did you go to church because you chose to or did they make you go?

RR: They didn't make me go. I just took it for granted that you do what your family did. It wasn't such a big deal, you know.

LM: Did your family consider you creative?

RR: I don't think they would have used that word. Yes, I think they thought I was unusual, but they were not very demonstrative. They showed their affection in many ways, but they did not just say, "We think you are wonderful."

78

Two aspects of playwright and biographer Frank Hogan's early life seem to have influenced his development: his Catholic upbringing and his subsequent rebellion against it, and his powerful sibling rivalry with his older brother, Bill. Like Paul Torrance, he mentioned competition during the interview; however, unlike Paul, Frank withdrew from competition until he was an adult. His homosexuality was a strong influence as an adolescent and into adulthood. His family's political involvement has affected Frank. His subject matter is often political. Frank felt very different from other children, and he did not have friends or participate in games. Frank, the psychologist Carl Rogers, and the writer Tom Robbins, were reared in a restrictive religious environment, and all three rebelled against it. Education was stressed in the Hogan family. Frank is the youngest of four children.

FH: My mother's family was of Irish descent, had been in the country since the very early 1800s. My father's family came from Nova Scotia. His mother was English. His father was Irish. Both my mother's father and my father's father died when the children were very, very young. They went to grammar school together. Both were extremely poor. My father went into the Spanish American War and started writing her from there and came back and didn't contact her for years. Then he got into politics and became a city councilman, a member of the Massachusetts House of Representatives and a city assessor at Cambridge. They were married in 1909. A big fancy wedding. Years later, when my sister, Marian, was debating whether or not to marry a man she was engaged to, my father advised her, "The worst thing you can do to yourself and to him is to marry a man you don't love. I woke up the morning after my wedding and realized that I'd married the wrong woman." Their first child was a girl, Margaret, who died when she was 14 months old from whooping cough. Margaret would be 2 years older than my brother Bill. That would be 1910, when she was born, so she died in 1912. Bill, my brother, was born in 1912. Dorothy, my older sister, was born in 1914, both in April, he on the 14th, she on the 16th. Dorothy died about 15 years ago of cancer after 5 years of absolute hell. I am 2 years younger than Dorothy, born June 6, 1916. My father was born on June 3rd. We're both Geminis. Then Marian is 3 years younger than I am, born May 16, 1920. We were raised in East Cambridge, when my father was in politics. East Cambridge, at that time, was a melting pot area, very, very mixed.

We were Catholic, raised Catholic, my mother having great pretensions of religion. I'm not sure how much of it was true. My mother and father, neither one had any education beyond public grammar school, which I suppose was not so unusual in that day. So really, their drive was to get people educated, one way or another. There is a ritual in the Catholic Church, which you may or may not have heard of, of visiting seven churches on Holy Thursday. And we used to be able to go to seven different Catholic churches, of seven different nationalities, without walking more than 20 minutes in any direction.

Bill went to Cambridge High and Latin School, to Boston College, and then to Harvard Law School and then got into politics. Was put into politics by my father. I don't think Bill was a very good politician. Dorothy went to secretarial school. Marian turned out to be an absolute--if you're looking for more interviews, you should talk to her. She went to MIT [Massachusetts Institute of Technology] and took her master's in meteorology and then formed her own--the first--private weather forecasting company in America. I went, as we all did, to Sacred Heart Grammar School, then it was insisted that I would go to Catholic high school. At the end of my first year at St. John's High, I won my first fight--rebellion--with my parents and was "allowed" to go to Cambridge High and Latin, a public school. I remember my mother saying to me that first report-card day (I didn't do very well), sarcastically, "I hope you're happy, now." I laughed and said, "Yes, I am." And I was because I was out of the grasp of the nuns and didn't have to pretend--or to be--a goody-two-shoes altar boy any longer. And besides, I'd discovered sex, but the family, of course, didn't know that. In fact, I didn't know that sex was what I'd discovered. I was never a good student. I can remember two things about grammar school. The first day that I went to school--you've got to remember we were living in a tough neighborhood--and my mother got me dressed in a Little Lord Fauntleroy white linen suit. Don't you laugh!

LM: I see your predicament.

FH: Yeah, immediately. White linen trousers and a starched Buster Brown collar and a great big red bow necktie, silk. My father took one look at me and said, "I'm not going to be seen on the street with that kid!" Well, they had a fight over that, of course. Which isn't the greatest way to start school. We lived not far from the school, only a block, and being a Catholic school, they couldn't just start school with school--you had to go to mass first. The church was a gigantic, semi-Gothic kind of thing. And, as we arrived at the church, the place was loaded with kids, the oldest at the back, the youngest at the front, and so my father and I go down the aisle. Father Higgins, who was a big, tall, giant of a man with lots of white hair, said to my father, "That boy cannot go into the first grade. He's not old enough. He has to go to kindergarten." My father said, "He's going into the first grade." I don't know what the hell is going on, of course. I know there's a fight though. So, the big priest said, "No! He cannot go into the first grade," and my father said, "He's not going to go to someplace where he'll be playing around and making paper dolls. He's going into the first grade, or I'll take him out of here and put him in the Thorndike School--and you don't want any Hogan going to a public school." I was thinking, "Gee, that would be wonderful. That would be just great." How could I dislike the idea of a Catholic School at the age of 5? I suppose I was--and wanted to be--different from the rest of the family. But, my father won. He beat the Catholic Church right in its center aisle, in front of the altar where he and my mother had been married.

LM: Were you happy as a child?

FH: I have no idea. I guess to some extent. Home life was pretty good, as a matter of fact. One thing that always happened the first day of school...my brother was 4 years ahead of me and very bright. He was always number one in the class. He was always president of everything and still is. And the first day of school, the nun would say to me, "Oh, you're Billy Hogan's brother. You must be a very smart boy." And it wasn't until very recently that I figured out what would happen. On the first report card, I would be number 2 or 3. On the next, I'd settle back to about 13th or 15th and would stay there for the rest of the year. I finally discovered in analysis when I was close to 40 years old, that I did this deliberately. I was absolutely not going to be like my brother. Bill was a great athlete, a good athlete. Young Bill, my nephew, was a good athlete. And I would have nothing to do with that, ever. I always had the ability to write, to draw, play the piano without ever being taught anything about any of it. This was both tolerated and looked down upon in the family. My mother was afraid I was going to go out to Hollywood and marry five or six women. Little did she know that I was going to turn out totally opposite from all that.

My mother and father would fight...the arguments would explode right in the middle of dinner for no reason. Then, they wouldn't speak to each other for 4 or 5 days. We, the kids, didn't know which parent to talk to--or get caught talking to--kind of like taking sides--and they'd talk to each other through us. Partly as a result of that, I don't fight about anything. There's nothing worth fighting about. I just do and think as I want. Someone wants to disagree--good. Let 'em. Being a nonfighter is quite a weapon. It drives people crazy. This will answer part of your thing about happy childhood. We had dinner every night with the whole family. While we were not ever rich or wealthy, we ate well, we lived well, my mother worked hard.

Bill is 4 years ahead of me. He was graduating from advanced class the year I was graduating from grammar school. For the first and only time, they combined these two graduations, and he gave the graduation oration. When I was graduating from high school, he was graduating from Boston College as president of the class. Both graduations fell on the same day. His in the afternoon, mine in the evening. We went to his graduation commencement that day, and then my uncle drove me back to be in time for my graduation, and my mother, father, sisters were to follow. On the way home after graduation I said something about, "I looked for you people and couldn't see you at all." My mother said, "We were there, sitting such-and-such a place," and my father said, "We weren't there; we stayed over at Bill's graduation for the supper." I can still hear my mother's wailing, critical, "Oh, Bill..." at my father and his telling her, "Well, we weren't there and he might as well know the truth." My father had a heart attack around that time, and I think I saved his life one night by slapping him across the face and pouring a shot of whiskey down his throat, getting him into bed. The heart specialist said he had 2 months to live. The family doctor said he could cure him. He lived 35 more years. Meanwhile, the heart doctor died.

My mother was manipulative--attributing to my father words and attitudes, restrictions, disciplines which were hers not his. Withholding letters to Dorothy from her boyfriend because he wasn't Catholic...getting people to interfere--breaking up friendships between Marian and a couple of her boyfriends--not letting my "friend" into the house when he came to visit when I was sick. Not telling me he'd been there. There was, I think, a contest between Mother and Father to see which one each of us liked more.   Is that manipulative?

LM: Did you feel like other children?

FH: I didn't feel like other children in any way.

LM: No way at all?

FH: No way.

LM: How about different from other children?

FH: I always knew I was different.   I felt different, in the broadest sense of the term.   Aunt Tillie used to come down to the house quite regularly, and she would help my mother with the wash and that sort of thing...she walked me back to school after lunch.   And I, as usual, stood there. And she said, "Don't you ever play with these other kids?" It was true. I didn't. I would never have noticed this unless she pointed it out.   My mother would ask why I wouldn't go skating, go down to the park and go skating.   After my parents had worked so hard to get skates.   The skates were never my own.   They were hand-me-downs.   Not that I wanted skates.   But I was made to feel evil--guilty--because I didn't want to skate.   I just hated it. I hated the whole idea. Mother liked skating; I didn't.   I eventually taught myself to skate out in the backyard.   Marian says she can remember Ma and Pa standing in the window and laughing every time I fell down, and I wouldn't get up while they were watching me.   And I taught myself to swim eventually.   Much to my anger at the time...we used to go down to Nantasket Beach in the summertime, and there was a raft in the bay. I had swum in the ocean and was kind of pleased by having taught myself to do that, but I had never been in deep water. When I wouldn't dive in off the raft, my father threw me in. I told young Bill Hogan, my nephew, that recently when I was up in Connecticut, and he said, "Was it good or bad for you?" I said, "I don't know. I don't have any idea." I can remember how angry I was. I was furious. When we got home that Saturday afternoon, after he'd tossed me in the bay, he explained to my mother he'd thrown me in "because the other kids were laughing at me--and you don't ever let people give you the 'he-haw.'" He believed that. Lived it. Funny, I recall a priest in confession--when I was a kid and confessing that I'd played with myself, saying "You don't want to do that, the other guys will give you the 'he-haw.'" That always seemed, still seems, a dumb reason for doing or not doing something. Let 'em laugh. I was just different.

LM: You said earlier that you were not unhappy.

FH: I think I didn't know enough to be happy or unhappy. I didn't think about that.

LM: What is your fondest childhood memory?

FH: Funny, I don't have any that I am particularly fond of. I have some I don't mind. Oh, yes. One time, when we were going to the beach and started up the hill, my father said, "Watch that hill. It's just like everything bad that is going to happen to you in life. As you go up the hill, it gets smaller."

I can remember another time at the beach. My mother's mother was staying across the...the only grandmother we had, the only grandparent we had...and she took me out for a walk. We went down around the bay, or on a pier out over the water, and she bought me some chewing gum or something. Anyway, the idea was that I was allowed to throw the wrappings into the water and watch them as if they were boats getting carried along by the current under the pier. This seems to be very important, that day with my grandmother. For some reason, I was occasionally sent down to her house to stay for dinner. She was always very busy baking, doing bread and that sort of thing, and making mashed potatoes for my uncle and aunt when they came home. She would put lots of butter on top of those mashed potatoes, and then she would give me the spoon to lick. It was great.

And I have a lot of good memories of Aunt Tillie. She, I think, was probably my favorite relative. When I needed money when I was going to art school, I called her, and she loaned me the $50 I needed. I paid her back. But she said, "You're not in trouble, are you?" I said, "No, I'm not in trouble. I just need tuition money."

Novelist and artist Tom Robbins's upbringing was also influenced by his family's religion, and like Frank Hogan and Carl Rogers, he rebelled against it. Also like Frank, he spent much of time alone, but unlike Frank, he also spent time with friends. Tom began writing as a child. He describes both his parents as somewhat creative. Tom was the eldest child.

TR: My mother and father were always stinging each other, fighting for ultimate control. There was a lot of stress in the house. There was a lot of Southern Baptist pseudo-Christian repression. I have two twin sisters. I had a third sister who died when I was 7. She was 4. My twin sisters are 7 years younger that I, so we were never close.

LM: So you were the oldest. And the only son.

TR: I was treated with a lot of love and reverence by my mother. My father was a mechanical, electrical genius. I have no mechanical aptitude whatsoever.

LM: And your sisters, what are they like?

TR: I don't really know them very well. The older I got, the greater the gap. My other sister was born before my twin sisters. She died before they were born. My mother prayed that she would have twin daughters because she felt if she had only one, she would always be comparing her to the sister who died. She prayed for twin daughters and she had twin daughters--that's pretty amazing.

LM: Very amazing.

TR: Well, it isn't really. The universe always provides if you know how to ask right.

LM: Who else in your family would you describe as artistic or creative?

TR: My great-great-grandmother, Polly Elrod. She was one of the first pop artists. She lived in a cabin back in Appalachia in the mountains of North Carolina. Coves is what they call them. The particular place where she lived, the official name of it, was Buffalo Cove.

She chewed tobacco and in those days, when I was still a child, tobacco came in unwrapped plugs. Occasionally, it was wrapped in cellophane, but mostly it was unwrapped. And the way you would distinguish one brand from another would be a little tin tag with prongs on the back that you actually stuck into the plug. There was Red Apple, and that plug was red and shaped like an apple, and there was Red Dog; it was kind of a greyhound-type dog; and there was Red Jay, which was shaped like a jay bird and had the features of a jay bird, but it had black letters that said Red Jay Plug or Red Jay Chaw. My father and his father walked back into Buffalo Cove from Blowing Rock. It was like a 2-or-3 day walk to visit my father's great-grandmother Elrod. She had a stone fireplace, homemade fireplace, and it had been shaped with mud. Into the mud, she had stuck these little tin red jays so that this entire fireplace, which took up one whole wall of the cabin, was covered with these little tin red jays. I love it. A pop art tableau.

LM: What about your dad? When you were describing him earlier, you were talking about his being a mechanical genius. Was he creative about that?

TR: It was mostly skill. But he went to the World's Fair in Chicago in 1939, and there was a device there, flat metal device of some sort. They put a silk scarf over the plate, metal plate, and then they put a frying pan over the scarf and cracked an egg in the frying pan. The egg cooked, and the scarf did not burn or scorch. This was one of the attractions at the World's Fair. My father stood there and watched it for awhile, thought about it on the train on the way home, came back to Blowing Rock and built one. And people came from miles to see it.

My mother was creative. My mother was offered a scholarship at Columbia University in creative writing and journalism...anyway, writing. She had grown up in South Carolina. She was born in Charlotte, and her father was a Baptist minister. She grew up in little towns, and she was terrified of going to New York City, so she didn't go. She went into nursing training instead. But she wrote all the stuff in the annual for her class in nursing school. She contributed children's stories and poems to Southern Baptist magazines.

I think my one sister has creative ability. She has talent, but talent is a dime a dozen. Talented people are a dime a dozen. There were people who were in college with me who were better writers than I was, but they didn't have the discipline and drive, and that's what it takes. So they dropped out.

LM: What is your fondest childhood memory:

TR: Circus...going to the circuses...and sleeping next to the generator at the power plant.

LM: The power plant, the one you were talking about because of the sound?

TR: The sound and the warmth and the smell.

LM: And the circus was more visual?

TR: Well, there's a lot of smell involved there also.

LM: In what ways were you different than other children?

TR: Well, I lived more in fantasies. Didn't really like group activities and still don't.

LM: Did you spend a great deal of time alone as a child?

TR: Yes. Oh, I had friends. I spent a lot of time alone. I spent a lot of time with friends, too. It took me a long while, for example, to get into athletics. I finally did in high school and was the high scorer on my high school basketball team, but I didn't really try out for sports until I was a junior in high school. I was shy.

When I was a kid, I had a talking stick. I used to go out in the back of the house and make up stories, endless stories and fantasize, and when I was real small I actually said them out loud. Later on, I would just say them to myself. But I would...I kept up a rhythm with the stick with which I beat the ground. It is sort of hard to explain. I'm sure that it sounds totally insane, but it seemed perfectly normal to me. Even today, sometimes when I'm writing, and I get excited about the story, I'll get up and sort of pace the room, and I'll find myself slapping my thigh for emphasis occasionally, whereas what I used to do was hit the ground for emphasis. And there was never any grass in large patches in our backyard all during my childhood.

LM: Would you keep a rhythm with the stick? Or would you use it for emphasis like you do your thigh?

TR: Yeah, it was more for emphasis, but there was kind of a rhythm too when I would get real excited. And naturally, I had to keep that all to myself. It was a solitary enterprise, because I would have been teased right off the planet.

LM: Did your mother or father ever ask you about it?

TR: They made comments about it from time to time. They never grilled me about it or made fun of it.

The talking stick and thigh slapping exemplify an interplay of the body and mind in the creative process. Kinetic awareness and creativity are addressed in later chapters by Wendy Palmer and George Leonard. The talking stick is also an example of a ritualistic behavior. George describes some rituals he uses in creativity in Chapter 8, addressing the creative process. Tom continued and described some of his childhood antics.

TR: I had friends. My little friends and I had hideouts in those mountains. Even today, I love hideouts. I'm in ecstasy when I can be somewhere and no one knows where to find me. Particularly if people are trying to find me, I like to hide out.

Two things happened in the 2nd grade. There was a school newspaper. I went to a large consolidated school where all the grades were in the same very large building, and there was a newspaper, but only the high school students worked on it. And I just went to them and submitted some copy when I was in the 2nd grade and got my first byline.

And then there was some kind of stage play. It wasn't like a three act stage play...maybe it was. But, as I remember it, it had a whole lot of musical numbers. It was almost more in the order of a review. There were lots of costumes, but it didn't have a unifying theme. It was quite a large production, and it involved all the school. They had me in some god-damned daffodil or something, a tulip it was--because there was a Dutch theme. I just threw a tantrum, because I wanted a speaking part and, by God, I got it. They made me...well, among the lower grades, I had the longest speaking part. I can't imagine doing that really being a shy little Cancer.

LM: It's that Leo cusp.

TR: Maybe. It's a secret theatrical side. I know a lot of people who would accuse me of that. But let's don't get into that. And then we moved to another town in North Carolina the following year. And they did a skit for the entire school. It was real short, like during assembly. Maybe only 10 minutes. I was brand new in this school and brand new in this town, and they came to me and...it was a one person skit...and they came to me and wanted me to do it. Now looking back on it, it was probably in my records from the other school.

The inventor of the Bell helicopter, philosopher and writer Arthur Young grew up in an affluent, creative environment. Feeling like other children or different from them was of no importance to him. As was true for Rowena Reed and George Leonard, Arthur had an unusually happy childhood. All 11 respondents displayed creativity at a young age. Arthur was the oldest of five sons.

AY: I must have had an easy birth, because I went to some kind of therapy in which I relived my birth, and it was a lot of fun. I had a wonderful mother. My father was a painter, artist. I respected him very much, but he was pretty nervous and grouchy. I had four brothers and I would say a very happy childhood, because we lived in the country, and we did all kinds of things on our own initiative. I was the oldest, so I was generally the one to invent some new kind of game. We had all kinds of games. When I went to school, I'd already learned to read. I got very good marks in school the first year. That was before I caught on that that wasn't the thing to do. So then I held back.

LM: You said you have four brothers?

AY: Four younger brothers.

LM: Did any of them go into what you would consider creative activities?

AY: Yes, my second brother went in for abstract films.

LM: When you were a child, was your experience one of being like other children or different than other children?

AY: I must say, I didn't know that I was different or alike. Seemed to me that everything was different when I encountered the world at large. Each person was different. When I got to college, it was rather disturbing that everybody was doing this...at that time, it was wearing plus fours, and you more or less had to drink, or else pretend to, to keep up with the times. In other words, you had to be collegiate. I had an older cousin who impressed me very much, because he had been kicked out of three colleges for drinking. He would boast of it. He took great pride in it.

I decided to go to Europe for fun in 1926. Now this is scarcely childhood, but I'm talking about the question of being different. So I invited my older cousin and my younger brother, Chris, the one who made the movies, and we all went to Europe and had a good time. The dollar was...well, you could do a lot on a dollar. At any rate, we took the boat to, whatever, tourist class. The first thing my cousin said was, well, let's go up to the first class deck, and I'll show you how to pick up a girl. We were hidden behind the lifeboat. He picked up this girl. I was very impressed with that. Then later, I talked to the girl myself. She said, "What an odd person your cousin is." I thought he was the epitome of normalcy, you know, the absolute standard person. And when she said what a strange person he was, and I could see she was normal, more like myself, I suddenly dropped all this nonsense about being collegiate. Real people weren't necessarily collegiate. That was a great release for me, to be unburdened by the fact that I had to be like other people in college, because I think they were equally perplexed by it, but they didn't let on. I found it again when I decided not to stay with my collegiate college friends and instead found it more interesting to have artistic friends. They were different from the collegiates. They weren't necessarily intellectuals--that was a different category again. But I found myself more at home with...you could say, Bohemians. They played the piano or did paintings or knew about literature, as against the collegiates who were always...well, sort of affecting boredom. That was the vogue of the times.

LM: Reminds me a little bit of when I was in college. That seemed to be the vogue at the time then also.

AY: You sort of have to discover where you are most comfortable, even if it involves going against what most of the others are doing.

The visionary and counselor Patricia Sun described her childhood as lonely. Like Paul Torrance, she remembered feeling quite different from other children, and like Wendy Palmer, Patricia Sun demonstrated unusual awareness and sensitivity early in life. As also was true for Wendy Palmer, God was an important force in her life at an early age, which may be common among people who experience extremely difficult childhoods. Also like Wendy, Patricia had a sense of a personal relationship with God that has continued into adulthood. Like Tom Robbins, Paul Torrance, Carl Rogers, Wendy Palmer, Frank Hogan, Norma McLain Stoop, and Niels Diffrient, she spent much of her time as a child alone. Like Tom Robbins, Paul Torrance, and George Leonard, Patricia Sun reported experiencing a lack of support and true education in school. As did all 11 respondents, Patricia Sun evidenced creativity at an early age. She was an only child.

PS: I was just thinking of an experience that I had with my mother when I was a child. It was...I knew that plants and animals responded to how you felt about them, and if you loved them a lot, they grew better. I had what's called a green thumb, and I just knew plants could feel when you loved them. I remember telling my mother something about, you know, if you love a plant, it will grow better. And she said, Patricia, don't ever tell anybody that.

When I was in school, I had an IQ test once, and I remember feeling very sad because I could tell what answer they wanted, and I often felt it was a dishonest answer. I had that battle all through school, and sometimes I would disengage and wouldn't play, do just enough to pass. Other times,

96

I would make an effort to see if anybody was listening. They usually weren't. But I remember a question on an IQ test that asked could a rose feel. I remember feeling very heartbroken; I answered it no, because that's the answer they wanted.

LM: You mentioned your mother. Were there other people in your home?

PS: My father.

LM: Any brothers or sisters?

PS: No, no.

LM: How old were your parents?

PS: They were very young when they had me. My mother was 18, and my father was 19. I have always felt that I had a very painful childhood, but I never really felt that my parents didn't love me. I just felt they didn't know how to. I felt their pain all the time. In other words, I felt their craziness, I felt the parts that were confused, and I didn't know what to do with them except be quiet and be as helpful as I could, just wait until I grew up, and it would be different. So, it's sad. It was a very lonely childhood, because there wasn't anybody to talk to about all this stuff. I mean I remember when I was 5 and 6 years old wondering about God and realizing that there were a lot of people that didn't believe in God. People would say, "Do you believe in God?" and "Are you a Communist?" with exactly the same energy. There would be a nasty, suspicious, anticipating meanness in the question. It always shocked me. I felt very bad about that. I cared very much about whether there was a God. I used to think about it and try to figure it out. I would think either you believe in God now, or you don't--and you will later, so who cares? And besides, God gave you the intelligence to doubt there is a God, so God certainly doesn't mind. Then I realized that people who were demanding about God to others really did not believe in God themselves, and their fear about that caused them to persecute others.

LM: It seems as if your childhood was lonely, and yet you have maintained your ability to be creative, to be original, to be exceptional. Why?

PS: I think I often ask not so much why was I creative, I assumed I would be. I asked why had I been treated badly? Why were people crazy? Why did they harm me? Why did they go unconscious? Why did they lie? Why did they go blank? Why did they project onto one another? It was clearly their own thing. I mean, I could see it was clearly their own thing. They were just pointing their finger at everybody else. I didn't understand that, and I did feel very sad as to why that was happening to me. But also part of the answer I got was so that I would be smart, so that I would be wise and figure it out. It's been priceless for me, because it caused me to figure people and myself out. If I had had an easier childhood, a happier one, a less uncomfortable one, I think it's very possible I just would have gotten into the world sort of at a normal level--inventing things or designing things--not have the profoundness of caring about people and what they are doing...I mean, I wouldn't have geared my problem solving energy to try and understand why people hurt themselves. I could just make a lot of money and enjoy life and not really produce something with purpose. So, I don't regret it.

When you were asking about my best feature, I was wondering if you were going to ask me what was my worst. The thing that I work on most all the time is forgiveness. Because I certainly am a human being, and I don't like it if somebody treats me badly. I don't like it when people treat other people badly. I never have said you should like it, I don't think you should. But there is a difference between not liking it and becoming stuck in it and vengeful about it. Truly forgiving can, in a very miraculous way, give you the power to really undo the problem.

LM: So you use adversity a great deal?

PS: Absolutely, when it is there. It is best to heal it if you can. Adversity shows us where we are missing information.

LM: What is your fondest childhood memory?

PS: Healing animals. Drawing. When I was a little girl, I used to tell fairy tales. You know how kids used to go into the garage and hear mystery stories. I used to sit in the garage, and kids would come, and I would tell fairy tales. I love fairy tales, and I love science fiction. I think it is because your mind and imagination can be uncluttered.

George Leonard, humanist and writer, had an extremely happy childhood. He was successful in a creative field at 17, conducting the second largest swing band in Atlanta. His family supported his endeavors and were lenient. George sees playfulness as the greatest gift he received from his family. Both George and Tom enjoy a highly playful nature. George was the oldest child. George's cousin was his mentor.

LM: Do you have a fondest childhood memory?

GL: Yes, music. Music is 51% of my life, and actually I could say music is 100% of my life, because according to the Pythagorus, it's 100% of everyone's life. I've given a lot of my life to music. I started playing the piano accordion when I was 9. My father one day said to me--I'll tell you one thing about my father. He would always say to me, "They [the state] can take everything away from you, but what you have inside, they can never take away. That's one reason I want you to start taking music lessons." It was really important to him.

I was about 15 I/2, one summer in Monroe, Georgia, and I had a radio on, and way down, you know, Monroe was a long way from Atlanta in those days (now it's very close), and it was really quite isolated. It had a population of 5,000 souls, and there were another 5,000 blacks around the edge of town who were not considered souls. At II:30 one night, on the radio, I heard Benny Goodman playing from Meadowbrook Ballroom. These magic signals do come through the air, and they reach people down in Monroe, Georgia, in the summer. I was totally transformed. It was one of my peak experiences. I got it.

At age 16, I got a clarinet. My cousin had a clarinet, and my cousin is important to my story. He is 5 years older. He was going to the University of Georgia at the time. I got this clarinet, and he showed me basically how to hold it, and that one summer I taught myself how to play clarinet. In fact, I worked out some fingerings which are not the standard fingerings to get certain notes on the clarinet. Within a year and a half, I had my own swing band, and it was very successful. We began playing in Atlanta. We started our first big job at the Piedmont Driving Club, and within a very few months (things can happen fast when you are 17), we were playing for some of the biggest dances in Atlanta.

LM: You said a minute ago that in your family you were given playfulness.

GL: Yes, I was the oldest child, and my father and mother were both very permissive. They adored me. I felt tremendous love. Then my aunt moved in with us, my maiden aunt, because my mother was a typical neurotic. She had a 37-year long nervous breakdown. She was often in bed. She seemed a vague, dramatic feminine presence. My father was a strong, soulful man. My aunt moved in to take care of my mother. She totally spoiled me. My aunt, mother, and father all supported me. I mean anything I wanted, I could get. I became very creative, very young. I went through a series of hobbies. I got totally involved in every one of them. My first memory at 3 or 4 was Lindbergh crossing the Atlantic, because my aunt would get on the street car and go downtown and get me every aviation book out of the children's department of the public library. By the time I was 10, I had read every aviation book in the children's section.

I was spoiled but I was never greedy. I always thought I was very fortunate. I never asked for much. In fact, my father later said, "I wish I had given you more because the younger kids got more material stuff." Because my father and mother were just starting out. But I had everything I

wanted.   So I went through these hobbies.   I
started bird watching.   In the 5th grade, I was
president of the Bird Club in my grammar school.
Then in the 6th grade, I started collecting snakes
with John Crenshaw.

LM: Did your mother like that?

GL: Everything I did they loved.   They thought it
was wonderful.   One time my partner and I had 97
individual   snakes,   and   that   represented
approximately 50 species.

LM: Did you keep them in aquariums?

GL: Out in the back yard.   My father wouldn't let
me keep poisonous snakes, so we would keep the
poisonous snakes over at John's house. I always
had a chemical laboratory.   Make fiendish
concoctions and blow up things and what was
next? A ham radio.

I had a younger sister and two quite younger
brothers--really two families.   One of the great
influences of my life was my cousin, Ed, who was
5 years older.   For three summers--I was 13, 14
and 15--we spent the summers in Monroe.   I
learned very little in school, incidentally.   I was
rebellious at school, and also my family was
permissive about my not going to school.   In fact,
when my mother had her nervous breakdown (I was
in the 2nd grade), I went so little that they finally
called my family.   They were going to take me off
the rolls because I was hardly ever there.   If I ever
felt bad, I had a cold,   I just wouldn't   go   to
school.   Oh,   they liked to have me at home.   I
loved to be at home.   School was a   boring place,

you know. My sister and I, we often talk, we very rarely went to school on Monday or Friday when we were in high school. We wanted to get things ready for the weekend. And when I had my band--I had already started my band in high school--I had rehearsals and stayed up late at night doing jam sessions. But this cousin--the summer I was 13 was a very key summer in my life--because he started teaching me. He was my mentor.

Much like the playwright Frank Hogan, the poet and editor Norma McLain Stoop, defined her childhood as happy, but described it as difficult. Like Paul Torrance and Frank Hogan, Norma suffered a long illness as a child and attributed expanded creativity to the time infirmed. Norma's childhood was spent in an affluent and demanding environment. Her parents demanded she be "the best" and expected her to perform for guests. Like George, she was educated in a nontraditional manner as a child. Norma began writing and dancing when she was quite young. She had a competitive relationship with her mother. Like Wendy Palmer, Tom Robbins, and Carl Rogers, Norma prefers the company of the opposite sex, perhaps because creative men tend to have more feminine interests and creative women more masculine interests than their less creative peers (Barron, 1968; MacKinnon, 1975; Torrance, 1962). She had an older sister who died at the age of 2, before Norma was born, and she has a sister 8 years younger.

NS: I was born in the Panama Canal Zone. I was supposed to be born in Paris.

LM: You were supposed to be?

NS: But my mother was on a cruise, and I was a 7-month baby. I was born in, I think it's Ancon, the capital of the Panama Canal Zone, which made me an American citizen. When I was, I don't know how old, l0 days old, whatever, I went back to

Paris. My mother was half Spanish and half French. My father was Scottish. He was an American, but my mother liked living in Europe. She planned to come to the United States.

I had an older sister who died when she was 2 years old. Well, I lived in Brussels and Paris until August 1914. Mother and I came to the United States on the last boat that left after the start of World War I.

LM: I've gotten confused. You had a sister who was 2 years older who died?

NS: She was dead by the time I was born. When I was a baby, I had French governesses. French is my mother tongue. I spoke French, German, and Spanish until I came to the United States. I had a French governess until I was about 12 years old. All of this shaped me more than anything in the world, because I read history books put out in France, and if you were brought up on history books put out in France, you know entirely different things from what is in history books put out in the United States.

One of my governesses, who was originally from Russia, had me do barre exercises when I was about 4 and 5, which extended my body. My mother was a terrific pusher. When I was 5, I was practicing the piano 4 hours a day, and I had to learn a poem every evening. Daddy would come back with a newspaper around 5:00 or 6:00, and I was put in a room with the door closed for half an hour to learn that poem and come out and recite it. If it wasn't perfect, there was hell to pay. I had to remember it. I would be asked for it when guests came over. I was a performing little dog. I had to play the piano for guests and recite poems for guests. I always had to do everything better than anybody else.

LM: I was going to ask if they had any more children yet.

NS: Yeah, one sister was born when I was about 6 and died shortly after birth, because she was again a 7-month baby. I lived through it. She was what was called an incubator baby, and she died in about a day. Then my present sister, whom I love very much, is extremely creative. She is 8 years younger than I am.

When I was 12 years old, my mother decided I ought to go to boarding school. So I took a test. I had never been to school, period. Everything I had learned was from these governesses. I think toward the end, I had a couple of American ones. I took a test to get into Penn Hall, which was a private school in Chambersburg, Pennsylvania. I passed everything with flying colors except math. I was a 3rd-grade level in math, so I was tutored all summer. The joke is that I took algebra my first year in school and got a 99 average.

LM: When you were at home as a child, were you happy?

NS: I think I was wildly happy. My sister doesn't. If I got anything below an A, I was considered by the family to have flunked.

LM: But your own memory is that you were happy?

105

NS: I think so. I had some things happen. I had the flu during the 1918 epidemic, which was my biggest creative boost. I was terribly sick, and I was in bed for one year after that. The beauty was that Mother or Daddy, I forget which, gave me two books. All I was allowed to do was read. Those two books not only shaped my life, but shaped my poetry, shaped my writing. Bullfinch's <u>Age of Fable or Beauties of Mythology</u> and Bullfinch's <u>Age of Chivalry or King Arthur and His Knights.</u>

LM: Was your family religious?

NS: Not at all. Daddy was religious in a backhanded way. In other words, he was religious, but he didn't go to church. I had to go to Sunday school every Sunday.

LM: As a child, you went to Sunday school. How did you feel about that?

NS: I loved Sunday school. As a matter of fact, the nearest church was a Baptist church, and I came home one Sunday and said, "I'm going to be baptized next Sunday." My mother and father nearly died.

LM: How old were you then?

NS: I was close to 7. My parents had a fit, but I didn't get baptized. They wouldn't allow it, and for many years, I wanted to be a missionary.

LM: How do you think you were like other children? In what ways were you similar to other children?

NS: I always liked boys. There was a vacant lot right next to the house we lived in until I was about 12. I used to play baseball with the boys. I never liked girls very much.

LM: So you were a tomboy?

NS: Yes and no. I was a tomboy, and yet I was not a tomboy. Let's see how I can put it. I was somebody who played piano and wrote poems and all that kind of thing in the daytime until 5:00. When the boys got out of school, we used to play baseball. As a matter of fact, one of the people I played with was Douglas Fairbanks, Jr., because his cousin, Alan Evans, lived across the street from me.

I never did much of what I'm doing now until I was 59 years old. Never wrote a review, never wrote a feature article, never wrote any journalistic-type stuff.

My mother was very beautiful, and she knew she was beautiful, and she thought that every man in the world was in love with her, which they pretty much were. When I was 19, I had to tell everybody I was 17 so that my mother would seem younger than she was.

LM: At that age, you don't want to be younger. That's no fun.

NS: Not only that, she spent her life saying, "I have blue/black wavy hair. Why is your hair jet black? Blue/black is much prettier. Why do you have such big feet?" She had size 3 1/2 shoes. Even at that age, I was wearing around 6. I'm now talking about when I was 16, 17. Whenever I had a date, she would come down and try to steal him from under me. Daddy, I adored. My sister is exactly the opposite. She likes Mother better than Daddy. But see, she wasn't competition for mother, because she was 8 years younger.

LM: Do you see yourself as more like others or different than others?

NS: I always find something that I have in common with everyone.

LM: Did your family think of you as creative when you were growing up?

NS: Not particularly, because they had me performing. You forget. First of all I studied piano, and when I started growing up and they found out my fingers were not right for the piano (you can see very easily), I had to go on to violin, which my fingers were perfect for, but I was afraid I'd get a thing under my neck. So I dropped that and I wanted to be a harpist. My father said you can't take that to somebody's house with you.

Mentors

Relationships influence human development in both childhood and adulthood. One especially important relationship is that of the mentor. Wendy Palmer, Carl Rogers, Paul Torrance, Patricia Sun, Tom Robbins, Frank Hogan, and Niels Diffrient did not have mentors. Norma McLain Stoop had a mentor, but not in poetry. Arthur Young had several mentor-like relationships. Rowena Reed and George Leonard had mentors. Rowena's mentor was her husband. George's cousin was his mentor. George's relationship with his cousin began when he was 13. No one else had a mentor so early in life. Following is a segment quoted from my interview with Patricia Sun.

LM: Did someone in your life ever give you direction? I'm wondering if you have ever had a mentor.

PS: No. The people I have learned most from are my children. I learned from them because it was very immediate and very real.

LM: Have you been a mentor?

PS: I don't know. I suppose I know I'm a model for people if that's what you mean. I don't play the role of a mentor like a teacher in a sense of I don't have people who come study with me. I won't even set up the organizational situation where that could happen. People ask for that. I think I am a ... I know I'm a teacher. I know that I show things and share what I've learned. I know I'm a role model for people because people tell me that all the time. I'm kind of a loner. I enjoy learning things myself in the sense that any time I've asked questions when I was younger and somebody gave me an answer, I would find the answer so inadequate.

Patricia continued to tell of an experience of hers that addressed this issue.

PS: I was on a radio program in Canada once. I was with a Buddhist priest, and the interviewer had asked us both questions, and we were giving fairly consistent answers one to another. I could tell that he liked me very much, the priest. He was enjoying my answers. As we got to the last question, right before we were going off the air, the interviewer said, "Well, I have one last question." He said, "Do you need to have a teacher to become enlightened?" And the priest said yes, and I said no at exactly the same moment. So it went like "yes/no." Suddenly the priest looked at me very worried, you know, like we disagreed, and I put my finger like in an ok sign and said, "That's wonderful. That's the perfect answer; that's the whole answer--yes/no. Whatever fits for you."

Several people, such as Niels Diffrient and Carl Rogers, did not have a mentor but did have helpful relationships with people they considered teachers. Paul Torrance is another example.

LM: Did you at any time in your life have anyone who guided you or directed you?

PT: There are many people who have helped and who have kept my creativity alive. In the 4th or 5th grade, I had a teacher who taught three grades. She encouraged me to do a lot of creative writing, imaginative writing, and so forth. I think that was important. When I spent one summer studying with Moreno [a teacher of Paul's and the person who developed psychodrama], it was very encouraging and facilitating. He made me more aware of my creativity as a strength than anyone else had done.

LM: Would you classify any one of them as a mentor?

PT: No, not really. Now, I would say I've had some great teachers. I don't think I've had anyone who was as strong as a mentor. I've had a number of people, who for a short time had taken interest in me, encouraged me. There hasn't been anyone who has had a persistent influence. There were times it would have helped.

Paul told me of a longitudinal study he conducted.

PT: Having a mentor does help. I don't know whether you've seen my little book based on mentor relationships. I think it is the first time anyone has offered any statistical evidence that having a mentor pays off.

In the book Paul mentions (Torrance, 1984), he describes a study he conducted in which he found evidence to support the theory that having a mentor facilitates success through creativity. His subjects, though successful, had not reached the level of creative production of the 11 respondents in this study. Of the 11 people interviewed in this study, 7 did not have mentors. They are Tom Robbins, novelist; Carl Rogers, psychologist; Paul Torrance, educator; Frank Hogan, playwright; Wendy Palmer, aikido instructor; Patricia Sun, visionary; and Niels Diffrient, industrial designer. The poet and editor, Norma McLain Stoop, did have a mentor, but in singing, a career she did not pursue. Industrial designer Rowena Reed's husband mentored her. George Leonard, writer, had a mentor relationship with his older cousin beginning at the early age of 13. Arthur Young, inventor, considers a few of his teachers to be mentors. Only 2 respondents, George and Rowena, had one extremely close mentoring relationship in their lives.

One explanation for the difference between Torrance's findings and mine might be that having a mentor helps most people succeed, but not to the level of the respondents in this research. Perhaps a mentor might limit the extremely creative, exceptional person and help the more average person to excel. Another explanation is that having a mentor might be rare, and that for 2 of these 11 people to have had one is unusually high.

111

Summary

It appears that creatives begin their search for the true self in childhood. This time that is mysterious to adults, partially blocked from conscious memory, marks the onset of their life long quest as meaning makers. How is it that creative adults maintain the creativity naturally present in all children that too frequently is forced from us by a society that demands "right" answers, "right" behaviors, and uniformity? As was demonstrated in this chapter, it is true that the childhood experiences of the respondents were diverse and it is true that commonalities existed.

All eleven respondents experienced a psychologically distant relationship with their parents. This distance sometimes existed in a supportive, warm environment, as was the case for George Leonard, and sometimes in a stressful, difficult one, as was true for Patricia Sun. This distance may have fostered independence, which appears to engender creative thinking. For these creative children, time in solitude was often experienced as an oasis; however, in no way do I suggest imposing emotional distance between parents and their children for the purpose of fostering creativity. A respect for privacy and recognition of the child as a unique and valued individual might accomplish a similar outcome in a warm, loving environment.

In addition to this psychological distance, all the respondents reported experiencing their childhoods as extremely unusual. Sometimes they reported an extremely happy childhood, as did George Leonard, and sometimes, as was the case of Patricia Sun, they reported painful memories of childhood.

With the exceptions of industrial designer Niels Diffrient and inventor Arthur Young, the respondents perceived themselves as experiencing some sort of adversity during childhood. With the possible exception of visionary Patricia Sun, none of the respondents were abused or neglected as children. I expect most children experience some sort of adversity, and the variable differentiating creatives might be the methods by they coped as children. Novelist Tom Robbins, psychologist Carl Rogers, Aikido instructor Wendy Palmer, poet Norma McLain Stoop, industrial designer Rowena Reed, writer George Leonard, and inventor Arthur Young reported some of their childhood experiences as inspirational or creatively facilitative.

The question "In what ways were you alike and different from other children?" was never satisfactorily answered. Most of the respondents saw themselves as unusual children, and most of them attached meanings to and experienced feelings about these perceived differences. It may be that the experience of being different was actually an experience of individuality, and someone else with a more objective viewpoint would have considered them less unusual than they considered themselves. People other than the respondents in this book with whom I have spoken also have experienced themselves as being unusual or different than other children. It may be that most children perceive their individuality as unusualness, and that children who remain especially creative into their adult lives make more meaning of the perceived differences.

Several respondents expressed the need to remove themselves and their feelings from the judgments of others. Doing so also may have fostered independence in thought. Writer Frank Hogan exemplifies this idea in his discussion about being different than other children. Another theme expressed by several respondents, especially Wendy Palmer and Patricia Sun, was the importance of creative individuals seeing adversity as opportunity and attributing value to it. Often creative people suffer an extended illness in childhood, as did writer Frank Hogan, poet Norma McLain Stoop, and

113

educational psychologist Paul Torrance. Wendy Palmer had to adapt to the illness of her mother.

Another striking similarity among all the respondents is that each manifested creativity early in life. Novelist Tom Robbins reported his belief that all creative people begin expressing their exceptionality in childhood. I agree with Tom. It also may be true that these children pass through phases during which they are more and less creatively expressive.

The majority of the respondents were first born or only children. Niels, Paul, Rowena, Tom, Arthur, and George were first born. Patricia was an only child. Norma's parents had a child who died at the age of 2, before Norma was born. She has a younger sister. The findings of this research support the theory that creatives are more likely to be oldest or only children; however, being first born is not a requirement, as is evidenced by Wendy, Carl, and Frank.

In this chapter the respondents have described some of their childhood experiences. These memories and other forgotten or suppressed thoughts, feelings, behaviors, and perceptions formed aspects of their personalities-- personalities encompassing creative excellence.

CHAPTER 5

SELF-PERCEPTIONS

To understand those experiences that facilitate creativity requires discerning how those experiences are perceived by the respondents. Chapter 5 includes responses to questions intended to reveal the personalities of these creative individuals. The questions addressed the respondents' perceptions of themselves as individuals.

The primary areas of investigation presented in this chapter are: (a) Self-perceptions and identity; and (b) Similarities and uniqueness in creative individuals. The research questions answered are: How do creative people characterize themselves as human beings? What personality characteristics enable creative people to persist with their endeavors? Do they see themselves as risk takers, rebels, and nonconformists? And how do they see themselves as similar to and different from other highly creative people and people in general?

Characterizations

Novelist Tom Robbins sees himself as a Hermes type in that he does not enjoy group activities. Like Rowena, Tom is intolerant of boring people, and when he finds himself in a group of boring people he creates some sort of mischief. He is a private person, has few friends, and prefers the company of women to that of men. Some people describe Tom as aloof and hard to get to know. Although he feels warmth for others in his heart, success has made it difficult for him to be open to people, because he experiences people as either wanting something from him, wanting to hurt him, or both. Like Paul, Tom has felt misunderstood. Following is Tom's response to my question about how he characterizes himself as a human being.

TR: I'm definitely a Hermes type. I learned that on my trip to Greece where we studied the gods and goddesses and how they manifest in our psyches today. It was very clear to everyone in this study group from the beginning that I was a Hermes type. Hermes does not like group activities, doesn't function well in groups. And cannot stand to be around boring people, and usually will cause some kind of mischief if he is in a boring group or around boring people at all.

I keep a low profile. I have very little social life except for volleyball. Ninty-five percent of my social life is involved with my volleyball team. Most adults don't like me. I don't like to be in a room sitting around with men talking about things that ordinary men talk about. I'd much rather be with women. I have some close male friends, but very few. And I have never had very many. I don't like going to the tavern and hanging out unless it is with one of my special friends.

LM: So you are very particular about how you spend your time?

TR: Extremely particular. I'm a very private person. I don't like...well, I'm never bored when I'm alone. The only thing that bores me is other people.

LM: And it seems most people are the other way around. If you were to imagine someone who knows you very well, what would he tell me about you?

TR: I don't even want to think about that. I'm in a stage of my career, and I don't think of it as a career because I think that is a very funny word. I like careen better than career. But whatever it is that I do, I'm at a stage where I get written about by people fairly often--in fact it would be a lot more often if I allowed it--and I try to avoid reading. it. A guy in Idaho actually wrote a book about me, and I've never read it. I hate reading about myself. It makes me uncomfortable and frequently depresses me. Makes me sad to read about myself. I don't even like talking about myself.

LM: Then this is difficult for you.

TR: Well, right now it feels ok. Tonight I'll probably be depressed about it.

LM: I hope not. [pause] How have you been perceived by your peers? And you can define your peers however you like...maybe your friends, your volleyball team...?

TR: I don't know. I have a feeling that they think that I'm...that they enjoy me, but they think that I'm sort of aloof and hard to get close to.

LM: Well, a double Cancer.

TR: That's true, and sometimes it makes me sad. I wish I could be more openly warm, because I feel it in my heart. I've experienced a lot of envy and the kind of senseless and rude attacks that come from envy. And a lot of resentment. You go to any social event...and one reason I live where I do is to stay away from literary events. But I go to them once in a while, and they aren't always literary events...an opening of an art gallery or something...

and you'll find that people either want to stab you or butter you up. And some both at the same time. It's like once you've become successful, you don't change, but other people change. And then I guess that causes you to change. I don't think I changed at all until the other people changed first, and that made me very wary.

LM: Because you had to respond and protect yourself.

TR: Yeah, it just made me more reclusive. I don't ask to be treated differently as a result of my success. I like to be treated differently because I like to think of myself as a different person, but that has been true all my life. The fame has its notoriety, as I would prefer...has its advantages. I've gotten to know people that I never would have known under other circumstances. Rock and roll stars and movie stars, and I like hanging out with those people...some of them, not all of them. Some of them are jerks. I like people who are creative and who are doing something with their lives.

LM: More on the edge, do you think?

TR: Yes.

Tom thinks his most outstanding quality is his imagination. I had expected him to say his wit. Tom reported that his wit and fun loving nature are sometimes burdensome to his friends.

LM: What is your most outstanding quality?

TR: Intensity within tranquillity is the quality I aspire to. I think my outstanding quality is my imagination.

LM: And your wit.

TR: Well, Robert Bly said I use too much of my wit. He gets really snappish with me. "The trouble with you, Tom, is that you live too much in your wit." A friend...one day we were walking down the street, down here by the grocery store, and she suddenly whirled on me and said, "The trouble with you, Tom, is that you have too much fun!" So I get accused of that from all quarters.

LM: I always thought it was impossible to have too much fun.

TR: Well, some people obviously don't.

LM: If you could change something about yourself, what do you think you'd change?

TR: My voice. I want to sound like Richard Burton or George Sanders. He had a way of saying, "I travel alone, and I find the company excellent." That sounds ridiculous when I say it, but he could say it and send chills up your sides.

LM: In the past, have you felt satisfied with yourself?

TR: No, not too often.

LM: Do you now?

TR: No. Satisfaction is a form of paralysis.

LM: Prevents change, growth. So you wouldn't want to feel satisfied?

TR: I'd like to feel a little more satisfied, yeah. But I look back...each year I look back to the previous year and think, "Boy, what a fool I was." And now I've gotten...this has happened so many years that now I'm sure...I know that next year I'm going to look back and think, "God, what a fool you were."

LM: Other than poetry, when you write you intend it to be a publishable book?

TR: Yes, I'm a professional, and when you write...and again, when I say professional, I don't do it just for money, it's my careen...and so when you spend most of your life at your desk, 6 hours a day, 5 days a week, then you don't sit around and write stuff for fun to amuse yourself. At least I don't.

LM: Have you felt misunderstood in your life?

TR: Constantly.

LM: Does that have an effect on you?

TR: Yes. And I really hate it too. I hate it almost as much as I hate injustice.

As was true for the artistic individuals I interviewed, Tom was afraid if he examined his work too closely his intuition might suffer. He described himself as an intuitive writer. Because it is important for him to provide his reader with a special reading experience, Tom likes to keep the plot secondary to the book itself. For Tom, reading a book is an experience that can not be duplicated.

LM: How do you see your work as fitting into society?

TR: Boy!...I'm an intuitive writer. I operate much more from intuition than from analysis, and therefore it makes it kind of difficult to analyze what I do. I don't know that it is at all healthy for me to get so analytical about what I do. I think it might impede the intuition. I have never thought about it, and I don't think that it would be good for me to think about it.

LM: How do you respond to the fact that your public quickly and easily consumes your work after you put a great deal of time and energy into it?

TR: Well, I try to write my books in such a way that they can't read them too quickly. Because I keep plot secondary to the book itself, all my books have plots, but they don't depend on the plots. Many people read them more than once. It's more common than not for a person to read my book two or three times. And probably people have read them eight or nine times. And some people keep them by the bed and just read in them like a Bible or something. But when I think of all the harm the Bible has done, I despair of ever writing anything to equal it.

So part of a purposeful plan of mine is to provide a reading experience--an experience that can only be had from words on the page. Whereas if plot was primary, as it is in 98% of novels, you need to read it only once in the first place. Because no matter how good a book is, once you know the ending.... What I'm getting at is if the plot is the primary thing, if you're only interested in telling a story, and I'm not putting down stories, stories are wonderful--probably the first sentence that a human animal ever uttered was "Tell me a story." I really love stories, but in my books I try to keep the story secondary, so what I do cannot be duplicated in any other medium. If all you want is just a story, you can go to a movie, or turn on TV, and you get the story without having to work for it.

I asked Tom to account for his uniqueness and for his originality.

TR: As a child I decided when I grew up, I either wanted to be French or eccentric, and I could never pronounce French. [Pause] My parents certainly enouraged it. They gave me a lot of support both financially and emotionally. My mother always wanted me be be a writer. My father wanted me to be a pharmacist.

LM: How do you account for your orginality?

TR: I insisted upon it.

LM: Why?

TR: Well, at a fairly young age I took a look around me and...oh, brother! I don't want to be one of them. Plus I never want to be just another member of the team. I am a team player when I play ball with my group, but I manage to make comments and jokes while the game is going on. So even when I am physically being a team player, I'm pretty different than other people. Although on my team it is pretty hard, because they all are pretty crazy.

They all joke while we are playing. Even though, I'm sure a part of it is...I don't think of myself as a particularly egotistical person; in fact the man who is credited for discovering me, a West Coast editor for Doubleday, told me after I'd published my second book--and he was instrumental in getting my first one published--he said, "Tom, you know I have to tell you that I never thought you'd make it as a novelist because your ego is too small." But there is a part of me that doesn't like disappearing into a group. I insist on standing out. That is a part of the Hermes personality, and whether it is motivated by something more profound than egotism I can't say for sure. I'd like to think it is.

I was interested in what these people perceived as the reason for their success. Tom believes he is filling a need.

LM: How do you explain your success in this competitive world?

TR: Because I think there is a need...I am fulfilling a need in society. Or a very small minority of society. But I think people take life and themselves far too seriously. Life is much too serious to be taken seriously. They take art too seriously and get caught up in ego, fear, anger. A lot of people--many, many people--deep down inside know that's its all wrong, but they don't get much reinforcement in that knowledge. So when somebody comes along and reinforces the playful side, which is not a frivolous side at all.... In fact, it may be the wise and expedient side because the universe itself is playful.

The universe is made up of combinations of seemingly irrevocable and random playfulness. We have learned that evolution is not all business, is not all purposeful; part of it is purposeful, and part of it is simply adventure and games. So to be playful is really to be more in tune with the evolutionary process and more in tune with the workings of the universe than to be somber and serious and responsible and tight assed. So you are really more wise and more natural, more realistic. I am more of a realist than John Updike. And the more we learn of quantum physics, the more we learn that this is the way the universe really is, the way it really operates; and all this tragic view of life is unrealistic and is out of tune with the natural world. People feel that deep down inside, and when a writer comes along and awakens that sense, then it makes them feel good about themselves and changes their lives. It affects the way they live their lives.

LM: A purpose of yours would be to help people to remember?

TR: Yes, I think the purpose of the novelist is to meditate upon the ever-changing world and in the process awaken people to their own personal sense of wonder. I'm schizophrenic enough--I guess that's the word--being born on the cusp of Cancer, July 22nd--I am on the whole, much more Cancer than Leo, but there--I am an extremely ambivalent person, and have many areas where I have opposite opinions about the same thing. And there are areas in my life where I am a radical. I consider myself a bohemian, anarchist radical, and I like that image; but I must admit, if I'm honest with myself, that there are other areas in which I am extremely conservative.

When interviewing poet Norma McLain Stoop, I thought that she did not want to answer my questions in a manner that would lead me to believe I understood her. It seemed being unlike what I expected was important to her. My impression was that she was concerned about the image she projected, and this concern sometimes appeared as contrariness.

Norma reported that she likes herself and she described herself as outgoing. Unlike Tom and Paul, Norma has not felt misunderstood. She feels satisfied with herself, and stated that, given the opportunity, she would not change a thing about herself. Choices have always been important to Norma. She stressed the importance of the act of making choices over the choices themselves.

LM: Do you see yourself as being unusual?

NS: No.

LM: So you see yourself as being more like other people than different from them?

NS: No.

LM: How are those things both no?

NS: But you see, that's what life is. Most things that are exactly opposite are actually the same.

LM: Have you felt misunderstood in your life?

NS: No, never.

LM: Did you as a child?

NS: No.

LM: If you could change anything about yourself, what would you change?

NS: I don't think I'd change a single thing. I like myself. That's why I like other people. If you don't love yourself, you can't love anybody. I like myself very much, and that's why I like other people.

LM: I was asking you what someone who knows you very well would tell me about you. As a human being, how do you think someone else would characterize you?

NS: Gregarious, outgoing. I think that is what most of them would say. I like people. There are some people I don't like, but there have been very few. Choices are important to me. My choices. I mean, this is a cliche, but it's very true about me. I prefer to make the wrong choice than no choice at all, and, as a matter of fact, I think it's irrelevant whether the choice is the right choice because you are never quite sure.

One reason the act of choice is so meaningful to Norma might be that it provides her with a sense of control. Choice may be important to Norma because by choosing she becomes the author of her life. Whatever the reason, Norma emphasized choice as a fundamental experience.

Throughout the interview with industrial designer and educator Rowena Reed, I found her reluctant to talk about herself. She seemed more interested in talking about her work, art, thoughts, or in listening to my ideas. Like Norma, Rowena sees herself as outgoing and is satisfied with herself. Like Tom Robbins, Rowena avoided introspection and defined herself as intuitive. Also like Tom, she is often bored by people, but unlike Tom, considers herself stimulated by the people she does not find boring.   She described herself as liking to get to the bottom of things, conventional, particular, and thorough. Rowena thinks her work has been hampered by her good disposition and her conventional ways.

> LM: What would you say is your most outstanding quality?

> RR: You ask me about myself. I don't give myself that much   introspection.

> LM: Here I am, making you think about yourself.

> RR: Yeah. I don't know my most outstanding quality.

> LM: You just mentioned that you are persistent. That might be one possibility. You mentioned that you are talented, and you are intelligent.

> RR: I like to get to the bottom of things.

> LM: So you are curious.

> RR: I'm thorough. I recognize the importance of small relationships as well as large. I think I'm particular, and I think that's good.

> LM: Have you in the past felt satisfied with yourself and with your life?

> RR: Well, overall, yes.

> LM: Do you now?

> RR: Yes.

> LM: How would you characterize yourself?

RR: I'm very intuitive. I'm an introvert. One has to be, I think, to do any serious work. But I'm very stimulated by people.

LM: So you are gregarious, but introverted.

RR: Yes, I think I am gregarious. For instance, I can be feeling just so-so, but when I get in front of a classroom, I'm galvanized. I see all those people and think "Isn't this fun?"

LM: Maybe you are a motivator?

RR: Oh yes.

LM: My guess would be that you probably are a thinker.

RR: I would hope so.

LM: Do you see yourself as being more intelligent or more creative?

RR: I think I'm almost on a 50-50 scale.

LM: You are about as creative as you are intelligent, and as intelligent as you are creative?

RR: It's hard for me to tell. I haven't had an IQ test. I don't know, but I know that I'm intelligent. I can tell by the results I get. I wish I had been more ruthless. Picasso was not a very nice person in the conventional sense. When you think overall, he was the nicest of anyone of his time because he contributed so much to the art world. He wasn't particularly nice to the people around him. He wasn't very nice to the ladies in his life and all that.

LM: So you feel in some ways your work has been hampered by your good disposition?

RR: Yes, by my conventional ways, I suppose. I think that could be said. I hate second-rate people. I can't stand them. There are so many people who I think wish to be...they don't wish so much to be creative, they wish to be thought of as creative. They will try to choose a profession in the arts or theatre or someplace where they have an opportunity to do that. Their talent is mediocre. And then that person will find out in middle life, and then it's kind of late to be starting something. I think as we grow up, we find a place in life; and in that sense, my field is different from other people's fields, but I don't think personally I'm all that different. Other people have similar backgrounds, education, and ambitions. You know, there are different levels. I'm inclined to classify people by their different levels of intelligence; I'm sorry to tell you that. I have two columns. One is talent for visual sensitivity, which would be mediocre, unusual, or not so good. The other way I classify is IQ. I think they are both necessary in development of abilities as an artist. I think I've grown more compassionate as I've grown older, because I've grown more understanding, and one should.

LM: How are you viewed by your peers?

RR: I think they respect me.

Like Rowena, fellow educator Paul Torrance is persistent. He is devoted to work. Paul described himself as a workaholic, although he said that is a term used by other people to characterize him. For him, his work is his recreation. Paul

129

responds to social needs, is concerned about others, and expresses integrity and persistence. Although he said he would like to avoid losing his temper, I find it hard to imagine that losing his temper is something he often does. My experience of Paul leads me to describe him as a soft-spoken gentle man who is intelligent, creative, dedicated, loyal, and hardworking. He has been dedicated to a vision. Lately his life has been filled with hardship, because of his and his wife's illnesses.

LM: Could you name a few people you think of as creative?

PT: Edison and Franklin.

LM: How are you like them?

PT: I guess I see myself...well, I think like Edison in that he spent long hours at work and didn't get much sleep and was very eager to take a nap when he needed it. But he also knew how to use groups to get ideas and help develop ideas. I think the creative way in which he worked is one that is familiar to me. Franklin, so many of his ideas and inventions involved things in which he tried to fill some void. His work tried to fill a need that had been expressed by his fellow man. And I think a lot of things I have done were to fill voids.

LM: What would you say is your most outstanding quality?

PT: I don't know. Just so far, just being able to hang in there. There are times when I want to give up. Especially when a lot of bad things happen and nothing good happens. Fortunately, so far I haven't been overwhelmed to where I couldn't take another bad thing. And then something good happens, and that gives you a new start to hold together and not fall apart. I guess I've always been a workaholic, which is the way people would describe it. I have never thought of it in that way, and I still don't think of it in those terms. Most of the time I've been doing things that I enjoyed, so my work has been pretty much my recreation. I've always worked long hours, and I think that goes back to being brought up on a farm and getting up at 5:00 to milk the cows before going off to school. And so I still get up at 5:00 o'clock in the morning. I guess I would have to say in terms of persistent characteristics that I have shown persistence and hard work and ingenuity, concern about others. I guess those are some of the things that have persisted.

LM: I might add scholarship and loyalty.

PT: Yes, I think so. Although the scholarship seems to have faded out.

LM: And strength--personal inner strength?

PT: I guess so.

LM: If you had the ability to change something about yourself, what might that be?

PT: I guess it would be avoiding losing my temper.

LM: Have you, in the past, the majority of your life, I suppose, felt satisfied with yourself and with what you were doing?

PT: No. Well, there are things about which you feel satisfied and know they are good and that you've done a good job.

131

LM: So there have been moments with a sense of satisfaction?

PT: Yes.

LM: What do you see as the major benefit of living creatively--of pursuing a creative career, a creative lifestyle?

PT: Well, I think it gives you pleasure and gives others pleasure too.

Psychologist and writer Carl Rogers described his personality in the following pages. He was quiet, yet determined and thought his persistence served him well throughout his life. Both Carl and Norma stressed discipline. Like Carl, Rowena, Patricia, and Norma basically feel satisfied. Carl described himself as very disciplined, sensitive, physically active, and moderately adventurous. He preferred not to be interrupted; however, he could change his focus quickly. Like Tom, Carl found ways to circumvent obstacles. He was intense, gentle, and said he had a whim of steel. Like Tom, Carl was a loner and preferred the company of women over that of men.

LM: What would you describe as your most outstanding quality?

CR: I suppose I'd have to say persistence, because I think that when I think something, I believe something, I'm pretty persistent in following it through, even if it means going it alone.

LM: As a child, you felt different. Now that you are an adult, do you still feel different from other people?

CR: No. There are enough people that I feel very congenial with and we share similar ideas and goals, that I don't have that feeling. I feel different from the pack, but not different from others, if that makes sense to you.

LM: If I were to ask someone who knows you very well to describe you to me, what do you guess he would say?

CR: I think he would say he is a very disciplined person, not in a sense of a rigid schedule or anything like that, but when he works at something, he really works at it. Quite sensitive to the feelings of others, that he is capable of forming very intimate relationships, but also is quite a loner. It's easier for me to be close to women than to men. They would say he gets a hell of a lot done. And also makes transitions just in nothing flat; that is, be working at something and a phone call comes in about something entirely different, and I shift gears. So those are some of the things they would say. I'm active physically. I am moderately adventurous.

LM: What helps you work?

CR: Well, let's see. I like it best when I can concentrate on one thing and not be interrupted. But if interrupted, I can change the focus quickly and be as focused on the second thing as I was on the first. I'm like El Greco in the fact that moderately early in my professional life, I began to have a hypothesis about relationships and so on, about therapy, and I have consistently pursued that. People could pick up many of my works at most any stage and say, oh, this sounds like

Rogers. A few years ago I was working at something--I don't know what--in the studio, and all of a sudden it came into my mind a full-blown sentence. "You walk softly through life." There is a kind of psychic experience or mystical experience; I thought, "Where the hell did that come from?" It had nothing to do with what I was doing. Then I thought, "Well, it makes sense because that's what I've done is sort of walk softly through life." When I was a boy, I read Indian stories, frontier stories, trappers--those are my favorite stories--and they would walk softly through the woods, and you wouldn't know they were there. I feel that has been the way of my professional life. I've tried to avoid professional fights with anyone. At the moment, I should look out.

I was told early in the game that psychologists couldn't do psychotherapy; that was medical. So I didn't do psychotherapy; I did counseling. If you did enough counseling, did enough research in counseling, then obviously it was psychotherapy. For the most part, I've gone around obstacles and gotten to the place...it's like the island-hopping technique in the war. The Japanese are well fortified on this island and practically impenetrable, and so you go around to the next one and cut off the supplies. That's a pretty good analogy of my professional life. My experience has been like the man who used to wear terrible-looking ties. One of his colleagues said, "You shouldn't wear such awful ties." He said, "Well, it's just a whim of my wife's." The man said, "Well I know, but you shouldn't wear them."

134

He said, "You don't know my wife. She has a whim of steel." I think that pretty well describes me.

LM: A whim of steel.

CR: Because it is true that I am a gentle person. But also, if I want to go someplace and people for no good reason block me, they are in trouble.

LM: Do you feel satisfied with your life?

CR: Yes, no question about that. I feel I've been very fortunate and feel I've had some real lucky breaks, though I don't attribute my career to lucky breaks. I feel very blessed by the fact that something that I never dreamed would have any influence outside of just one-to-one counseling and therapy has had a larger influence. It's weird and wonderful. I feel very satisfied in my professional and personal life. I have very close relationships with three women.

LM: Have you for most of your life had that satisfaction?

CR: No.

Inventor, philosopher, and writer Arthur Young did not quite know how to answer my question about his most outstanding quality. His wife Ruth was passing through the room as I asked the question. She responded and then left to talk with a visitor elsewhere in the house. Much like Rowena, Arthur did not want to become too introspective. He described himself as inquiring into the nature of existence.

AY: I don't know. What is my most outstanding quality? How would I know anyway? I mean, I don't know what I project onto other people.

Ruth [Arthur's wife]: You can think outside of your time. Most people are so caught up in their own period. Arthur is able to think newly on any subject that comes along.

LM: Could you name a few people you consider very creative for me?

AY: Peggy Huddleston, Veblem, the mathematician, Courant, Eddington, Mary Benzenberg Mayer.

LM: How do you see yourself as being like these people?

AY: Inquiring into the nature of things, wanting to know about what's going on in the world, what are we here for, what's the purpose of existence.

LM: You are all curious?

AY: Yeah, I suppose so. Although Veblem never involved himself in the nature of consciousness, but he made basic contributions to mathematics.

Visionary and psychotherapist Patricia Sun listed her most outstanding qualities as curiosity, courage, and kindness. Unlike Tom Robbins and Rowena Reed, she has always been fascinated by people. Patricia described herself as able to be thoughtful and determined if the task at hand was worthy of her effort. She described herself as a problem solver. She reported that others often describe her as strong, thoughtful, and determined. Throughout her life she has felt as if she were different than others.

PS: I guess my most outstanding quality, and I have 3 come to mind that I like to hold, they are curiosity, courage, and kindness. I am a problem solver. The more important the problem, the better. You can build a little paper box or you can build a Taj Mahal. You might as well go for the big thing if you can do it. I have always been fascinated by people, and I am sorry there is so much sadness in the world. What I have learned about solving problems is that you get the most done when you have courage and use kindness. So they are related.

LM: As a child did you feel more different that others or more alike?

PS: More different.

LM: Do you as an adult?

PS: Not as much. Still, but not as much. I realize now I just came a little ahead of my time or a little bit aware in a different way. I accept grace as the reason, not any particular thing I did. I didn't do anything to make it so. The only thing I give myself credit for is that I did stick my neck out. I do have courage, and I do stay focused. But again, that's the only thing that makes sense to me; I really can't take credit.

LM: If there were someone else here who knew you very well, what would he tell me about you?

PS: It's funny. Of course I've heard people who were close to me, and the first thing that popped into my mind is that I am strong. I see myself as thoughtful and determined sometimes, if it were worth it. But always on a scale of worth.

LM: If you could change one thing about yourself, what would it be?

PS: Oh my. Everything I go to say is in the process of change already. I would be able to read my body better, give it more attention, because it's a part of my conditioning to ignore my body, because I've gotten away with it, and because I can heal my body very, very quickly. I don't give it all the attention I should.

LM: Have you felt satisfied with yourself in the past?

PS: Oh yeah, and dissatisfied, but...

LM: But in a general overview?

PS: I think so.

LM: And now?

PS: Yeah, I think I work very hard. I know how much I care. So I think so. Not that I don't have plenty more that I want to do.

Industrial designer Niels Diffrient has an innate comprehension of objects in the physical world, and his development was influenced by this ability. Like Tom Robbins, Niels described himself as more creative than intelligent. He described his work as flamboyant in concept but not in execution. He views himself as conservative and low-key, and named endurance as his most outstanding quality.

Niels used an interesting metaphor to describe himself. He said that he has gone through life like a piece of fly paper, picking up whatever stuck. Unlike Norma McLain Stoop, Niels said he never made any choices in life. He said he has the ability to generalize and philosophize, and to use reason and knowledge both visually and verbally. He also described himself as equally good mechanically and artistically.

ND: I'm not a flamboyant designer. I'm flamboyant in concept. Not in execution. This chair right here, which has probably gotten more publicity than any other single chair, has a flamboyant concept. But the execution is highly conservative. It's like winning at sports without sweating. To come up with a good concept, then do it low key. When I was younger, I was more flamboyant.

I always had the feeling that I was like a piece of fly paper going through life. I only picked up what stuck to me. And it had nothing to do with me. I never made a single choice myself.

LM: What is your most outstanding quality?

ND: Endurance. I'm willing to wait for things to happen. I rely on it. In my particular activity, it's hard to pinpoint a specific capacity, like musical or mathematical skill. It's more generalized. Though I can draw well, I'm not a better drawer than a lot of other people. I can draw, but that's not an outstanding quality. I don't know; it's hard to say. I know I've got something that allows me to deal with the world and come up with answers to things, but the only way I've ever been able to categorize it is a kind of ability to generalize and philosophize about conditions, and then reason and knowledge, both visually and verbally, and a high level of visual competence. And I'm equally good at mechanical things or artistic things.

LM: That's convenient.

ND: Yes, it is. Well, I originally thought I would be an engineer, so I have inherent capacity, though I never studied engineering. It doesn't seem to be any mystery to involve myself with anything visual. I mean, I can do architecture, at least on a modest scale; I can do it as readily as designing a machine. As long as it's a physical thing, I somehow seem to be able to comprehend it. If someone describes to me the basic elements of a technical situation, I somehow seem to be able to comprehend it.

LM: Do you have a strong ability to problem solve?

ND: Well, that's a part of it. But one might be a problem solver in some other field as well. My tendencies lead me into the areas I'm in, dealing with the physical world. I expect I could get pretty good at designing any aspect of the physical world. I haven't run across anything yet that I couldn't do well. But I'm better at some parts than others.

Earlier in the interview Niels said he had a rich fantasy life as a child. To my question about fantasy, he responded that he fantasizes about everything. He said he has difficulty because he fantasizes about all of the things that could go wrong as well as right. He remarked that often he feels as if something other than his conscious mind guides him. He does not consider himself a self lover, although he does see himself as realistic and intelligent, but he would not describe himself as an intellectual.

LM: As a child you had a rich fantasy life. Do you still?

ND: Oh yeah, some. Not as simple as my childhood anymore, but I fantasize everything. The problem with fantasy life is that it works two ways: it works to the good and it works to the bad. You can have fantasies of good things and you can have fantasies of bad things. I would say a person of my sort has a great deal of trouble being courageous, because you fantasize everything that could go wrong. I can control my acts, but not my thinking. I can't remember the way I want to remember. I remember when my mind is ready for me to remember. I feel most of the time that something else is guiding me, at least not the conscious me.

LM: How do you conceptualize yourself as a human being? How would you describe yourself, characterize yourself?

ND: Well, I'm not a self-lover. That is, I don't have a love affair going with myself. I mostly characterize myself as being unsatisfied with myself. On the other hand, about that, I consider myself very realistic and in tune with the real conditions of the world. I'm not particularly good at reacting to them, but I sense them very readily, and I feel very intelligent, though I'm not intellectual.

LM: Do you think you are more creative or more intelligent?

ND: I guess I'd have to say more creative, because I'm not fully outfitted as an intellectual. I'm not the type to be a quick wit, or anything like that. I love the world. I love the country I live in; I love many things. That's part of the driving force that makes me even more dissatisfied. I see so much potential for designing a better world or a better person, in my case, that I'm just constantly designing stuff.

I think Niels was correct in describing himself as realistic, because it seemed to me that he presented an accurate portrait of himself. His self understanding has probably contributed to his success.

Writer and aikido instructor George Leonard sees his playful nature and his creativity as important aspects of his character. He thinks everyone is creative.

LM: What is your most outstanding quality?

GL: I would say creativity. I consider myself very creative. Somebody asked me once what I'd want put on my tombstone, and I said that I'd invented a new frisbee. I think that one of the main things is to just assume you can be creative. Assume and think you can do things. Creativity is play. Incidentally, when I sound like I'm bragging about being creative, I'm doing this very consciously; but I'm absolutely sure that everyone is. When I say I, I don't think I'm anything special, except maybe I had an upbringing that allowed me to play and encouraged me to play. I think every human being has almost the same creative ability. One thing I want to do is an article called "Toward a More Vivid Peace." I feel that one reason war has an attractiveness to it is that peace is so dull, and it's a basic spiritual emptiness--especially the Yuppie way of life which is just greed and consuming. "The one who dies with the most toys wins." That whole thinking. It's very dangerous. I like to create games. You don't have to go off to

142

war to feel tingly and alive. So, that's creating games, but let's go on with your questions.

When asked how he characterizes himself as a human being, George responded that he has a Don Quixote aspect. He continued to say that while he is less pompous than he used to be, he still has an aloof quality. Several respondents described themselves as aloof.

I was struck by the simple life styles the respondents chose for themselves. None of the respondents made the accumulation of wealth a personal goal, or valued it as a goal for others. Several respondents, including George, spoke of the dangers of the materialistic life-style many Americans are living or striving to live. George described his life style as simple. Much like the other respondents, George is disciplined and hardworking. He described himself as conceited and arrogant; however, I experienced him as warm, outgoing, caring, and maybe a little arrogant.

> GL: Well, I think I'd be untrue to you and to myself if I didn't mention a certain Don Quixote aspect. I mean I can see myself as a ridiculous knight on a mule tilting windmills, I can definitely see that part. My whole life could be a caricature. If you wanted a caricature, you'd have Don Quixote. Actually, I guess we are all tilting windmills. Maybe everything is a windmill. A lot of the things we worry about, a lot of them could be thought of as windmills. In the late sixties I was in some encounter groups. That was wonderful. You don't have any accurate mirrors on the world, but those are pretty accurate, because everybody tells you what they really think of you. At that time I got quite a bit of consensus that I was very pompous and aloof. I think I've changed quite a bit since then.

I think aikido had a lot to do with it. It gave me back my left side--my right brain. I used to be pretty strongly left-brained, if you are following that model. Esalen and aikido gave me back my left side for which I am glad. I don't think I'm as pompous as I used to be. Probably have a touch of it. There is still a certain aloofness. Like Annie and I, we don't have people drop in. We stay sort of apart. We're rather satisfied with a simple life. We both live this unbelievably simple life--get to sleep by 10 at night. Many people think it's dull. I think it's very, very exciting. Incredibly packed, altogether too full, never enough time in the day. I'm still working very hard on an 8-day week, where I get an extra day. Just my fitness schedule--I teach twice a week, train twice a week, and run three times a week. If I have to go off on trips, I do miss times. I always feel bad. I'm conceited. I'm willing--I really don't think I'm more conceited than anybody else, I'm just willing to talk about it. That's my guess. Maybe I'm more conceited. Maybe some arrogance, I don't know, helps me.

Throughout this part of Chapter 5, questions about the respondents' perceptions of their own personalities are addressed. Adjectives like persistent, determined, and enduring are mentioned again and again. In response to the question about his most outstanding quality, Paul, for example, replied, "...just being able to hang in there." Carl described himself as focused and disciplined with a whim of steel, and Niels named endurance as his most outstanding quality. About as many respondents felt satisfied as dissatisfied with themselves and their lives.

Courage

I also wondered if courage would be an important aspect of the creative personality. Counselor and visionary Patricia Sun said that her life looks more courageous than it feels. She thinks that courage is sometimes the result of innocence and naivete, and that the openness of innocence has power. She thinks that openness grows from the expectation that you and the world are good, and from the capacity to love.

> PS: I remember sometimes reflecting on my early life, and being sole supporter of three children, and what I did, and how I lived. Looking back on it, it looks kind of courageous; but when I remember how I felt when I lived it, there was just nothing else I could do, and it really wasn't particularly courageous. It was just the most sensible thing I could think to do.
>
> I think that intuitive side has an innocence. I think naivete has a power; I don't mean ignorance; I mean naivete, openness, an expecting that you are good and the world is good, and things will work out--even as you know it's not, even as you know things aren't always good. You still have an inherent belief or feeling or knowing of that. I believe that's true. I think when we get disconnected from that place is when we do cruel, harmful things. That courage, interestingly, comes from the word heart, and innocence, authenticity, comes from heart, comes from a capacity to love the world, to love life, and to expect the best from people.

Unlike Patricia Sun, educator and creativity expert Paul Torrance did experience a need for more courage than others. He defined himself as a minority of one, and for that reason he has felt that courage has been a significant aspect of his life.

LM: Have you needed more courage to be a minority of one?

PT: Yes, I think so. That is just one facet of it because I am a part of the majority in quite a number of ways.

LM: My guess is that you have made some sacrifices in order to live your creative life. You are shaking your head, so I guess you agree.

PT: Yes, yes.

LM: Can you describe any of those sacrifices?

PT: All alone I kept my research going out of pocket. That has been a sacrifice. I could have done the research at foundations willing to pay, or the Institute of Education, or some others, and done the kind of research they wanted done. It would not have been the kind of research I wanted done, and it would have kept changing because the quotas for research are very whimsical. At the end of your career you start counting to see where the money has gone. I'll make out alright. I should have saved something, but I never have managed.

Inventor and philosopher Arthur Young's perspective was more like Patricia Sun's.

AY: I don't have much courage. In fact, I don't know what you really mean by courage. The vast implications of the universe seem terrifying to me, but ordinary things don't.

LM: Most scientists don't talk about the things you've talked about. They would be excommunicated if they did.

AY: Oh well, I have nothing to lose in that respect, but maybe things like first testing the helicopter. I'd never flown an airplane, so I didn't know if I could fly a helicopter, or whether it would fly. So it was very much an uncertain thing. But I did it very carefully.

LM: But you were risking your life.

AY: I didn't think of it that way. I always thought I'd break the helicopter or something. I don't think of myself as courageous.

Arthur's response, "I didn't think of it that way" typifies this group of respondents' perceptions of their own courageousness. They reflect a certain naivete. Novelist and artist Tom Robbins thought perhaps he manifested a little more courage than other people.

TR: No. It hasn't seemed that way to me. Maybe I have. I don't know that I've needed it. I guess I have manifested more courage than most of my peers because, as I said, there were people in my school who were better writers than I, but they never made it. Because they didn't have the courage to develop the discipline and the drive. They got married and got a mortgage and took a big bunch of bananas and caved into it. I think that lacks courage.

Industrial designer and educator Rowena Reed thinks one must be courageous to be creative.

147

LM: So you are a courageous person.

RR: I think so.

LM: Do you think being courageous is necessary to be creative?

RR: Yes.

Playwright Frank Hogan described himself as courageous and related an example of a courageous experience.

LM: Have you needed more courage in your life than you think most people need?

FH: In some ways. I think that to be homosexual and go into the service, Coast Guard, Army, Navy, whatever, and there were thousands of us in the service during World War II...and to get to the point of running the lives of 350 guys, telling them when their boats were going out, when they were going on liberty, and getting on well with them all, I think that's quite an accomplishment. I think it took a hell of a lot of...I don't know if you'd call it courage or not, but it took a hell of a lot of something.

Poet and editor Norma McLain Stoop did not see herself as courageous.

LM: So you see yourself as courageous?

NS: No, not at all.

LM: But you said you're never scared.

NS: I'm never scared--not because I'm courageous, but because I'm stupid. I think I can do anything.

Industrial designer Niels Diffrient has never thought of himself as courageous, although others have described him as being so. His description of himself exemplifies the attitude of the group. It is as if most of these individuals agree they are not courageous; they just place themselves in situations where they must behave courageously, once again separating who they are from what they do.

ND: Well, because I've never thought of myself as courageous, I've practiced what I call in my mind the falling-off-the-limb attitude of getting on. In other words, I crawl out on the limb and saw it off, one way or another, and I figure when I'm falling I'm going to do something. It's like being afraid of going to the dentist. You get someone else to make the appointment for you, but then you go.

LM: Do you think you have more courage than most people?

ND: I didn't think so, because in my lifetime I've never been a front runner in the courage department. I'm not the type who always throws himself into the ocean to save someone or anything like that. But not long ago somebody wrote an article about me for a magazine, called a lot of my friends in the field for their opinion of me. And one of the people I admire most, George Nelson, listed courage as one of my qualities. I almost wept to think that he thought I was courageous, because I thought I did these things out of sheer doggedness.

Although a number of the respondents did not report thinking they are courageous, others have described them as such. Some of those possessing courage do not know it or, from an internal perspective, would not define it that way.

Costs, Benefits, and Recognition

Creative careers provide costs and benefits, as does the recognition that often accompanies the creative life. Rowena Reed said that one of the major costs of her career has been social. She has not been especially affected by the desire for recognition. Rowena thinks her work could influence people.

> LM: I'd also like to ask what have been the costs of choosing a creative career as opposed to a more normal kind of career.

> RR: The costs in life? I guess there have been a great many, but I have not minded. One doesn't have such a variety of friends, and sometimes there isn't time to do things like travel as much as would have been nice.

> LM: So, your social life?

> RR: I've had a different kind of social life. It's been more narrow, with my peers. Yes, I would have liked it to have been broader.

> LM: Your life has perhaps been more focused, and you therefore have missed out on variety?

> RR: Yes, because I'm not interested only in artists, although I'm interested in them primarily. I think I'm interested in very unusual people. I was spoiled by my husband, who was really a very unusual person, and I consciously or unconsciously would measure people by him. I have not met enough people like that.

> LM: In what ways has a desire for recognition affected you in your work and life?

RR: Not very much.

LM: It hasn't been a desire particularly. What about a desire to be unique?

RR: I never gave that much thought. If I am in any way unique, it is just a natural evolution. Not because I have tried to be.

LM: Do you see your work as being a social change agent in any way?

RR: Well, it could be in the way art is. You never know that until 20 or 30 years after.

LM: Would you like it to be?

RR: Yes, I think it would be fun.

LM: In what way would you like your work to change society?

RR: Well, it could open people's eyes to the fact that art is much more than illustration or story telling.

LM: That your art may have an influence on the way art is perceived by others?

RR: Yes.

Although he had a strong desire to effect change, psychologist and educator Carl Rogers was most effective when he did not make effecting change his goal. He did not try to be different than other people, but often was.

CR: I don't think I consciously tried to be different.

LM: Do you hope your work is an agent for social change?

CR: People have said, "Oh my God, you're not a scientist; you're an evangelist," and I laughed and thought there was some truth to that. I would like to get a message or idea across or something like that. When you say you are trying very hard to be a significant social change agent, I realize that's what scares me about the peace project, that I seem to be aiming directly toward that, and that's what could make it fall on its face somehow. I have been a social change agent, and I like that fact. But I have done it mostly by indirection. So it's a double answer. Yes, I would like to see society change in a lot of ways. I would like to see education change, but I suppose my books in education have had an evangelistic role. On the other hand, I feel I've been most effective as a change agent when I've not aimed directly toward that.

Paul Torrance has wanted to change education, but has not desired uniqueness or recognition. His uniqueness is something he has learned to tolerate.

LM: You were talking earlier about being a recognized person. Has recognition been something you've desired?

PT: No, I don't think so.

LM: Was it a by-product?

PT: Yes, I think so.

LM: Have you, as a human being, experienced a desire to be unique?

PT: No, not particularly. I don't think I've tried to be different. I just have been.

LM: That was not any kind of decision.

PT: No.

LM: It just occurred.

PT: I think it's a thing that I was able to accept to a certain extent. I don't think that I've ever learned to accept it completely, but I have recognized that and learned to tolerate it.

LM: I wonder if you have not had the desire because you were so unique.

PT: Yes, that could be.

LM: Have you felt misunderstood?

PT: Yes. I gave up a long time ago trying to get people to understand me. So I've come to tolerate being misunderstood.

LM: Do you think feeling misunderstood had any affect on you?

PT: Yes. It makes you be as straightforward as you can be in what you say. It makes you work on the improvement of your communication skills. So I think it has that kind of effect, because no matter how clearly you say it or how many times you say it, there are still going to be people who don't understand you.

For both aikido instructor Wendy Palmer and visionary Patricia Sun, recognition has been desired for some reasons and not for others. Wendy sees the double edge of recognition, and therefore tries not to allow it to affect her.

LM: Do you desire recognition?

WP: That's a good one for me, because I have a double edge about it. I'm very afraid of being recognized; it's one of my big fears in life. At the same time, I want to be appreciated, so I put myself in a bind.

LM: What about a desire to be unique. Has that affected you?

WP: No, that doesn't affect me at all. I don't mind other people copying my material. I don't mind borrowing from other people's material. Our uniqueness as individuals comes from the moment, not the material.

LM: What about a desire to be a social change agent?

WP: Mostly in that I change myself. If I can do it for myself, then I can be an agent. If I can do it for myself, it doesn't matter if I change other people. The irony of it is, if I do it for myself, I do affect others.

Like Paul Torrance, Patricia Sun desires recognition of her work because she wants to institute change. Also like Paul, she prefers to appear less unique than she is.

LM: Have you had a desire for recognition in your life?

PS: Yes and no. Being Pisces/Leo, you might get that in 2 parts. There is this part that says yes! There is this part that says no! Just let me sit on a mountaintop and beam at everyone. What I found I had to give up...for a long time I did not get recognition for what I did, because one of the things I had great talent for doing was giving away my ideas. Of course I realize that giving away my ideas was a priceless thing to be able to do, but at the time it annoyed me. I would think of something and start to present it, maybe even present it. People wouldn't hear that I'd presented it, and then in a day or 2, they would say "I have this wonderful idea." They'd tell me what I'd just told them. It used to frustrate me a little, not seriously, just a little annoying, like "Hey, come on." Then I realized it was really wonderful. That what had happened was that I had gotten the point across. The person had owned it and was off and running with it. That was a more powerful way to receive it. So I'm kind of good at planting seeds that have the whole thing in it, and I think that's good. So I get enough recognition. I learned a long time ago that you don't need recognition for what you did; just enough to have connection. I'm happy with that.

LM: What about a desire to be unique?

PS: I'm already unique. I don't need a desire. It's been enough of a hassle. I really see people as unique. I often see things in people others don't see. They will make a general thing and I will see this other unique thing, because I like uniqueness. I don't go for homogenization of the world; I find delight in seeing uniqueness and a little bit of eccentricity is interesting, in the sense of, well, there are more opportunities--it's different.

LM: It's fun. It's nice.

PS: Yeah, exactly. It's interesting. Actually, to answer your question, I do a lot of stuff not to look unique.

Norma McLain Stoop and Frank Hogan, both writers, expressed a strong desire for recognition and uniqueness. Tom Robbins, also a writer, expressed a desire to be viewed as unique. Norma thinks her current desire for recognition is the result of her childhood desire for recognition from her parents.

NS: I've always had a desire for recognition. I wanted my parents to recognize how good I was. I've always had it, and it affected me.

LM: Did your parents recognize how good you were?

NS: Very much so, but in completely different things.

LM: How has the desire to be unique affected you?

NS: Tremendously.

LM: In what ways?

NS: I don't want anybody else to look like me, and I don't want to look like anyone else. Every woman in the U.S. wants to look like a movie star; she wants to look like a particular one; she wants to look like everyone else, or there wouldn't be magazines like Mademoiselle and Glamour. In Europe when a woman has a flaw, she emphasizes it, because she wants to look different.

LM: How about in your work?

NS: I want to be different.

LM: Has your work been different because you wanted it to be different?

NS: Sure. I don't know if it has been. My poetry has been. The way I sing has been. The way I dance has been. I was writing for markets when I did my reviews and articles.

One of the reasons recognition is important to Frank Hogan is that it wasn't a part of his family's plan for him.

LM: In what ways has a desire for recognition affected your life?

FH: I would assume it probably is essential, simply because it was the thing I was not supposed to have, in the family plan.

LM: Because you were not supposed to have it, having it became important to you?

FH: I didn't know this, but I think it's true. I'd say I was trying to defeat the family plan, not defeat it, escape it, and by escaping it, defeat it anyway. The plan was unlikely to work, and it certainly was not going to work on the basis that I was going to be a nobody, which is what the plan entailed. If you translate that as recognition, sure, certainly. But I didn't call it that. Again, I was not putting tags or names on things, because I did not know what names to put on them. I was stupid.

LM: Though you didn't name it and it was not conscious, you might have had that motivation.

FH: Absolutely, that's right, yeah. I'd go along with that.

LM: In what ways has the desire to be unique affected you?

FH: Well, it's part of the last question, really. Being unique gives you recognition.

LM: One thing you said earlier, to sum it up, not to quote it, is that you put a lot of energy into being different from your brother.

FH: Oh yes, I think that's true. At times it was pretty negative. I remember one day down at the beach. There had been a terrible storm and there was a barrel floating around in the middle of the rough stuff. Another kid and I were a good distance away from it. He was a good athlete, baseball player. He was trying to throw stones from the road into the bouncing barrel. I just picked up this stone as natural as could be and just plunked it right into the bottom of the barrel. He said, "My god, why didn't you play baseball?" I said, "No thanks."

LM: Because your brother did?

FH: I think so. I think so, yeah.

Like Frank, Tom Robbins described a desire to be recognized for being unique. Tom wants his work to be recognized, but unlike Frank and Norma, does not desire personal fame. Again, Tom commented that he does not want to be associated with groups, that he wants to be unique.

In the following quotations, Tom described a way of life to which he aspires. In his interview, Tom introduced the term outlawism, which I found helpful in other interviews.

LM: Do you think the tantrum and the big row you threw at the other elementary school had to do with recognition?

TR: Probably.

LM: To be recognized for being unique?

TR: Yes. Like the story I told you about Rheinhart when asked if he was an abstract impressionist, and he said, "To heaven, but not with them guys." And I guess that's sort of the way I've always felt. I don't want to be identified as a part of a group. I want to stand out. I don't know why that is. I've also practiced the black marble technique which I guess is something different. It doesn't really have anything to do with what we were talking about.

LM: What's the black marble technique?

TR: Well, Joseph Wambaugh is a L.A. policeman who has written a number of commercially successful police novels. He wrote one called The Black Marble about a precinct in L.A. where they had some kind of container with marbles in it. They were all white except one which was black. And at the beginning of the shift they would all draw marbles, and the one who got the black marble had to go out on vice in this really sleazy, awful, really dangerous district. And one guy came on the force, and he found out what they were doing, and he asked for the black marble. It wasn't that he liked it... It's kind of hard to explain, but I understand in my heart totally why he did it, and I'd do the same thing. If there is something really bad no one wants to do, I'll volunteer.

LM: I think I understand. I may not.

TR: Well, it has metaphysical and perhaps karmic aspects. It's kind of hard to explain. It's kind of like outlawism, too. It's a turn of the tables. I think one way to deal with life is...in a situation...is just to turn the tables. Whatever life hands you, if you don't like it, instead of resisting it or fighting it, you just turn it around.

LM: Do you see yourself as an outlaw?

TR: Well, that would probably be pretentious to say. But I definitely identify with the outlaw's sensibilities, although I don't consider myself as alienated, although I'm not very social. I'm not a criminal. There is a difference between outlaws and criminals. I feel very much at home in the world, and I feel pretty much at home in society. Let's say I feel at home in the world, and I like the world, and I like being here, but I have insisted most of my life that my stay here will be on my own terms, not society's. I guess you could just as easily call that extreme individualism instead of outlawism. I like the word outlaw better than individual.

For Tom, it is important to live on his own terms, not society's. In the following quotations he recounts experiences that provide metaphors for his philosophy as well as examples of his dramatic quality.

TR: In my first book I wrote about one of my experiences in the service, an autobiographical account. As a protest against the food, I bought a giant tube of Colgate toothpaste. At that time, you could buy uncolored margarine; you had to color it yourself. It was white, and you would get dye, probably a carcinogenic dye, that you would mix with it. It looked like lard because it was white. I took a razor blade and slit open the bottom of the toothpaste tube and got almost all the toothpaste out. Then I filled the tube with the uncolored margarine. This took days, but there wasn't much to do in the service. This was in Nebraska. So I filled this tube up with uncolored margarine, and I took it to the mess hall and--the reason I was annoyed with the mess hall was they kept serving raisin bread toast for breakfast.. This didn't bother me except when I was on midnight shift, because that was the only time I'd eat breakfast. You'd go in, and you'd get this toast with gummy raisins, sweet and gummy, to mix up in your mouth with your eggs. It really was offensive from a culinary point of view. So, I was complaining about the raisin bread toast, and they were mad at me for complaining about it. So this one day I went in, and I got a big stack of it, and they realized something was up. I stationed myself at the most central table in the mess hall, and out of this little brown bag I took this tube of toothpaste and squeezed it out on the toast. I did this very slow and dramatically, so that by the time I had the toast covered I had every eye in the mess hall on me. Then I commenced to eat it with great relish. They sent for the Air Police to arrest me. And they did arrest me.

LM: Is it illegal to eat toothpaste?

161

TR: No, it isn't. They found nothing they could charge me with. They tried to charge me with creating a disturbance and things like that, but couldn't find anything that covered it, and let me go.

Then I made, in the same mess hall, I made a snowball during winter and brought it in and put it on my tray and just asked for gravy. They brought in the mess hall sergeant. He was furious. But they were never able to do anything. We had an inspection one morning, and the notice on the bulletin board was "All foot lockers must face the isles." So when they came in, everybody's foot locker was facing out except mine which was facing at this oblique angle. He really got red in the face and asked me what that was all about. I pointed out that the only isles I knew about in Nebraska were in the mouth of the Platte River, and I was facing them as best I could.

LM: They didn't have much of a sense of humor, I gather.

TR: Well no. Authoritarian people never do. But there was nothing they could do about that either. I was the only person who followed this directive explicitly. I got called in and talked to by the officer in charge. But there was nothing they could do. So I managed to get through the Air Force without a black mark on my record. I was the only man in my outfit who didn't get a re-enlistment talk, so I consider my military a success.

LM: Do you still find ways to get around or out-do authority?

TR: Oh, you have to. It's the only way to deal with authority. If you try to fight it, you just get ground into the pavement. It is ridiculous to take authority on head-on, unless it's a minor authority, which you could realistically beat. But I don't find authority any problem, because it's so easy to outwit. The way to handle authority is sabotage, not direct confrontation. Direct confrontation is just a manifestation of the death wish. But you can outwit them and sabotage them at every corner. I didn't like the military part of it because I dislike authority, mindless authority. If I'm out rafting in white water and the guide says back paddle, I'm gonna back paddle without question, because he knows far more than I do--he's an expert. But to take orders from politicians, policemen, preachers, and military officers rankles me. But I found a way. I mixed a little Gandhi doctrines of passive resistance with some Dada and surrealistic tactics to avoid clashes with authority.

Risk Takers, Rebels, and Nonconformists

Tom thinks risk taking is an important aspect of creativity.

LM: Risk taking?

TR: Very important.

LM: How have you used risk taking to further yourself?

TR: I think any artist has to take risks. If you don't you are going to be mediocre. One risk I run is that there is a very thin line between playfulness and cuteness. Because I believe in playfulness and think it is a profound manifestation of wisdom, I try and bring playfulness to my work. Sometimes I cross that line into cuteness. I am aware of that, and don't like it, of course, but it is a risk I have to take. When I fall on the wrong side of that line, there's a school of piranha who are ready to leap on me; you know, reviewers and critics point it out without pointing out the times I didn't and did manage to be playful without being cute. So that's one risk I run all the time. I think that just the subject matter of the book I just finished, and the way I chose to deal with the subject matter is very risky. I think I took a lot of risks with this book, plus changing my style somewhat. When you have a style that has become known and accepted by a certain readership, it provides you with feedback and recognition and certain economic benefits; the temptation is to repeat yourself. It happens to the best of us. It happened to Hemingway, for example. That's the safest thing to do on one level.

LM: What about the process itself of risk-taking? Is it something that has value because of the process itself?

TR: Oh yeah, it keeps you on the edge. That's what I meant when I said I believe in the Bonnie and Clyde tantra. One man and one woman out on the edge taking risks. Where he has a map to the treasure, and she drives the getaway car. That's another way of approaching divinity, of making contact with the divine, of remaining transparent to the translucent.

164

Tom Robbins described himself as an outlaw. Poet Norma McLain Stoop seems to be strongly affected by others, an attribute that surprised me. Most of the respondents reported that others had little if any affect on their work. Norma did not work for 33 years because her late husband did not want her to. She still defined herself as a risk-taker, rebel, and outlaw. She related an experience in which she took a risk by publishing her photographs.

LM: Do you consider yourself a rebel?

NS: Tremendously. I've always been a rebel. I've always been a rebel except for the 32 years I was married. Nobody would believe it; my husband would not wear a pair of socks unless I knitted them. People who know me now don't believe I could ever be that kind of woman.

LM: Do you consider yourself a risk-taker?

NS: Oh tremendously. I don't think you live if you don't take risks.

LM: Has being a risk-taker been influential as far as you as a professional are concerned?

NS: Absolutely. I've taken risks every step of the way. For instance, right to start with, well, back in....Risk-taking, ok. I told you about my photographs. If that wasn't risk taking--I'd never taken a photograph in my life and I had the nerve to hand <u>Dance Magazine</u>, who has the best photographs in the U.S., my stuff.

LM: What about as an outlaw?

NS: Sure. How many 75 1/2 year old women go to a discotheque and dance crazy?

165

Some of the respondents distinguish who they are from what they do, like educator and creative thinking expert Paul Torrance, who says he is a conformist, but takes risks.

LM: Do you now or have you in the past seen yourself as rebellious?

PT: No, I don't think so.

LM: Have you ever had the experience of living outside the norms?

PT: No, I've been pretty conforming.

LM: Would you consider yourself a risk taker?

PT: Yes, I think so. Not greatly. I don't think I had enough courage to be much of a risk taker, but I've taken more risks than most people do. My style of writing and my style of teaching and the type of research I've done.

Aikido instructor Wendy Palmer describes herself as highly antiauthoritarian. All the respondents who commented upon authority described its effect on creativity as hampering. Wendy identified with outlawism.

LM: Do you see yourself as a rebel?

WP: I've been known... I am antiauthoritarian; there is no question about it. Even to myself.

LM: Maybe you are an outlaw?

WP: I've been called that. Yeah. I mean I'll even make an agreement with myself and break it just on principle. My joke with my ex-husband was

"Just don't tell me not to have an affair, because you are in trouble. If you want me to stay monogamous to you, just give me an open rein. But if you ever say don't do it, you can count on it." I'm like that. I even do it to myself.

Visionary and psychotherapist Patricia Sun did not describe herself as an outlaw or rebel, although she speaks of her individualism and her ability to transcend social laws. She uses the rules when they work and makes new rules when they do not.

LM: Have you ever seen yourself as a rebel or an outlaw?

PS: No.

LM: You put your energy into looking less different.

PS: It is a very unproductive place to put yourself in if you want to get your thoughts across. I've certainly always been an individual, and I never took social laws too seriously, except if they could hurt me. I did my adapting as a teenager. I had to be good, so I got married early.

You follow the rules when it's the most productive thing to do, and when it's not productive to follow the rules, I find...I remember something my mother said to me that I love. She said, "Nothing succeeds like success." So I found that if I ignore the rules and succeed, I set new rules. So it didn't matter. What gets us in trouble is our worrying. We carry that as an energy and people pick it up and they say, "Oh, you can't do that." If you are worried, somebody is going to stop you. I didn't worry about that, and wouldn't define myself as an outlaw or outsider, although I always felt a little different from everybody, so a little of that is true.

Writer and aikido instructor George Leonard--like Patricia Sun, Paul Torrance, Carl Rogers, Frank Hogan, and Tom Robbins--would like to effect social change. George described himself as a cultural outlaw, which is the way Tom Robbins used the term.

LM: Do you see yourself as a rebel or outlaw?

GL: More outlaw, but not so much of an outlaw. I see myself as very conventional. Because all the externals of life are very conventional. I don't break many laws. I'm not an outlaw, but I am a cultural outlaw. I did a lot of stuff on the Civil Rights Movement, more than anybody at Look.

LM: I remember. You marched.

GL: Yes. And did the California issue [for Look], and all hell broke lose. My colleagues, many of whom I thought really liked me, they hated me. Tried to get me fired. It was the damnedest thing that happened in my life.

Industrial designers Niels Diffrient and Rowena Reed see themselves as conservative and law abiding, but also as risk takers and rebels. Frank defined himself as a risk-taker, rebel, and outlaw. Throughout life, Niels did what he needed to do without much regard for others. He was not aware that other people or authority might not like what he was doing. He experiences no personal use for authority, and often perceives authority in much the same way as novelist Tom Robbins, as a senseless, uncreative force.

LM: Do you see yourself as being a risk-taker?

ND: I do now. I've never thought of it before. Mainly because the motivation to do for many years was so all-encompassing that I followed the urge with little or no regard for what it might have seemed like to others. I think I was something of a bore. I probably was not always the most pleasant person because I did not realize the social consequences of some of the things I did. I just didn't. That was just the only way I could see to get done what I wanted done. I don't think I've ever been consciously rude or mean to anyone. I'm not that way. But I realize in retrospect, some of the ways I was when I was a youngster--I didn't care about authority or anything. It wasn't because I was thwarting authority. It just never occurred to me. I didn't even think there was an authority.

LM: When I first began the interviews, I was asking people if they saw themselves as rebels.

ND: Again, I don't feel like one, but I've been one. And when I was younger, I was quite rebellious. Not so much in an open way, like fighting or anything like that, but authority is one thing I can really find myself bristling against. I think the thing I hate most in this world is bureaucratic situations where the authority is a nebulous nonperson, and yet exercises a senseless, uncreative force on people.

LM: A word that has come to me is outlaw. People see themselves more as an outlaw than as rebellious.

ND: Not rebelliousness. I'm not against authority. You know, I'm basically very law abiding. I'm conservative in nature. So it can't be basic rebelliousness. It seems pure and simple that I don't want anybody to stop me from doing what I love to do most. And anyone who has the least clue of stopping me...I'll go to any extreme, because it's basically a form of murder. They would take away my real life, which is not just living and breathing. It is the one thing that throughout my entire life has made the difference.

Rowena Reed described herself as a rebel and a risk taker. She, like Tom Robbins and Frank Hogan, stated that courage is a necessary aspect of creativity.

LM: Do you see yourself as a rebel?

RR: I suppose so. Yeah, I do.

LM: What sorts of things have you rebelled against?

RR: Well, I rebelled against my artistic education, for one thing. Also, I've never been very articulate about it because I think other women are being so darned picky, so it wasn't necessary for me to sound off about conditions that are inferior for women. There are plenty of intelligent women doing their jobs and doing them well now, so I don't need to contribute to that.

LM: Do you feel you've been a risk taker in your life?

RR: Yeah, I've never been afraid of risks. The biggest risk I took was when I married, that was a complete jump into the dark. I've never been afraid of risk.

Playwright Frank Hogan described himself as an outlaw, rebel and risk taker.

LM: Would you define yourself as a risk taker?

FH: Oh yes.

LM: What about a rebel?

FH: Absolutely.

LM: How about as an outlaw?

FH: Well, of course. Keynes, you know, and Hogan, both were illegal, absolutely illegal. What he was doing sexually while he was running the Treasury was illegal.

Summary

The goal of this chapter was to provide the reader with an understanding of the personalities of the respondents. I experienced a strong sense of individualism in all the respondents, ranging from a statement of individuality to overt rebelliousness. Individualism supports independent thinking, which in turn is required in creative thinking.

Because independence and divergent thinking are required in creativity, courage becomes an important aspect of the creative personality. I experienced these individuals as courageous, even when they did not see themselves in this way. Each can be described as a risk taker; each displayed a sense of humor. The words best describing every member of this group include hard-working, caring, and determined. Each one is dedicated, although they are dedicated to varying visions.

I think that in concluding this chapter it is appropriate for me to note that I experienced every respondent as warm and interesting. During the interviews each one was open and willing to connect with me on a personal level. I liked all 11 respondents and have maintained contact with each one of them.

CHAPTER 6

LIFE ISSUES

This chapter's questions address the following primary areas of investigation: (a) Similarities and uniquenesses in creative individuals; (b) Life experiences affecting creativity; (c) Affective style of creative individuals: judgements, feelings, beliefs, and values; and (d) Interactions between creativity and God, sex, and money. In this chapter, the coresearchers are asked to respond to questions about a calling, the relationship between creativity and death, sex, God, money and criticism. They are asked about the adversities they have faced and about their success and uniqueness.

A Calling

Did the respondents experience a sense of a calling? Tom Robbins, Arthur Young, Wendy Palmer, George Leonard, Norma McLain Stoop, and Patricia Sun did. Niels Diffrient and Rowena Reed did not.

Even as a young child, novelist Tom Robbins felt a sense of a calling. Like Tom, visionary Patricia Sun remembers feeling as if her life were preordained when she was only 2 years old. Arthur Young wrote of this type of experience in his book The Bell Notes. Playwright Frank Hogan had difficulty with the word calling, but did experience his work being preordained. In the following quotation, Frank expressed the belief he had in himself. His early life was experienced as if he were waiting for something to happen, a personal transformation, in order to do the things he believed he was supposed to do.

LM: Did you have a sense of a calling?

FH: I don't think so. I know that goes against everything else I've said. I never thought of it as a calling. I suppose in a way, but calling is too strong. I don't cozy up to the word calling. I had belief in me. Looking back, it was as if I was waiting for something to happen before I could be me and do the things that I was supposed to do, whatever they were.

LM: Earlier you said you knew you wouldn't die because you hadn't finished your work, as if it were preordained somehow.

FH: Yeah. I think there is a kind of preordained thing. Is that what you mean by calling? Yes, I suppose preordained. I have felt that at times about my writing, that it was preordained. This is me. This is mine. This is supposed to be in here. It's mine.

LM: But as a child you never felt like you had been born for some unspecified but particular purpose?

FH: Except to get out of the house. And I didn't know that, believe me. I didn't really know that. I didn't know how many steps it would take, transitions, years, to become Frank Hogan.

Tom responded humorously at first, perhaps because he thought it arrogant to experience a calling.

LM: Do you have a sense of a calling?

TR: Yes, but I have an unlisted number.

LM: Or a special reason for being on this planet?

TR: Yes, as arrogant as that may sound. I've felt that since I was a small child.

From a young age, Patricia felt as if she had a special inevitable purpose in life.

LM: So you've had a sense of calling?

PS: A purpose, yes. It felt like an inevitable purpose that had something to do with helping people. I had a realization that I could see other people's points of view even when they were different than my own, and even though each is different, each could be valid. Even at 2. I wanted to write that down because I wanted to remember it, because that was important. There was something I was supposed to do.

Like Tom and Patricia, aikido instructor Wendy Palmer experienced a sense of a calling.

LM: Do you have a sense of a calling?

WP: Yeah. I think I do this work because I think I can't not do it. Even if somehow I came into $20 million, I might take a 6-month vacation. But I'm not sure if I would or not.

Neither Niels nor Rowena, both in the field of industrial design, experienced a sense of a calling. Niels had a sense of fortunate genealogical structure.

LM: Have you had a sense of calling?

ND: No. I have a sense of fortunate genealogical structure. Born into a family of peasants, if you will. Oddly enough, my brother and sister are quite intelligent. Both have advanced degrees, but in science and electronics.

LM: Are they creative?

ND: I don't know for sure.

Below is Rowena's response.

LM: Have you in your life had a sense of a calling, a purpose for being?

RR: Not a special time when I would say, look, I'm called upon to do this, this, and this. No. I would do it, and then after I had done it, I might be able to say it must have been that I should have done that because I did it and I did it well, and that's fine, but not before I did it.

LM: As a young person, did you have a dream or a vision about what you wanted your life to be?

RR: I don't think so. The whole thing is a puzzle. I don't live at the right time for me. I think I was ahead of my time, so therefore the time I grew up was very annoying to me.

Although Rowena did not experience a calling, upon reflection of a completed work she often experienced the feeling that this work was significant and perhaps necessary when viewed within the flow of her life. The term calling may seem pretentious to Niels and Rowena. Both industrial designers have an extreme sense of commitment.

Death

The next topic is death. In her book <u>Death and the
Creative Life</u>, Goodman (1983) says creative fulfillment
enables one to look to the future, unafraid of death, and
therefore to live more fully in the present. Her book was the
result of more than 700 interviews with people ranged widely
from failures through average, successful, and exceptionally
creative people, and her findings demonstrate that creativity
does affect people's attitudes about death.

I was curious about how people's creativity would be
affected by the confrontation with the knowledge that they
would die someday. The poet Norma McLain Stoop said death
motivates her to work. The knowledge that she will die pulls
her. She views death as a new challenge, but is frightened by
helplessness.

LM: How does the fact that you know some day you
are going to die affect you as a creative person?

NS: First of all, it makes me want to get an awful
lot done.

LM: Hurries you up?

NS: Pulls you. Secondly, I am very much looking
forward to dying. I've always liked a new
challenge, and, for all we know, this is going to
be a fun thing. A lot of people say it is; these
people that have died and come back. I'm looking
forward to it. It's a new challenge. The only thing
that frightens me is being helpless.

LM: The reason I ask you is that some people say
the reason that we create is to leave something
behind.

NS: That's terribly important to me, but I've got it.

Somewhat like Norma, Wendy and Niels find illness more frightening than death. Wendy relates to the world through her body, and as an aikido master, is physically present, graceful, and potent. She fears hobbling and struggling.

WP: Death is a necessity of life. I think it's not in dying so much as getting life. Death itself is not as frightening as when I see somebody, a very old person, hobbling down the street or struggling in or out of a chair. That's really frightening to me--to be in that state.

LM: Do you think you'd be living differently if you weren't going to die, or if you didn't know you were going to die?

WP: Never. Would I hustle?

LM: Would you?

WP: Not much more than I am now.

For Niels, retiring would be like giving up on life. He fears the interruptions of old age, and dreads the prospect of being sick or crippled. Below is Niels's response to my question about how death affects him. The older Niels grows, the more value he places on his time and the more carefully he chooses his projects.

LM: What about the knowledge that you're going to die someday? Does that affect you?

ND: Well, it hasn't. But as I approach 60, I begin to realize that maybe I should think a little bit more about how much more I can do. It's mostly a practical thing. I have no intentions of retiring or quitting or any of that. Once again, it would be like giving up life. But my projects take so long. If I choose a project, I commit 5 years to it right away. Well, how many more 5-year increments have I got, and what shall I do with them? It's like having just so much to bet. When you're down to the last five or six chips, you're a little more conscious than you were when you had a whole sack. That's about the only way I can see it, I think. And I have a lot more fear of the interruptions caused by old age. The dying part is not a real concern to me. It's the interruptions that precede it. I hate the idea of having to go to the hospital, be sick in bed, or being crippled by something.

It is a whimsical notion that one's life has been a tool in the historical evolution of the world culture. Many of the respondents expressed, as an answer to a direct question, some thoughts about their work being immortalizing to them. Below is educator Paul Torrance's response to the idea that we may desire to leave some creative work behind to provide a type of immortality.

LM: Rollo May talks about creativity and death in terms of the struggle for immortality. Do you experience that at all--a desire to leave behind something to immortalize yourself?

PT: Well, you are not supposed to admit that, but I guess in a way you do. I guess saving the archives and that sort of thing is part of that hoping that somebody will use it in creative problem solving.

Is immortality the ultimate reward for a creative person? Is it the prime motivator for creative work? Tom

179

Robbins thinks people are creative to prove their existence, because through creative work we leave behind some of our identity and uniqueness. He does not think work gives life meaning. He thinks life is meaningless and love gives it meaning. Tom's latest novel, <u>Jitterbug Perfume</u>, questions the concept of death as inevitable. In it, the two leading characters discover the secrets of physical immortality.

>LM: Well, I was going to ask if the knowledge of your own death...the fact that you're going to die some day...how that affects your creativity?

>TR: Well, it probably was a motivating factor. It probably is in all art. I've heard that people say that we create to justify our existence. I don't think that's true. I think that we create to prove our existence, and the desire for immortality, I think, is very simple for the creative person. Again, it's part of wanting not to come here and just disappear, but to leave something. Part of your identity and your uniqueness. But I don't know how I'll feel about that now that I've decided not to die. [laughter]

>LM: That does complicate things. Some existentialists talk in terms of death as the thing that gives meaning to our lives because, if we were never going to die, there would never be any push.

>TR: I feel just the opposite. I think that love is what gives life true meaning. See, life doesn't have meaning anyhow. We have to give it meaning. We could live, say not have a life span of 7l and 3 months--we could have an average life span of 200 years and life could be just as meaningful, if we gave it meaning.

Bell helicopter inventor and physicist Arthur Young's firm belief in reincarnation and the soul's immortality created a different perspective of death for him. He believes we are as old as the universe.

LM: Are you affected as a creative person by your knowledge that one day you'll die?

AY: Am I affected? Of course I'm affected. I should get to work on my will. But other than that, I wouldn't say I'm looking forward to death, because I'm enjoying life and so on, but I see that I can't go on like this indefinitely.

LM: Some people say that the fact that they know they are going to die someday motivates them to create things because in having something that they've left behind, something they created, they gain a certain kind of immortality.

AY: I don't buy that idea. I used to think it was a satisfactory answer, but now that I'm into reincarnation.... In fact, I never had any difficulty with the idea, just didn't know about it as a kid, that immortality is what it says it is. You're as old as the universe. Some souls are older than others, but maybe I don't know why that is. Some have made more effort, so they are in different stages, but fundamentally they are as old as the universe.

For Rowena, death has not been a strong motivation. She thinks everyone is in some way affected by the knowledge of death.

RR: I think everybody is affected by the fact that they have to die, not just creative people. I think creative people would resent it more than others because they enjoy life and feel the longer they live, the more they can accomplish creatively. Because creativity is the thing. One of the things about art today that makes it so unsatisfactory is the fact that the younger artists feel they can make a painting or a sculpture in a week or so. As far as I'm concerned, it's a sketch. It looks as if it had taken a week.

LM: Rollo May said that the reason we do creative work is to leave something of ourselves behind, a sort of immortality.

RR: That would be nice, and it would be kind of an immortality. I would agree with that. But that's not why I work. If I didn't feel that my work would be a part of me left, I would not stop working.

LM: Do you think it hurries you up at all?

RR: It should. It hasn't hurried me up enough.

LM: Some existentialists talk about death being the thing that gives life value. If we knew we would live forever....

RR: That's true. It's terminal. It's like the end of the race, and you say, well, if I don't do it by then...but I have given deadlines to myself. I hadn't expected to really live as long as I have. So I've just given that up. I've had several of those. I have thought, well, I won't live more than 5 years, and I'll take a 5-year lease on my loft. Really I did! Now I'm about to give myself another 5 year lease, but I'm not sure I'll make it.

The idea of being immortalized does surpass money as the ultimate reward, and it has the added dynamics of a recognition of spirituality and a life beyond worldly struggle. Like Paul, Frank is happy his work is being collected by a major university. He is motivated by the knowledge of his death. Knowing that he will die causes Frank to experience a sense of urgency, a desire to complete his work more quickly.

LM: We as human beings either unfortunately or fortunately have the knowledge that we're going to die someday. How is that with you as a creative person?

FH: I think it's very important. I'm very happy that Wyoming's Archives of Contemporary History is collecting my stuff. It tends, occasionally, when you get to be my age, to...a kind of urgency at times, a wish that things would go faster. In the very early days of the Maynard project, I was in the hospital, and I never had any question about the fact that everything was going to be great. I would lie in the hospital and think, "God's not going to let me die. I have to finish the Keynes project. So nothing's going to happen to me." I still believe this.

LM: Some people say the reason we create is to leave something behind.

FH: Max Geller, my psychoanalyst, says immortality. My character Mother Finn MacKool kills her whole family for immortality.

LM: Do you think that's true for you?

FH: I think it's the result, not the motivation. I don't think so. I suppose it must be part of the motivation. Sure, it's part of the motivation. I don't think it's the only motivation, though. Perhaps it becomes increasingly true.

The knowledge of death was not as strong a motivator for the respondents as I expected. It seems as if their lives are full and they enjoy living. All of the respondents expressed that their work is strong enough a motivator or purpose to continue living so they do not want to die, but they have no deep fear of death. Norma and Arthur expressed the idea of death as an exciting challenge. Several respondents, including Niels and Wendy, reported a fear of being infirmed and losing the high quality of life they now experience. As a group, the respondents are in love with living.

Sex

The following addresses the respondents' perception of the relationship between sex and creativity. The relationship of creativity and sexual energy has been addressed by theorists, especially those with a psychoanalytic orientation, who think that creativity is the result of sublimated sexual energy [see Chapter 2]. I questioned that aspect of the theory, and was curious what these individuals might say on the topic.

I asked the respondents if they had experienced a relationship between sexuality and creativity. Niels experienced less need to express himself sexually during those periods in which he found himself creatively productive. He does note that his wife, an internationally recognized artist, experiences the relationship between creativity and sexuality differently than he does.

ND: Well, I think there is a connection. If you love your work, the level of emotion is in the same category or at least related to the other kinds of love. You know, I only love two or three things in my life. My wife, my children, and my work. So it's not a hard thing...but I would say that when I am intensely involved in something, the sexual urge goes down. Now, my wife Helena, she's at her sexiest when she's just finished a big project, and it's installed, and she's acclaimed for it. Then she feels free.

LM: There have been a lot of theories about sexuality and creativity. Freud said it's all the same energy, and either you're using it properly through sexual intercourse, or you're using it improperly by being creative. Even though it's great for society....

ND: Did he say that? He was a mixed up old man.

By her own admission, Rowena Reed has not experienced sex as an especially satisfying part of her life; therefore, she could not see a positive relationship between sex and creativity in her life. She speculated that sex was important to Picasso. She theorized that sex is nice and normal and keeps one in balance, but it has not been balancing for her. Perhaps here is a case where Freudian theory is accurate. She is of the generation that had more orientation to the life Freud observed.

RR: I don't think that creativity is just a sublimation. Do you?

LM: No, I don't. How would you relate sexuality and creativity?

RR: Well, I think sexuality is a very important part of life, a very healthy part, a sustaining part. I guess I missed a lot of it. I've had a few experiences since I've been grown, but nothing terribly satisfactory.

LM: Do you find that your creativity is enhanced or diminished, either one, by sexual activity?

RR: I don't know. I don't think it has been enhanced all that much. It's a nice normal thing that keeps one in balance. From that point of view, creativity and everything else in life becomes easier. Maybe you can draw a direct line, but I don't find it to be true. Some people actually require more sexual activity than others. Picasso was such a person. I think it released certain creative impulses, and I don't think he could live without it. I'm interested in him, and I've read a lot about him. He was a pretty sexy character. I've also seen people, including students, where oversexual activity is debilitating. Physically, I mean.

Frank thinks good sex directly facilitates creativity. Sex has been an extremely important part of his life. He thinks that the more vigorous people are in general, the more vigorous they will be sexually. Frank found a great deal of support for his creativity in a sexual relationship. In Frank's case, freely expressed sexuality augments his ability to do his creative work.

LM: Was there ever anyone who facilitated your creativity, say between the time you were born and 18, before art school?

FH: I don't think there was anyone, really. I think I kind of lived that out on my own. I want to say this carefully, because ...I think that it was through sex contacts that I somehow or other realized that there was something out there which was what I was looking for.

186

LM: Was that more because of the type of individuals with whom you were having sexual activity, or did the sex itself somehow act....

FH: Sex itself.

LM: One of the reasons this is a particularly important question is that a lot of the older literature on creativity, particularly in the psychoanalytic school, says that we have this libido, this drive, this life force, and that we can use it the proper way, through sexuality, or we can sublimate it into artistic and creative pursuits.

FH: I disagree totally. I think that when you are using your sex drive, your creativity is at its best.

LM: A lot of sexual energy expended increases the amount of energy to be expended creatively?

FH: Absolutely.

LM: Do you think the more creative a person is, the more vigorous that person is sexually? Is there a correlation?

FH: Speaking for myself, yes.

LM: Do you think that in general?

FH: I guess so. Yeah, I think so. I think energy is energy. It renews itself. If you have it in your creative field, then you have it.... I think the sex energy is basic to it. I became active sexually in art school. I had been active before that, but that was just stuff in a subway john someplace. That was just cruising. I started to make relationships at that point. That was important too. There was a great deal of support for creativity that came out of that.

LM: You had an important, primary relationship, and that person....

FH: God, I would have killed anybody that called it a primary relationship. I knew a guy; I slept with him regularly...went to the theatre with him. My God, I'm the first person in the family who ever stayed out overnight, you know. And, God, the fights that used to go on in my house about my going out for the weekend. Oh! I thought they didn't know what was going on, you see.

Wendy thinks sexual activity is not directly related to creative output, because some people who are very sexual are very creative, and other people who are celibate are also very creative. It is interesting to note that celibacy is not the logical opposite of sexuality, impotence and frigidity are. A celibate must be cognizant of not having sex, there is no blotting out of sexuality, only a commitment not to act on it. She reported that generally, when her energy is high, she is both more sexual and more creative. Sometimes; however, other forms of satisfaction will reduce her desire to be sexually active. Probably, she does not see herself as dependent on a man, and he, in most cases, would be a requirement for sex. Wendy recalled a definition for satisfaction she once heard; that satisfaction means being well used.

LM: What about the relationship between creativity and sex?

WP: They said Bach had many children. He was obviously a very creative guy. Some Asian monks are completely celibate. I know celibate people who are very creative, so they are not necessarily interrelated at all.

LM: Have you found yourself more or less creative at times that you were more sexual?

WP: I would say that when the energy level is...when I'm on a roll and my energy is very expansive and I realize I'm in a very creative time...a lot coming forth...that sexuality is generally high too. But all energetic contacts are high at that time. Then often on the returning or receptive time, everything becomes less intense, so the sexuality would be less intense as well.

LM: So it's not your experience that when you're being especially creative that it takes all of your energy and there is no more left over for....

WP: That's also possible, because the combinations are endless. Sometimes when I'm out windsurfing all the time, I'm really into it; I come back in, and I don't have any need or urge or desire, whatever, that sexuality can fulfill. Someone had a great definition of satisfaction. They said it is being well used, which I really like.

Paul does not see a strong connection between sex and creativity, but like Rowena, thinks excessive sex could interfere with creative production.

LM: We talked about death and power and some of those things; the next area that I wanted to talk about is sex. Do you see any kind of connection between sex and creativity other than that is how we create other human beings?

PT: Well, right now I don't, and in my life I haven't seen any particular connection. I'm sure that sexuality could interfere seriously with creativity.

Much like Rowena, Patricia thinks that good sex is an important part of a healthy, balanced life and therefore does aid creativity. For her, creativity is especially important during her less sexual times. She also thinks that sex combined with intimacy is a part of a wholesome life. For Patricia, high intimacy sex enhances creativity.

LM: There have been a lot of conflicting theories about sex and the sex act and sexual love and how that fits in with creativity, or hampers creativity, or enables creativity, and everyone disagrees. What do you think?

PS: Well, I think that sex is such a wonderful thing that we have trouble accepting it. Of course, when I say that, I don't mean just sex sex; I mean sex combined with intimacy and connection. Sex is a biological thing. It's very real; yet we are not merely biological beings. We are also intellectual, emotional, feeling, thinking beings. There is nothing inherently wrong with sex. Sex is God-given and obviously important and wonderful, but we need to relax on it. Take it more like every other thing. Let it build towards the full potential it can have. It's interesting, in the Bible too, talking about chastity. Chastity just means pure, and that means a wholeness, that means not violating yourself. That's what you are supposed to be. It doesn't mean never have sex. It only means do it in a pure way. Do it in a way that really is aligned or loving.

LM: How do you think one's sex life affects one's creativity?

PS: Well, I think it's different for different people. I think it's nice if you have a good sex life, and obviously I would think you would have more creativity if you were content and healthy and alive sexually. It's certainly true that a lot of people sublimate drive and feeling that they have into creative pursuits, to get a high somewhere when they feel blocked sexually. I don't think it's the lack of sex that created the high in creativity. Creativity has its own high. It was the displacement of the lack, feeling a loss, needing to compensate it by doing something well, getting this alive feeling from somewhere. I think it's fine to be celibate, and it's fine to have sex. I don't think that's the question--that's missing the point. The point is the giving individual, their heart, their body, their innocence, their authenticity in their connection, and this could be married or unmarried. This is not the point as far as how it relates to creativity. I don't think it makes or unmakes creativity. That happens anyway. It certainly can appear to be intensified by people who torture themselves about sex as we have already seen in the world, but I don't think it was the torturing themselves about sex that increased their creativity. They already had it. They probably would have done it better and more sanely and more productively if they had a healthy sex life. It just kind of shows up as a real need to have it because they felt tortured sexually. And also, if they are really creative, they will be passionate.

LM: If you can, look back over your life at the times you've been more sexually happy or less sexually happy, fulfilled or unfulfilled. Has that had an effect on your own creativity?

PS: I don't think it has affected my creativity, no. Sometimes it's there, and sometimes it isn't. I know I'm very much more thankful for my creativity when it's not there. As I said, because I'm at least getting a high somewhere. I don't find myself less creative when I'm feeling sexually good. I'm perhaps more preoccupied with the person I'm involved with so I might be spending less time, but I don't feel less creative. I don't think anything inside has stopped. It might get delayed, because I'm putting my drive and attention into something else.

Patricia Sun's working medium is the spoken word. She intends to transform the energy of the group or individual. In formal words, she embraces the present situation in her psychic dynamics in order to create harmony and facilitate leaps in being and perception. During the questions concerning sex, she referred to this experience as working with one's inspiration. She stressed bringing feelings of intimacy, purity, and chastity into the action of sex. I am reminded of Carl Rogers's unconditional positive regard for a psychotherapy client as one of the necessary and sufficient conditions for change in this person's internal milieu. Might this be a necessary condition in one's creative projects as well? Each coresearcher has found ways of bringing intimacy feelings into the work of pushing the author's pen or the artist's pencil, or to reflecting feeling to a client, or to experiencing the inspiration when building a technological break-through.

Tom Robbins thinks sexual energy can be channeled into creative pursuits and that sexual energy indeed can add quality to creativity. Like Frank, Tom compared sexual energy with energy in general.

TR: I'll tell you what a painter friend of mine tells his art classes. He usually gets some pretty bad responses, especially from the women in class, but he doesn't care. He says you should always paint with a hard on, and I understand what he means. If you can arouse yourself into a state of excited tension, you do better work. So that might just be a metaphor, although there is something sexual about it. Especially if you are writing an erotic scene. If you can either be aroused before you start, or write the scene in such a way that it arouses you, then it would be much better.

LM: So you use the same energy for creating the book that you might use sexually?

TR: Well, not entirely, no. You can go down the rain chute with the umbrella down, but you can't go up the rain chute with the umbrella up. In other words, it doesn't work both ways. You can channel sexual energy into your work, into your creativity, but I don't think you can channel your creative energy into your sex. I think it's a different kind of energy. But I think of my muse always as feminine. I don't know exactly who she is or where she comes from, but I am certain that she wears lace panties.

LM: I always thought of muses as running around nude.

TR: That's not as erotic. I think of my muse as divine, but I also think that she shops at Frederick's of Hollywood.

There is disagreement about sexuality's relationship to creativity. Rowena Reed and Paul Torrance said that too much sex can deplete creativity. Everyone sees a balanced life, including sexual expression, as facilitating creative production. Tom Robbins can use sexual energy to improve his writing, especially if he is writing an erotic scene. Frank Hogan thinks sex may be the key ingredient to his creativity and suggested that he was first motivated to be creative by a sexual relationship. None of the respondents expressed the belief that a normal sex life depletes creativity, or that creativity is sublimated libido. It is more likely that a high degree of creative proclivity and a high degree of sexual proclivity, in an intimate and caring relationship, would coincide. Taking the respondents words as a whole, it seems that creative people can be sexually active people or they can be celibate. The question, "Can highly creative people be frigid or impotent?" remains unanswered.

God

The next topic, God and creativity, is closely related to sex and creativity. Both are powerful forces in our lives. Patricia believes that to continue our evolutionary process, we must incorporate the different aspects of ourselves, including our sexuality and God, into a whole, healthy, and sane individual.

> PS: When we recognized spirit was real and heavenly, then we polarized it against hell and earthliness and physicalness, so we had to mortify the flesh, we had to not love the body. Even though the realization was that the body was created by God, it was the temple of the spirit, we still denied our sexuality, our physicalness, our feelings, out of fear and somehow wanting to be one or the other, rather than understanding the wholeness of life.

For Wendy, creativity is a way of expressing the divine within into the field of action.

> WP: I would say that creativity is divine, the God within us. You know, if we're fortunate in the moment, as I've said before, when we look around us, we see God's creativity and the creativity of the divine spirit in the way the wind plays, nature, and that, hopefully, what we can do is be inspired by it and allow some of that spirit to come through us.

God does not seem to be a particularly important focus for poet Norma McLain Stoop. She thinks highly of personal spirituality, but thinks organized religion is harmful.

> LM: Does the divine have a place in your life?
>
> NS: You mean like God, religion?
>
> LM: However you choose to define that. Are you a spiritual person?
>
> NS: See, I don't think I am, but my sister thinks I am. I think that organized religion stinks. I think religion is great.

Rowena rebelled against the people who participate in organized religion because she found them limited intellectually.

> LM: Does the divine have a place in your life?
>
> RR: I really don't know. I think, deep down, it probably has, but I don't know. I've never really articulated that. I haven't gone to church for a

long time. I wouldn't mind going to church if I found a church that I felt was...kind of an intelligent church. Sometimes I feel quite close to my [late] husband for long periods of times.

LM: You feel connected?

RR: Yes.

LM: I've known people who have had important people in their lives die, who have that sense of strong connection and sometimes even guidance from that person on an unconscious level.

RR: I don't quite feel that. In a sense I feel that sometimes he is close to me, and I'm not far away. I'm able to imagine what he would like for me to be doing. I get that feeling, too, sometimes about my father. He was always a strong influence, although he didn't talk a lot.

Paul practices his religion, but finds it is less important to him now than it has been in the past. He still considers himself a religious person.

LM: Do you consider yourself to be a religious or spiritual person?

PT: Yes.

LM: Does divinity or spirituality, I don't know really what words to use, but does that have a large influence in your life, personally and professionally?

PT: For most of my life it has. It has been less in recent years.

LM: Do you practice any kind of religion?

PT: Yes, we are members of the Baptist church, and we have our own devotions every morning that we read from the Bible and pray.

Both Tom and Frank give the divine a central place in life.

TR: The divine is in everything, if only we recognize it. And when you start to see the divine in everyday objects, then the whole universe becomes alive for you.

In addition to a belief in God, playwright Frank Hogan reported experiences with divinity. In the following quotations, Frank described a spiritual revelation and psychic experience. He is religious, but like Norma and Tom, does not believe that organized religions are helpful. In fact, a personal spirituality without the support or interference of organized religion is a theme that occurs throughout these interviews.

LM: Do you see the divine as having any place in your life?

FH: Oh, absolutely. I am religious without being of a religion. When they asked me in the hospital, "What's your religion?", I said, "Deist." I guess that pretty well sums it up. I believe in God, and I believe in angels, and I believe in a lot of spiritual things. But I don't believe in religions. They've made a mess of it.

There was one incident in that hospital stay that I want to tell you, because it may be key in understanding what we've been talking about. On a Wednesday in September, 1981, I got terribly sick. I tried to reach my physician. I couldn't. I phoned a friend, and he came over and stayed the night with me. The following day, I was put in the hospital and the following Tuesday had a major operation. Because there were no semiprivate rooms available when I checked in, I was given a very tiny single room, with a john off to the right of the bed. On the night before the operation, I awoke in the middle of the night--early morning. Standing a short distance from the bed, in this very small room, stood a large oval of white light, shimmering and transparent. Sort of oval shaped, about 6 feet tall. Not frightening, quite reassuring, in fact. The night after the operation, back in my hospital room and bed--the operation had been done about noon--I woke. Lying on my back. Directly over my bed, suspended in midair, in a square of light, was a lady, all arms and legs, dressed in kind of a blue gauze, arms and legs churning like a pinwheel in a strong wind.

After being released from the hospital, Jim insisted that I stay at his apartment for a few days. One night, as I was getting into bed, I said, "Jim, I never told you about the white light, did I?" He said, "Did you see it too?" He'd seen it, not during my hospital stay, but the night when he stayed over in my house to be with me. He said, "I knew then that whatever happened, you were going to be alright." As for the lady with the arms and legs, two people who know about these things have, when I've told them, immediately identified her as Shiva, the Hindu god-goddess of life-death-reincarnation. I had discovered Shiva and Kali in the course of writing The Joshua People and glorified them in it. Perhaps that's why she-he appeared to help me out in my life-death struggle. Also, I'd had a prostrate operation, a matter which would be of prime interest to them.

198

After my father died, my mother went into a mental tailspin, wound up in a mental hospital getting shock treatments. I planned to go to Boston to visit her, but both Marian and Bill insisted, "Don't come, she won't know you, wait until she's better." But the shock treatments weren't working. On their advice, I decided not to go. Early Sunday morning, I dreamed that I was in a cottage which we had lived in for several summers at Nantasket Beach. I was seated in one of the wicker chairs in the living room. My father appeared in the dream and asked, "Where is your mother?" I told him I didn't know. "It's your job to know, isn't it?" he said. "Well, if she's anyplace," I told him, "she's in that little house down by the ocean." I woke, decided I would go to Boston, maybe take my father with me, I didn't know. Bill met me at the airport, drove me to the hospital. I saw my mother. She recognized me. Bill drove me to Marian's. She asked, "What made you change your mind about coming up here today?" I told her about the dream.... I came back to New York. That was Sunday. Tuesday, Marian phoned. The doctors had gotten through to my mother. The shock treatments which they were about to abandon had worked. They asked my mother what she remembered of the last 10 days. She recalled only one thing--that "everyday two men would take her down to that little house by the ocean...." Marian concluded, "I think your dream had something to it...."

Frank also described a more recent spiritual event in his life. Again, he stressed the importance of being receptive to messages and inspirations, and then following through with action.

FH: These are both important because of a third, and more recent event. I had a before-sleep message one night which said, "Everything you have heard up to the 19th...." I phoned a friend who knows about spirit things, numerology, etc. He said, "The first thing you should do is read both the 19th and 91st Psalms. Often, the numbers get reversed, but both have to do with communication between our space and the spirit of other worlds." As I said earlier, I don't know where the messages, inspirations, come from, but I tend to act on them, use them, write them, answer them.

None of the respondents classified themselves as atheists. Neither religion nor spirituality is a determining force in designer Rowena Reed's life. She attended church as a girl but was bored by the other people in attendance. She enjoys reading religious books and would like to find a church with interesting participants. Psychologist Carl Rogers rebelled against the influence of a suppressive fundamentalist religion foisted on him by his family, and that rebellion was the basis for an important developmental process in his life. For years he avoided the subjects of God and his religion. Recently he had experienced some reconciliation, and was questioning spirituality and seeking answers to questions about God and immortality. Frank Hogan and Tom Robbins also rebelled against suppressive religions. Frank was reared in a Catholic family. Tom's family was Southern Baptist. As was true for Carl, both Frank and Tom were influenced dramatically by their religions and their rebellions. Unlike Carl, Frank and Tom replaced religion with spirituality fairly early in life.

For Paul Torrance, Norma McLain Stoop, Patricia Sun, Wendy Palmer, Arthur Young, George Leonard, Frank Hogan, and Tom Robbins, spirituality has been a vital aspect of life. Paul Torrance is the only coresearcher who participates in organized religion. Spirituality is paramount for Patricia Sun. Myth, which Norma McLain Stoop considers the same as religion, has been important to her. A number of respondents, when asked about God, responded that spirituality or religion is influential for them, but they think organized religion is detrimental to individuals and society.

A number of possible explanations for this trend come to mind. The most obvious one is that the dogma of organized religion is a detrimental force to creativity; however, when a deeper look is taken, questions present themselves. It may be that creative people tend to question the given, whatever it is, and seek their own answers. Had Carl Rogers's family members been agnostics, would he have rebelled and adopted a religion? It is a question that will remain unanswered.

Evidently, rebelliousness appears more often in the highly creative than in the less creative personality. I also think it is important to note that most of the respondents experience a deep, personal connection to the spirit. My hypothesis is that the creative personality is a questioning personality, and it probably does not matter what spiritual concepts creative people are taught, because they will question those concepts and seek their own paths.

Money

Another powerful dimension in most people's lives is money. Each one of these creative individuals has been rewarded for their work, including monetarily. Convenience continues to allow the cultural and social definition of success to be found in money. A capitalistic economy will continually buy innovative ideas and products. I was interested in how money had affected these people both personally and professionally. I was especially interested in finding if their work had changed because of the influence of making money.

Only Norma McLain Stoop said that her work was strongly affected by money, because as she said, she always writes for a market.   I was surprised by the responses to the question about the first job they considered an expression of themselves.   Most of the respondents named jobs that were more mundane than I had expected.   They also named jobs they had at a surprisingly young age.

Tom Robbins' description of the first job he considered an expression of himself, a newspaper headline writer, is an example of the type of response that suprised me.   Money is important to him because it gives him mobility.   When he is being paid well, Tom works harder.   Money has become a symbol of the trust the publishers have in him and higher payment of money increases his motivation to write well, which increases his sense of pressure.   He expressed an element of denial about money having an influence on his work.   Perhaps he is haunted by the fear that his Muse is not for hire, that his creative impulse will refuse to come forth under the demand to write because of the contractual money agreement.

LM: What is the role of money in your work?

TR: Money gives me an intense Buddhistic calm. [pause]   Mostly it gives me mobility.

LM: Did your feelings about your work change when people started paying you well?

TR: It made me want to try that much harder to justify what they were paying me.   It gave me some fears   about letting them down, and so I worked even harder to try to do something that would be worthy of their trust in me.

LM: Did it make it more difficult to write?   Or easier?

TR: It put more pressure on me. They didn't put the pressure on me. I put it on myself, because then it became more imperative to me to...not necessarily to please them, because I think that would be wrong, because you have to write to please yourself, and hope that it pleases others. But just to do something that would be worthy of their trust and...exemplified by the money.

LM: So it was a matter of integrity?

TR: I guess...and pride, and not wanting to let anybody down.

Tom prefers to work with less pressure. He also enjoys surrounding his writing with an air of secrecy and drama.

LM: Did you ever in your life write anything and give it away for free?

TR: Oh, yeah. My inclination right now is, even though I am in a position of commanding what I consider to be extremely large advances, is not to ever get another advance. But just to go ahead and write at my leisure, and when I finish it...it's more fun that way. It's more fun also not just because there is less pressure, but also because it's more secretive. I like the act of writing to be charged with secrecy and drama. I like to think of myself going out to my work room like the Bronx Bomber, you know, going down in his basement and building these bombs when everyone thought he was a harmless bank clerk.

LM: When did you first start getting paid for doing something that you would consider self-expressive?

TR: When I was still a senior in college, I worked full-time, started out part-time and then went to full-time, on the copy desk of the <u>Richmond Times-Dispatch</u>, and even though it was an extremely conservative newspaper...there is an art to writing headlines, and I'm real good at it.

I was surprised by Tom's response to my question about when he first experienced security. He reported that he always experienced internal security, even when he was living on stolen vegetables. Perhaps what Tom means by security is the belief he has in himself that he will survive difficult situations, that he will create a solution to any particular life problem and move forward to the next phase of his life. This internal sense of security may be what allows him to be as experimental as he is. In his last book, <u>Jitterbug Perfume</u>, he changed his writing style even though he could have written another commercially successful book without the risk of change. Changing his writing style as he did is an example of how Tom has sought struggle, perhaps in order to prove to himself that he can survive change.

LM: When did you first find yourself leading a comfortable secure life?

TR: At birth.

LM: So you've never, even after college or when you began writing again in your 20's, you've never struggled?

TR: I struggled when I first moved here. For example, I was a midnight shopper. I would go out and raid fields late at night and steal broccoli and cabbages and cauliflower to live on. But it never seemed like a struggle to me. I've always felt secure.

LM: So you have inner security.

TR: I guess so.

A substantial proportion of the respondents expressed minimal ties with money as a motivating factor for their work. Evidently, real success in a creative field is not primarily measured monetarily. Frank Hogan perceived money as having changed him personally, but not his work. Here again a respondent has described a split between self and action.

LM: When did you first start to get paid for something you considered an expression of yourself?

FH: When I was about 13. I got a job as an usher in the motion picture theatre down at Nantasket Beach called the Bayside.

LM: Did your feelings about your work change when people began to recognize you and pay you for your work?

FH: Oh, sure. Well, the minute Tim Horan said, "Pick a couple of titles out of there," all of a sudden, I thought, "Gee, he must think I'm pretty good." Which he did.

LM: How did that change your work?

FH: I don't think it changed the work. It changed me.

The way in which Frank changed was in his realization that he was a skilled and talented writer, and as a result, he felt more self-confident. Like Frank and Tom, neither Paul, Carl, Rowena nor Patricia have allowed money to influence their work. In order not to have to change his work, Paul financed his own research.

PT: In the way I've done things, it hasn't made any difference how much I was paid. I've worked harder at some things at which I got no pay than I did for things for which I was well paid. I've had to choose to do things for which I would get money for survival purposes and to get money to do the research that I've done. I've put all the money that I got from royalties and speaking engagements into my research.

Like Tom, Carl felt secure even during difficult times. It may be that this inner security was what enabled him to challenge the accepted concepts in psychotherapy.

LM: How do you think that your life's work has been influenced by the need to obtain money?

CR: Very little. I simply was fortunate on that. There were plenty of times when I was hard up, but making money has never been a big thing, and I've never had a time when there was not enough.

Rowena does not believe fine art should be done for money. She made the choice to pursue her work in education and three dimensional design even though she could have made more money elsewhere. Currently she teaches only half-time at Pratt Institute to give herself time to write about three dimensional design, a field she originated. She has faced sexual discrimination in her work, and the result has been that she has often made less money than she would have as a male.

LM: What sort of experimental work have you done?

RR: This whole thing has been experimental. My whole life has been experimental work.

LM: Have you ever done work for which you didn't expect to be paid, just to see where it went, what would happen?

RR: Yes, the sculpture that I did, what little there was of it, was purely experimental, and I didn't get paid and would not have expected to get paid. That I would consider really bad--to do fine art for money.

LM: How have you dealt with that in your life, creativity versus commercialism?

RR: I think I made the choice. I could have made more money. I've done professional industrial design and made a lot more money than I did teaching, but I made the decision to teach.

LM: Your sacrifice was monetary?

RR: I've been restricted. I haven't always had everything that I wanted. I have less now than I've ever had in my life. When I was teaching full-time, I made more. Now I'm just teaching part-time. As I say, I came in at the wrong end of the stick as far as the teaching salaries. My successor at Pratt as chairman was offered twice the salary that I had.

LM: Did your feelings about your work change any when you began to get paid?

RR: Not especially. I was never really...I always knew that fashion drawing wasn't all that serious. I mean it was on a certain level, and it couldn't go any deeper. I enjoyed it. All women like clothes, and that was fun. You try to dramatize the clothes, and you got paid for it. It was amusing.

LM: Have you ever worked for free?

RR: No. I'm trying to remember if I ever did. Not that I would refuse, but it just didn't come up.

LM: When did you first begin to be paid that you consider an expression of yourself, your first job that you considered to be an expression of your personality?

RR: I guess I could always draw. I think it was somewhere between high school and college, maybe in the summer. I don't know exactly. I used to do fashion drawing. I worked for the newspapers. I was good at it, too. I won a prize to take a trip to Europe.

Like Frank, Tom, Paul, Carl, and Rowena, Patricia would not change her work because of money. She used to speak to groups for free, but learned that charging money was important because it allowed reciprocity. Any time she gets paid it is for an expression of herself. One of her primary goals in her work is to transform energy, that is to replace fear with love, and she can do that any time, not just when she is speaking before an audience.

LM: When did you first begin to be paid for something you considered an expression of yourself?

PS: Well, any time I got paid, it was for something I considered an expression of myself, even when it was something silly. I put myself into it. I still didn't do just like they wanted me to do. I always added something else. I feel that's fair, and anybody can do that. I mean, you work for the telephone company or an airline, and you work to bring in yourself, and you become good at it because, not only do you meet their obvious needs, but you help change energy as you do it. But I started getting paid for what I do now about 2 years after I started doing it. I did it for 2 years for nothing. During that time I realized I did it for nothing because I wanted to be a saint, and I realized that meant you didn't charge money. I was at a house with about 20 people. They were all asking me questions, and I basically was doing what I do. I didn't get to eat any dinner. This one man who was a bodyworker came up and said, "You know, I feel rude asking you these questions while you are trying to eat. I feel like I am grabbing at you. Why don't you have a workshop so I could pay you and feel comfortable asking you questions?" I realized in that moment that here was an ego thing in not charging any money. That it was a way to be superior. That really wasn't empowering the very thing I wanted to do. I wanted people to be comfortable and not feel indebted, because it is an unhealthy situation if they do. As I started meditating on it, I realized that I had to charge money. It had to be more than something frivolous, more than dinner and a movie, but not too much. Then, of course, I had money to live on and support my family, and that was good.

LM: What would occur in your life to change your work? You were talking earlier about many things you could have done and made more money, and instead you do what you do and make a moderate amount. Money has not been the great influence in your life. Do you think that might for some reason change?

PS: If it changes, it changes by itself. My purpose--and my overall purpose is to feel heaven

on earth--won't change. I'm really going for that.
That's what my life is for. That means I need to
enjoy my life, too.

Patricia would not change what she does to make more
money. She believes that whenever money becomes a problem,
money is not the real issue. Power and victimization are often
disguised as money issues.

PS: I would allow more money to come to me and
still do what I'm doing, and I would be doing what
I'm doing if less money came to me. I guess the
other thing on money is that I measure success not
by money. Money is incidental. Whenever we have
to deal with it, it's usually about some other issue
that isn't money at all. Somebody is using the
money to hold some idea about power or
powerlessness. So we have to be clear about it so
we can't keep blaming it on money rather than
their own power and ability. You don't do people a
favor if you let them not pay in a world where
that's how you express power. You compound their
belief that they are a victim.

Unlike the others, Norma said she writes strictly for a
market. It is important for her that others read what she
writes, so she, like Tom, always writes for publication. Having
her poetry read and her photographs seen is more important to
her than the amount of money she is paid. Norma is employed as
an editor of <u>Dance Magazine</u>; however, whenever I asked about
her work she would respond with a comment about either her
poetry or photography. When asked if she ever changes her
writing in any way because of money, she responded with the
following statement.

NS: For God's sake, what a silly question.
Everybody writes for their market. I write a

completely different article depending on my market. I write a completely different movie review depending on the group of people who are going to read it.

LM: The one place you don't do that is in poetry that is going to be published in university journals?

NS: Sure, I write for them. I write the kind of thing that I know they are interested in.

LM: So when you sit down to write a poem, one of the first things you consider is where you plan to publish the poem. Do you ever write a poem without that foreknowledge?

NS: Sure. That was usually when I was a freelance poet. Now let's see, the last poem I had published was about 3 years ago, because I don't sometimes send them in as I told you. The poems I've written lately were poems I had to write for one reason or another, but the minute I saw it, I said I'm going to send it to such and such eventually.

LM: You wrote it without knowing where you were going to send it, but as soon as it was written, you knew where it would fit.

NS: Yeah, I want people to read whatever I write; therefore, I write always from the point of view of fitting into a market.

LM: How has money affected your work?

NS: I cannot stand, my God, I'm going to lose friends, I cannot stand people who say, "I do it for myself."

LM: So you do it for money?

NS: I do it for people to see. People to see means doing it professionally, and doing it professionally means some sort of reward.

LM: Do you work harder if you are going to get paid more?

NS: I work much less hard. I work hardest on my so-called literary poems. That is the one place that you don't get paid. You very often have poetry published in an extremely good university quarterly, and you will get $10 or nothing; whereas if you write for Ladies' Home Journal, you get $5 a line.

Niels has been poor, and for him money is a safeguard against poverty.

ND: My need for money is to avoid being poor. It's not so much a drive to earn more for the sheer satisfaction of being wealthy as it is a safeguard against poverty. I remember well what being poor meant and it was a kind of a prison without walls. Once you've escaped, the only assurance against re-confinement is having money. Money also allows me to experiment with life and my need to design. It saves me from having to take orders from others that I think are life restrictive.

For Niels, money is important because it gives him freedom to experiment with life and design, freedom from having to take orders from others, and freedom from the fear of poverty. Arthur Young has not been affected greatly by the need to earn money. His helicopter invention has provided him with a comfortable living. Wendy Palmer said she would not change

212

anything about her work because of the influence of money. Even though George Leonard said he is motivated to write by the need for money, money does not strongly influence what or how he writes. Norma McLain Stoop was the only coresearcher to respond that her work is directly affected by money. She commented that her wish is for her poetry to be read and her photographs seen, and that she has no need for her readers and viewers to like her work. Recognition was enough of a reward for her; however, she always writes for publication and payment.

Several of the coresearchers have in common the realization of the necessity of having enough money to live a chosen lifestyle without pursuing their career goals with money as the symbol of success. Descartes's (1960) advice is appropriate to them; make a virtue from necessity, accept what you can not change, and act on that which is inspiritational.

As a group, the respondents work because they experience an internal drive to do so. They are committed to their work and responsible to their publics. If society, culture, or the economy rejects one of their projects, they move on to the next. They express the thought that they would have done that particular project whether there was money involved in its completion or not. If money is not the motivating factor in creativity, what is? Is there a unifying factor? For 10 of these 11 creative people, the primary motivation for working is not money, rather it is the sense of fulfillment they experience as a result of expressing themselves through their work.

Criticism

Being in the public eye puts the respondents in the position of receiving criticism. Criticism is similar to money in that both have the possibility to influence and even control creative work. I was interested in how these people respond to criticism, as well as how criticism affects their work.

Frank experiences a split between himself and his work. He said that criticism has affected him personally, but it has not affected his work. Earlier in this chapter he said the same thing about money. The following is quoted from Frank's interview.

LM: How do you respond to criticism? Especially from critics?

FH: Silence.

LM: How do you respond inside? I'm talking about when you have written a play and the critics review it, maybe good, maybe bad, and it's time for you to write another play. Does what they said affect what you write?

FH: It probably makes you go after it.... For myself, I think what I do is say, "I'm going to write what I want to write, make my peace with it, and say, 'Hogan, you are not a formula writer'."

LM: It doesn't affect you?

FH: Oh, I don't say that. It affects me--but not my writing.

LM: If you had never had a review in your life, you would be doing what you are doing right now?

FH: That's...well, I think you can't have production without reviews. The production is important. The publication is important.

LM: Pretend we live on another planet where they don't review plays. How would your work change?

FH: I would be doing what I am doing now. It does not change the general thrust of it.

The following is George's discussion of criticism. In another chapter, I referred to an example of creativity occurring during George's interview in which he emphasized the importance of considering nothing a mistake. The example follows.

GL: I have high respect for the vocation of the critic. Critics are the candle burners on the altar of art.

LM: The cattle branders on the altar of art?

GL: Candle burners; the cattle branders too. Sacrificial lamb. There is an example of creativity we just had there. I said "candle burners," and you thought I said "cattle branders." When I heard cattle branders, I could have considered it a mistake. But far from being a mistake, you said something of interest; if this little metaphor is of any interest, it is the other part of it. Because also on altars people burn cattle, lamb, sheep, in sacrifice. So now we have one full metaphor. The critics are the ones who burn the candles and sacrifice the author sometimes, burn the author. That's what creativity is--not taking anything as a mistake, jumping on every opportunity, seeing everything as a possibility, rather than saying no, that's wrong.

Earlier in his interview, Tom referred to critics as a school of piranha. He also said he rarely reads anything written about him. There was one time he liked what a critic said.

LM: On the cover of <u>Still Life With Woodpecker</u>, you comment on a remark of a critic. "Tom

215

Robbins writes like Dolly Parton looks." How do you respond to criticism from people who are not creative writers themselves?

TR: I try not to even read it.

LM: Did you ever figure out what that meant, I mean about Dolly Parton?

TR: Yes, I think I know what it means. I hope it means that my paragraphs have cleavage. I have a bouffant style, rather than a pixie cut. It was one of my favorite reviews. One of my favorite remarks ever made about me.

Because her role has been primarily that of teacher, Rowena has been protected from criticism; however, she expects to experience it in the future, when her book is published.

LM: How have you been affected by criticism?

RR: I have been in more or less a protected position. Wait until my book is published, then I'll get it from all sides. I'm not looking forward to it, but I'm not afraid of it.

LM: Do you think you will read what the critics have to say?

RR: Oh, sure.

LM: Do you think it will change anything you do?

RR: It won't change my point of view.

Over the years Wendy has become less affected by criticism. She thinks she has received both more praise and more negative criticism than she deserved.

LM: What about criticism. How are you affected by criticism?

WP: That's been changing. It used to be that I would fight against adverse criticism and look up to positive criticism. But, you know, over the years, especially during aikido, and there have been a lot of situations in which being a woman and having a lot of students is threatening to a lot of men who have spent their lives being recognized as aikido teachers, I feel like I've had it from both sides. I feel I have received more praise and criticism than I deserve. Over the years, I have become much less reactive. You know, in any crowd some people are going to love you and some are going to irritate you.

Norma, Patricia, Carl, and Paul are not greatly affected by professional criticism. The following is Norma's response.

NS: I never had anybody criticize my poety except my sister. Once I wrote a poem and she said, "That is the worst poem I ever read in my life."

LM: You never had a professional critic write about you?

NS: Write, yes. They never didn't like it.

LM: Still, how do you respond to people writing about your work.

NS: I don't care what they say as long as they have read it.

Patricia speaks to such a varying audience, in large numbers and in differing cultures and countries that she expects to be misunderstood sometimes. In the following quotation she described an experience in Madrid. She tries to express herself clearly, and intends for people to find meaning in what she says. Two of the purposes of her workshops are to shift energy and generate love.

LM: I guess you say things in workshops that people misinterpret, and then they say you said something entirely different. How do you respond to that?

PS: First of all, that goes with the territory. You cannot control what people will think about what you say. I make a tremendous effort to say things as cleanly as I know how. I really make an effort to do that. The most difficult workshop I ever did, was in Madrid. It was a meeting of psychiatrists and psychiatric nurses. At the workshop, a woman came up to me, very close to my face, and she was livid. She said to me, "I hate you, I hate you." She's right in my face, and I could feel the pain in her. I could feel the turmoil. I asked why. She said, "Because you can't love me, you don't love me." I said "Yes, I do. As I said it, she felt it. It was almost like her face cracked, and she fell crying into my arms, and I said "I love you."

Patricia's purpose in workshops is to help people experience love. Many people, especially those living in suppressive cultures, fear transcendental love. Patricia expects criticism and perseveres because sometimes, as occurred in Madrid, she succeeds in helping people open themselves to receiving higher or transcendental love.

Paul's feelings about criticism differ depending upon the amount and quality of information about his work his critics possess. Occasionally he will change his point of view and go beyond where he otherwise would have gone; however, he usually experiences criticism as harmful in the sense that it tends to prejudice people inexperienced in the field toward the critic's view rather than toward the intentionality of the researcher.

> PT: Yeah, I guess there is a difference. There are some critics who criticize what you do without knowing what you do. Then there are others who criticize what you do--they know what you've done, but don't understand what you've done. Of course, they are a little easier to deal with because the first group is frequently a very powerful group and will jump onto something without even looking into it. They don't know what you've done, and they attribute things to you you haven't done. That is difficult to deal with.

> LM: How do you respond to criticism?

> PT: Well, generally, I just grin and bear it.

> LM: Do you read other people's criticism of you?

> PT: Yes.

> LM: Does it ever inspire you? Or do you move forward...?

> PT: In most cases I've already proven that what they say is not true, but sometimes I change my point of view and go beyond where I would otherwise have gone.

> LM: So, sometimes it has helped?

> PT: Yes, it has been advantageous at times.

LM: But usually not.

PT: No.

Professional criticism had little meaning to Carl; however, he could become concerned when receiving criticism from someone who cared about him and whom he trusted to speak from their personal experience.

CR: I try to live my own experience, not by their criticism. I can be knocked off balance a little bit if it's someone close to me and who cares for me.

LM: I am wondering if most of your work isn't experimental, because of your sense of growth and change.

CR: Yes, in a broad sense it is.

Both Tom and Frank have found criticism hurtful. The other coresearchers were not greatly affected by it. It was rare for anyone to find criticism helpful, that is, a motivation to add to or change their work. The impression the respondents gave is that feedback does not affect their work. They value the idea that their work is all theirs, that it is personal, and that others do not contribute to it. Only Paul reported that criticism can be helpful, and for him it was a rare occurrence. The respondents recognize their position, expect criticism, and consequently have grown tough-skinned. Occasionally, positive criticism is experienced as entertaining or uplifting. Negative criticism sometimes, as with Frank, serves to motivate people to remain true to themselves.

There seems to be general agreement about criticism. No one particularly liked, needed, or appreciated outside criticism. We can assume that most people have the ability to form a critical faculty, especially those doing highly creative work.

As in Arieti's (1976) model, criticism must be a conscious process used for refinement of one's work. If the critical faculty remains in the shadow of consciousness, it could become destructive of one's creative work. This has not happened to any large degree to this sample of creative people, but they apparently know the struggle. Tom Robbins described critics as a school of piranha, waiting to slash and devour someone's inspired work. Tom seldom if ever reads criticism of his work. It could be that the respondents' critical faculties are so active that additional criticism is hurtful or destructive. If, as Arthur Young and George Leonard believe, everyone is equally creative in potential, then this critical faculty may be the key to some creative behavior.

Adversities

Another area in which I was interested is adversity. How had adversity affected the respondents? Writer Tom Robbins' social life has been negatively influenced.

LM: What do you see as the major costs and the major benefits of your creative career?

TR: It's very hard to have a family life. Or really much of a social life. In my particular case, I don't get to see films that I'd like to see, don't get to read as many books as I'd like to read. But probably the largest cost is social.

Industrial designer Niels Diffrient has not experienced much adversity in his work, or at least he has not defined setbacks as adverse. He felt more emotionally affected by his work at the time of the interview than ever before.

LM: What about adversity? How have you been affected by it? As far as your creative work is concerned?

ND: Well, I must say, I've been rather lucky. I haven't had any major adversities. As a matter of fact, I think I've been extremely lucky in that sense. I've had a lot of setbacks, but it's to be expected, minor things. I've had one failed marriage, that set me back a couple of weeks. When it failed I realized it wasn't the right marriage anyway. She ran off with somebody else. I didn't do that part. And it hit me hard when I found out, but the funny thing is, after the immediate shock was over, I suddenly felt released. I suffer the most...I have suffered the most in my current work--right now. I have been bothered the most by the fear of it not working. I can't remember ever being so affected.

Playwright Frank Hogan's greatest felt adversity was not having a mentor. He thinks he could have been more successful if he had a mentor to promote his work. He also considers his religion an adversity.

LM: You said your mother was critical of your creative outlook when you were a child. Do you think that facilitated your creativity or do you think it hampered it?

FH: I think probably my mother was afraid. First of all, this religious thing. The Catholic religion is really terrible for creativity. It truly is.

LM: Have you made use of adversity?

FH: Oh yeah, sure. Constantly. I've had a pretty chancey life, you know. Survival is a very good perspective to look at life through. I want to survive a long time.

222

LM: Have you used adversity in your work?

FH: No. I think my biggest adversity is the fact that I would have liked to have had a mentor-promotor. I would have loved that. I'm not sure I'm not too independent to accept the idea, but would have loved the right one. I'm going to have to learn to hype myself. I could promote you. I could promote anybody, anything, and I did. I can do lots of things. But promote Frank Hogan, no.

Throughout his life, psychologist Carl Rogers met opposition, and usually won.

LM: You have had a fair amount of opposition throughout your life.

CR: But usually have won. I realize there have been several points in which if I had been defeated....I don't know. I don't know how well I would handle defeat. I had a couple of real flops in my life of my own doing. They were quite upsetting, and I didn't know how to take them.

LM: Have you made use of adversity in your life?

CR: I suppose sometimes. For example, I went through a really horrible period with a patient--the one I was talking about earlier--and I realized after that, after some therapy, that my doing therapy was much improved, my creativity was much enhanced. Even though at the time, when some of the first interviews I'd ever filmed were being filmed, I was going through a lot of hell. I was sure these people were getting a last example before I went nuts. So there was some surprise that everything I did was considerably enriched.

For aikido instructor Wendy Palmer, opposition can be expanding or inhibiting.

> WP: In straightforward opposition, I'm really good. I think it's kind of whether the opposition hits one on the in-breath or the out-breath, and I mean that metaphorically. I think there are times when we are feeling expansive--we're in an expansive role, we are able to utilize the energy of the opposition in a creative way. If it hits us on the in-breath when we are going through a contraction, then it creates a feeling of claustrophobia and fear. Also, some of it is a character tendency. Some people are more accustomed to using opposition creatively and others are not.

Poet Norma McLain Stoop thinks opposition is necessary for people to gain clarity about which things are truly important to them. She enjoys a challenge.

> LM: What kinds of opposition have you met in your life?

> NS: Boy, have I met opposition. First of all, my husband was not the least bit interested in poetry, and he wasn't interested in my doing anything. I wrote my first poem when I was 7 years old. From then on, I wrote poems all the time, and prose, and short stories. Now, my husband had an operation for cancer of the kidney, and he was told he had a 50% chance of living for 5 years. I had just gotten what I wanted, an offer to sing in night clubs. See, I don't like doing any of this. I like to sing. Singing is the only thing I really care about. Photographs second. He decided to move to Greenwich, Connecticut. When he decided to move to Greenwich, it [my career as a singer] was over.

LM: Do you think this kind of opposition has hindered or helped?

NS: It is one of the best things. It doesn't seem so at the time, but because of the opposition, you know what you really care about.

LM: Do you generally make use of adversity?

NS: Absolutely. I feel sorry for people who don't. I don't think anybody appreciates--I hate the word happiness because it's not a true word. I don't think people appreciate good times unless they know the bad times.

LM: What do you see as the major costs of living the life-style you live?

NS: Tension and illness that is due to tension.

LM: What about the major benefits?

NS: Happiness, fulfillment. I'm bored to death once I've licked a problem, so I hope to God that I decide 5 years from now that I want to be a nuclear physicist because I like a challenge.

Educator and creativity expert Paul Torrance's disability segregated him, made him different.

LM: You have talked about trying to plow and not being able to get the rows straight.

PT: Yes, that was a disability, I think. It started with my handwriting on the blackboard and not being able to write in a straight line. Then when we got lined paper, I still couldn't get it straight.

225

I still can't drive a car because of it. And I still hang pictures crooked.

LM: Do you think this disability influenced your creativity?

PT: I suppose it may have. I think it kind of made me a minority of one. At least I attained some comfort in being a minority of one. To be creative, there are times you have to be a minority of one if you are going to have on original idea. And if it's too uncomfortable you're not going to do it. I have attained enough comfort to take that kind of risk.

Mystic and psychotherapist Patricia Sun views adversity as opportunity.

PS: I kind of use anything that most people call adversity as an opportunity to think differently and get a new orientation to the world. I believe it is an opportunity to shift and be more than we were. The reason people believe there will always be wars is that we are so attached to war as a solution. Until we really hate war enough to stop, we must use arms to defend our position. Until then, which is what I think is coming, we will have wars. We are making it difficult to have wars because of nuclear weapons and the ability to annihilate the whole planet. That style of solving a problem just won't work anymore.

Below is Tom's response to my question about being hampered.

TR: I was hampered by just about everybody. By teachers, by most of the women I've been involved with. Not deliberately, but by making the kind of demands you just can't make on a creative person and expect them to be creative. They can't turn you into Ozzie Nelson and still expect you to be Henry Miller.

Uniqueness and Success

In spite of adversity, hampering occurrences, and people, the coresearchers have succeeded in their creative endeavors. A number of guesses can be made and hypotheses developed about the reasons, but I wanted to know why these people think they are successful and unique.

Carl Rogers described the two qualities to which he attributed his success. He was a loner and he did not take himself too seriously.

LM: Why do you think you've been able to do what you've been able to do?

CR: Well, two things come to mind. One is that I'm a loner. I go off on what I think I'm interested in and I do it, and I don't consult with a lot of people before doing it. Well, it is, it is naive. So being a loner helps. Not taking myself too seriously. I think there are plenty of times, especially when I'm really intense about something, I say, "What the hell. It isn't that important." In some basic ways I can smile at my earnest endeavors.

Writer George Leonard told me why he is not more successful rather than why he is successful. He views himself as lazy, and with the exception of two of his books, he said he usually has written when he has needed money. It is interesting to note that Carl and George interpreted my question somewhat differently.

GL: I just feel I haven't accomplished as much as I should. I'm basically kind of lazy. I'm not an overachiever.

LM: It doesn't sound that way.

GL: I truly am. I love to lie around in bed. I don't work long hours, and I think I have not achieved my potential. If I had been a really hard worker, I would have achieved a lot, lot more. When I wrote Education and Ecstacy, I wrote passionately. I had to write it. The Transformation, I had to write. The Ultimate Athlete, The Silent Pulse, and The End of Sex I wrote basically because I didn't have any other job--I needed money. I wouldn't have written them otherwise. Now, once I got into them, I got very involved.

The ability to stay with a project for an extended period of time is the quality to which Paul Torrance attributes his success. He became creative because he needed and expected to learn and could not learn from his father, so he found ways to teach himself, which apparently became his method of working.

LM: You have clearly had a lot of success. How do you account for it?

PT: Well, of course, one thing has been working hard and long hours over a number of years. I think, in terms of my research, continuing to work on those sorts of problems has led me to do research that adds up to a body that has some meaning and strength to it, rather than jumping here, there, and everywhere. And being ingenuous, trying to make the best of what's available even though you couldn't do just what you wanted....using the opportunities and resources that you had. In my upbringing I got a lot of opportunities for practicing. My father was an extremely poor teacher, and so anything that I learned I had to invent or learn on my own. My mother was a better teacher; but I was a boy and expected to learn from my father, and my sister was supposed to learn from her....Being on my own so much, and being put off to do jobs by myself with no one around, I had to invent and practice it and do it my own way rather than the way someone had taught me.

Rowena would have been bored had she not actualized her potential.

LM: How do you account for your originality?

RR: How can I account for that? You have it or you don't.

LM: You think it is inborn?

RR: I'd have to think about that. I believe so. Because I have students who in the first year of their art education will demonstrate originality.

LM: Why do you think you have been able to do things others have not?

RR: I suppose because I wanted to very much, and because I would be bored not doing something. Isn't that the real reason people do things? Because ordinary life is so mundane and boring? Don't you find a lot of women lead boring lives? Of course, I think it is hard on women. I think they have not been urged. Now they are. Of all my college friends, I am an oddity. I can't think of another who had a professional career.

LM: So maybe you had more guts?

RR: I suppose. I thought I had a lot of guts. See, I didn't get everything from my husband. My father had great drive.

LM: And you internalized some of that drive.

RR: I must have inherited some of that drive. And my husband had great drive. I had two examples. I couldn't have any women role models, there weren't any. I suppose there were, but I didn't know them. They were scarce.

Philosopher and inventor Arthur Young does not think of himself as exceptional, but rather as acting when others do not.

AY: I really don't think I am exceptional. I think everyone has exactly the same resources and they tap them to different degrees.

LM: So it's your action?

AY: Yes.

Tom does not feel compelled to write novels; however, he said had he not written a novel by this time in his life, he probably would feel frustrated.

TR: I think I was probably compelled in the beginning at a very young age when a fairy came to my cradle and touched me on the forehead with a stone. I don't know which one. You know more about that than me. Or maybe it was a sausage. But I haven't felt real obsessed. If in this stage of life, I'd never published a novel, I probably would have an undercurrent of unhappiness. I don't think

I'd be destroyed by it as some people are. I have too happy an outlook on life. But underneath, I would be unhappy. I am perfectly willing to go for years without writing anything. But I'm not sure I'll make it, because in the past when I've gone too long, I've gotten pretty crazy. But I could paint as well. An interviewer asked me once, if I could not write, what would be my second choice. I said jewel thief. There is probably similarity between being an artist and being a jewel thief, the way I practice my art anyway.

Patricia named genuineness as the quality that led to her success.

LM: How do you account for your originality?

PS: You know, I really don't know. Although I don't think of reincarnation as a linear thing, I sure do know things I didn't learn here. I think at some level any human being can tune into the life of any other human being.

LM: How do you explain your success?

PS: I think it is because I deliver the real thing. You have to be it, you have to generate it, you have to make the psychic connection. It has to be felt. I also perceive it as a part of my work not just to tell people how or what to feel, but to really connect with them on that intimate level, using both hemispheres, having your clairvoyance operate. It calls to itself. If I use clairvoyance to communicate with you, your clairvoyance rises to match it. When you use it with me, mine rises to match it. When you send me love, mine rises to meet you. When I send you love, your love rises to me.

Norma's statement about not thinking she is exceptional is similar to Arthur's statement. Like Paul, Norma commented on making use of what was available to her. She thinks fun is the most important element in her life. A theme, common to all the interviews, is one Norma expressed: that by not fragmenting herself she is more likely to be successful.

LM: Why have you been successful?

NS: Because I was determined to be. Because my mother and father said, "If you don't get an A, you flunked." That's why I've been successful.

LM: Is that how you account for your exceptionality?

NS: I don't think I am exceptional. I think I have just made use of the things I have at hand. I think fun is the most important thing, I really do. I think you are a bore if all you think about is your poems or articles, or the weather. I don't worry about anything I can't do something about. That is one of the things that has made me successful. I don't fragment myself. My own work, I have control over. What I decide to do, I have control over.

Summary

The life forces under the influence of Scorpio-- sex, death, and money, are emotionally charged and potentially related to creativity. As does the Phoenix, the creative must rise from the ashes, soaring to new heights of awareness and

232

productivity. In addition to the relationship between creativity and sex, death, and money, this chapter addressed other involvements of Scorpion energy: criticism, adversity, and the experience of a calling.

Of the nine creatives who responded to the question about a sense of a calling, seven reported feeling as if they were called to do their creative work. I was struck by this finding. If a creative action is, at least in its initiation, the inspiring, or breathing in of divine movement, then some underlying, dynamic, perhaps even unconscious motivation might pull the individual soul in a particular, predetermined direction.

Four of the eight who were questioned on the subject view death as a motivational force in creativity. Eight respondents were questioned about the relationship between sex and creativity. Two think the relationship between sex and creativity is a strong positive one. Two think too much sex could debilitate creativity. The others see a slight positive relationship, usually because they think that a healthy sex life is a part of a healthy life in general.

None of those interviewed consider themselves atheists. For several, spirituality and a relationship with God are paramount and they expressed their belief that the divine and creativity are closely associated.

Writer George Leonard said that he has written 3 of his books because he needed the income. At least the project was initiated on the premises of work for money. As the actual writing of the books began, he was able to immerse himself in the project on a familiar level. Of the people interviewed, only poet Norma McLain Stoop alters her work because of money. Norma talked as if she peaked her feelings of intimacy with her perception of what kind of piece a particular publication would accept. Of all the respondents, Norma appeared to express different   motivations and purposes for creativity. None think criticism is generally helpful, perhaps because they are so critical of their work, demanding high standards for themselves.

CHAPTER 7

CREATIVE INDIVIDUALS LOOK AT CREATIVITY

The primary areas of investigation addressed in this chapter are: (a) Attitudes about creativity; (b) Affective styles of creative individuals: judgements, feelings, beliefs, and values; (c) The role of intuition in the creative process; and (d) Similarities and uniquenesses in creative individuals. Chapter 7 presents the respondents' ideas about concepts related to creativity. The concepts of creativity and intelligence, and the influences on creativity by the unconscious, art, and golden ages of creativity are included in this chapter. These concepts are discussed both theoretically and personally by respondents. This additional information adds depth and continues to form a more wholistic picture of the respondents as creative personalities.

Creativity Defined

This chapter begins with philosopher, writer, physicist, and inventor Arthur Young's definition of creativity. He stressed the 2 principles involved in creativity: the spark, and the development of the creative idea. He thinks the spark or insight comes to the individual's conscious mind from an outside source, such as the collective unconscious, and he believes hard work and a faithfulness to that insight are required in order to develop the idea until it becomes a reality. That insight might be good or evil, and the receiver must make a judgement about using it. Arthur thinks information can sometimes be an encumbrance because the knowledge of the wrong information can and does limit perceptions and choices. He said that creativity does the person, versus the person doing creativity. He also thinks we are all creating all the time, and the difference between the more mundane and unnoticed creativity and the exceptional is related to a personal vision.

LM: How about if we get to the question that you expected from the beginning, your personal definition of creativity?

AY: You could use the analogy of the masculine and feminine contribution to the baby--the sperm is a very small thing and the mother supplies 99 and 99/l00% of the substance of the baby. There are two principles involved in creativity--the initial spark of the idea and the development that requires nourishment. I mean you could have an idea for a helicopter and not do anything about it. Or if you did do something about it, it would take years of work. I find that creation consists of just what Edison used to say. It's 1% inspiration and 99% perspiration. There is a great deal more work than there is original spark.

LM: Do you think that most people get these insights and just don't do anything about them?

AY: I wouldn't be surprised. I think the insights come from God-knows-where, so what really counts is your faithfulness to them, trying to do them justice, or trying to express things that come as flashes. I think that is the valuable part when we are trying to articulate what belongs to the spiritual world, divine thoughts, or something. Of course there is nothing divine about a helicopter, but ...

LM: But maybe it's how the angels get around.

AY: I think I really believe in the angels. The angels may be angles, that's what I talk about in The Geometry of Meaning. You use the expression, "What's your angle?" What is your daimon? There is a sort of attitude that might make it impossible from the point of view of your friends or society, but you are acting out your angelic component. In some cases, it might even be destructive, but it's still coming from elsewhere. It's not just coming from your diet.

LM: It's an expression of the higher self, or is it a possession?

AY: It might be difficult to distinguish them. I think I'd rather not say it's a possession. They say Wagner was so obsessed with his work that he would insist on cornering everyone and reading these long, tedious operas to them. But he was so possessed in what he was doing that he didn't consider other people. Often, you have to follow your star and disregard the consequences.

LM: I guess that's where I was tapping into the possibility of courage, being courageous enough to disregard the consequences?

AY: Well, it's also, I mean you could read it either way of course, and just say that so-and-so is inconsiderate. But in any case, the creativity is something you don't do--it does you. It's the other way around. You don't account for it or there isn't something you can do to make yourself creative. It's almost like a garden. You can't make the plants grow, but you can weed it and give them a chance to grow.

LM: I've had experiences in my life when I've been doing something and gotten into that creative flow, and it seemed as if the project took on its own life, that it was no longer something I was doing. Is that what you are talking about?

AY: Yes, I've heard that when writing novels and plays, a character will take on his own life. That isn't what happens with me, but as I try to argue with myself, the ideas grow, and they come out of the process of putting it down. If you don't try to do something, this thing is stillborn, if it doesn't get going. But it keeps growing if you give it attention.

LM: We're talking about the term creativity. Another term often talked about is intelligence. Then there is a third term that has been used to describe you and a few other people, and that is genius. What do you think the relationship between these things is?

AY: Again, there is a question of definition. Nowadays the word intelligence has an almost reversed meaning. Roszak last night was talking about artificial intelligence. That's not what the ancients meant by the word. They had two worlds, mundo sensibles--that's the sensible world, material. And mundo intellectus was ... it wasn't intellectual in the modern sense. It was in the sense of intellect of the old sense of choosing between, knowing the right thing from the wrong thing, and that's different from intellectual games. Computers are intellectual games at best. They do not choose things. So when you say intelligence, which one do you mean? The intelligence involved in creativity is the older meaning of intelligence.

Sikorsky has an emblem on his helicopter of the bumble bee. The inscription says that according to the theory of aerodynamics, the bumble bee can't fly, but the bumble bee doesn't know about aerodynamics, so it goes ahead and does fly. It isn't that ignorance is an advantage, but information can be an encumbrance. You may know the wrong things.

Everybody is creating all the time anyway, and some people are creating what's the customary thing. Others have vision that goes beyond the period in which they live. Their creations may last longer. Of course they've had a vision that was not distorted in the way that the age was. ... I don't know which particular tribe it was, but I've heard many times that when the Indians or primitive peoples saw white men coming in sailing vessels and unloading, they didn't see the ships; they saw the rowboats because they had canoes which were of comparable size . They couldn't see the ships. The things that I've found in my theory, which you might say was inspired by the theory and I got from the ancients, people today don't see. I'm perfectly amazed by the way ordinary, lay people talk about the world. They talk about it the way they've been taught to think about it by science. I mean, anyone looking out the window or looking anywhere sees these things, like, isn't that wonderful, that plant? What's making it grow? Animals, plants, minerals, surely there is something going on there that's important. But nobody pays any attention to that. Now they are talking about particles and cyclotrons; what happened to the big bang 40 billion years ago? Nobody is looking at nature. What is this mystery right in front of our nose?

In their interviews, both Niels and Arthur reflected on how creative people can become so absorbed in a project that they ignore others or seem rude to them. Focused attention is an ingredient that was continually presented in these interviews. Arthur used the metaphor of a well tended garden to present his belief that we can make ourselves more open to creativity; however, we cannot make ourselves creative. This theme is expressed by most of the respondents throughout the interviews.

Arthur stressed the need to be especially open to those things with which you disagree, or to those that were unexpected. He thinks that in order to make discoveries one must first form an opinion. He defined creativity as being essentially self-discovery, and thinks that giving one's self permission to know the answer facilitates creativity. He also thinks outside resistance may facilitate creativity.

> AY: People are always saying. "Well you must be broad minded." Well I don't think so. You can't do a thing by being broad minded; you have to say I think it's here, and then you look there and it isn't there. Well then ok, then you look somewhere else. But you can't just sit there and say oh I'm sure it's here someplace. You have to say I think it's there. I think it's the things that you inherently don't agree with that you should give attention to. You can't afford to use your gut-level thinking all the time. You use it some of the time. Every now and then you have to open the door and let something new in. I think I have done that more than most physicists.

In the following quotation, Arthur describes himself as being open to conflicting ideas. He tells a story about how resistance once helped him explore radio.

AY: [I am] open [to conflicting ideas] and I don't like to give in, but when I do change, I change. I'll tell you a story about my father because my first interest was radio. I met an older boy in school who knew all about electricity and so on. He taught me how to make a radio. We had a ball. He made a radio telephone. This was way back in '22, maybe '2l. There was not such a thing as broadcasting. My father forbade me to have the radio. I had it anyway. I'd get up at 4:00 a.m. and take some instant coffee and put it in my mouth to wake me up and start sending to some people off in Ohio or something. I was fussing with these tubes because this thing had these vacuum tubes, and they made a light. I did not turn on my regular lights. I suddenly realized that my father was right behind me in the dark. I asked why he didn't bawl me out. I was waiting for it. He asked why. I said, "You told me not to have a radio and here I have it." He said the best way to encourage genius is to discourage it. By forcing me to do it on my own, it really gave me more incentive. Then you remember the story in Genesis. God forbade them to eat the fruit. He didn't support them. Why didn't He support them? If He wanted them not to do it, He wouldn't have put the tree there. That was there to be eaten. But He didn't want to do it by supporting them, because then they wouldn't have that very important initiative. That gumption to do it in spite of things.

In the quotation which follows, Arthur expresses his belief that people ask questions when they, on some level, know the answers. For this reason he thinks it is helpful in education to stimulate question asking, and then not answer the questions, thereby stimulating students to discover the answers within themselves.

AY: Another thing is about asking questions, getting students to ask questions when I am teaching. Sometimes I don't answer the questions, just go around the room getting them to ask a question. I didn't answer it. After you go around two or three times, they begin to answer their own questions. What I suspect is that people would not ask a question unless subliminally they had the answer. So the process that you want to encourage in the process of self-discovery is to find that you can answer the question if you give yourself a chance. I don't know what you have to do, but spit it out so that ... you may surprise yourself by what you know. Give yourself permission to know the answer.

Arthur thinks open-mindedness and allowing are important attitudes if creativity is to occur. He also thinks people must direct their focus and expect success.

In his interview, playwright Frank Hogan stressed courage and willingness, and the determination to bring an idea into realization with the knowledge that others may not like the creative product. He, like Patricia, thinks our educational system may destroy creativity. Earlier, he defined creativity as revolution. I asked him to elaborate. The following is his response.

LM: You were talking a moment ago about creativity and revolution. I was going to ask you to define creativity, and you did to an extent. Is there anything you'd like to add?

FH: Yeah, I think there's another step in there. I think it's revolution, but then there's the added thing of the courage to be the rebel, the courage to write it, the courage to paint it, the courage to do it, whatever it is, plus the determination to do it, plus the willingness to spend the time, money, and energy to make it work. Then, when it's all done, to accept the fact that people don't have to like it. You are deliberately setting out to do something which is not necessarily acceptable.

LM: In what ways do you see creativity and intelligence as being alike and different? Do you see them as two distinctly different things?

FH: No, I don't think so. I don't think I see them as different things. I think they are companion things. I think it takes a degree of intelligence to be creative. Again, I'm not quite sure, perhaps, what you mean by intelligence. You think back, on the other hand, to primitive art, and there's certainly intelligence there, not educated intelligence. I guess that's the distinction I would make. I don't think education is the key to it. Matter of fact, I think education can destroy it. I think too often it does. I think every 3 year old is probably more creative than they are at 13, or 18, or ever again. And that's too bad.

Like Arthur Young, the psychologist and visionary Patricia Sun thinks creative people are more open to allowing insight to come through them than are less creative people. She stressed the receptive function of the creative person and thinks the creative personality encompasses an innocence and naivete. In order to facilitate creative thinking, she said we must respect the wholeness and integrity of the individual. Also like Arthur, she emphasized the importance of accepting the formulation of unusual solutions and mistake-making as a part of the creative process. She defined creativity as love and openness. When asked to discuss the concepts of creativity and intelligence, Patricia began with a description of evolution, growth, and change. For Patricia, creativity and the evolution of the species are closely intertwined. Like Frank, Patricia believes our educational system can hamper creativity. She believes our society especially hampers our natural psychic abilities.

> PS: I think that the first 6 years of life, you're like a little sponge. You're absorbing at a profound rate an immense amount of information, awareness about culture, reality, judgments, survival, and emotions. You are extremely psychic then. What you are doing is you're learning to speak your language, your personality, you are creating your whole value system, everything is being absorbed by you being receptive to what's around you. One of the things you absorb is that you can't be psychic. You absorb that you cannot do this. Only crazy people can do this. They think they can do this, but it isn't possible. Both the ability and the fear of the ability are universal phenomenon.

Patricia speaks of Einstein's mystical side, his openness to allowing insight to come to him, in much the same way Arthur talked about being open to insight. Like Arthur, Patricia sees value in encouraging people to give unusual answers.

> PS: Einstein I admire a great deal. I empathize with Einstein, not necessarily in the sense of accomplishment, but in the style of thinking. He had that mystical bent and cared to bring it into the world in a way that it was palatable. He chose physics, and I chose sociology or psychology or people, but there was a caring and openness to the mystical side that I value a great deal. I think it is the essence of creativity and genius. Genius comes from genesis, which means creation,

something that wasn't but then is. I have often read descriptions of how he discovered things or how he thought of them, his childhood, his feelings about school, all of which I have sympathy with. I like him a lot. And of course Jesus. I admire Jesus very much, not that I feel--I feel that is what creativity is, it is great love and openness. I don't see it as an academic thing. I see it happen sporadically in people, you know, and I guess that's the way it does happen. Not a lot of people do it a lot, but everybody does it some.

Intelligence to me is a kind of flexibility to have complicated and various perceptions, and there is intelligence such as an idiot savant, who has an incredible ability in one area, and to the rest of the world seems to be an idiot, or very dumb. I think everybody has some special ability and it gets lost in our homogenized academic system. I don't think intelligence is one thing. I think it is a huge conglomeration of things, and creativity is the ability to move to that place where you allow the genesis of something that was never before to come to be. That is not a matter of figuring out. That is a matter of letting it in. School is set up to give a homogenized answer and not to think. It's geared to get the right answer when there almost never is a right answer. I find intelligence is a capacity to perceive and creativity is a capacity to let go enough to let something come into you that lets you deliver something new to the world. It is related to innocence, and openness, and spontaneity.

LM: You said that creativity happens, but we don't really do the things we need to do to support it. The thrust of what I am doing is looking for what we can do to support creativity. Knowing that now, do you have anything you would like to add?

PS: Yes. I think that what supports creativity is respect for dignity and integrity. Integrity means wholeness. So respect for the uniqueness, the dignity, and the integrity of different human beings supports creativity. For instance, the image I have of a school is not a lot of children sitting at desks reciting back what they were told, but an exchange between a person who has a lot of information and new, unique minds, all having a slightly different perspective on the world from the experiences they have already had, filled with curiosity, wanting to know all different kinds of things, not necessarily the things the teacher has on the agenda to tell them. And that for teaching to occur, you have to begin where they are. You have to begin to feel a respect for their dignity and be open to how their minds are working and what they are interested in. How we support creativity is let people give unusual answers. If we think it's unusual, ask more questions rather than saying it's the wrong answer. I can remember when I was a little girl wondering about when we would go to the moon. That was not only not thought of, you were ridiculed; it was stupid thing to say, that we would get to the moon. I did say it and was told it was stupid. Having respect for people gives them the opportunity if they have a dream or perception to follow it, build it, and nurture it rather than be brutalized for it.

LM: Let me throw some sand into the gears. What I see is two polarities operating in creativity. One is all the things you said. With someone who is growing, if you support their notions--good, bad,

246

workable, and unworkable--if you give them a chance to go with whatever they are thinking or doing, they will become more creative. The outcome doesn't matter so much. The process should be supported. On the other hand, you have just talked about how much you have learned from adversity.

PS: Authoritarianism is unsupportive to creativity for it tries to find safety through black and white rules. Things aren't black and white, except occasionally. There is a whole lot more there, so what you think of as sand is...there would be adversity, there would be crisis, there would be difficulties. First, let's try and undo the polarity. You don't necessarily support the notion, you support the exploration. I mean it's a difficulty when you think you've got a hot idea and you are given free rein to work on it. You work on it for 6 months, 6 years, and you find out it was all wrong. Or it had a whole bunch of holes in it. Every place you learned there previously was a hole. Through really looking, you now have a new orientation so that it is still supportive with creativity. We want immediate results on everything. We won't trust that things are unfolding as they should, that the thing called adversity is just not our getting what we think we ought to get. A lot of times we aren't supposed to get what we think we ought to get. Sometimes in getting what we want, we do violate one another in an intrinsically unhealthy way, and in doing that, we learn that it isn't a good thing to do and why. The why adds a whole other dimension to your knowledge. That's why our legal system is such a mess. We keep trying to make rules to cover the holes with little concern for the truth. What we have to do is have ethical people.

And we get ethical people when people see the value and the freedom of being ethical, and there is. Because there is a kind of messy hell when we are not.

Both Patricia and Tom said that authoritarianism suppresses creativity. Patricia stressed the need for learning to occur organically, because of a need to know. Like Paul, George, and Frank, she thinks schools prevent children from developing creativity, but that with changes, schools could foster children's creative abilities.

LM: So if we could, in fantasy or reality, have the sort of supportive environment where you could have respect and dignity, you would be free to use that potential in creative ways.

PS: But, it's more than a supportive environment. I go for getting more conscious about it. If something didn't work in this environment, we'd move to another one. In other words, the environment is, in fact, the state of mind of everybody that's in it. If one schoolroom likes to study one kind of thing and you want to study another, you can go to another kind of schoolroom. It's that freedom. Of course, I think we could teach children to read and to write in a more exciting and effortless way by not having it so structured, by responding to need. I learned a second language when I lived in Mexico. I learned Spanish. The first three months that I was exposed to learning the language, I didn't understand anything. I was trying to memorize different words, and I had a small vocabulary, but when I got near people who went [sound effects representing fast talking, Spanish-speaking Mexicans], I felt like I wasn't learning anything.

Except at the end of 3 months, I suddenly started to understand things. There were 3 months where it looked like nothing was happening. If anyone had asked me, I'd say no, I don't know how to speak Spanish, and I'm not learning it. At the end of 3 months, I suddenly realized I understood it very well. At the end of 6 months, I was dreaming in Spanish, and then I knew I knew it. Even if I don't speak for 20 years, my Spanish comes back. It's in there. It's in there because I learned it organically. I use that expression meaning life force, that natural order. Not a coerciveness, it grows out of a need. I didn't sit down at lessons and get told how to talk Spanish. I listened to people who talked Spanish, and I wanted to know what was going on. I was very frustrated. I didn't know what was going on, and when they laughed after going [sound effects], I felt annoyed. I wanted to know. It's that I-want-to-know place that causes you to learn. It takes time and has a period where it looks as if nothing is happening.

LM: Ok, if we had all this, if all this existed, then we wouldn't have the sorts of adversities you had as a child and learned from.

PS: We'd have new ones.

LM: So you think that would always fill itself up?

PS: Yeah. I just think that the new ones, though, they would be more aligned with our nature. There is a difference between an adversity, that is not getting things the way you want them, and poisoning the well. There are times when the well dries up and you gotta move, you gotta dig another one, and you gotta look somewhere else. That's one level of adversity. That level of adversity will always be, and it's good. We need it, and it will always come, and we will learn from it. We will also learn from this extra level of adversity which we create, when we poison our well. We do have to realize why it's not smart to poison our well. We have to know that, not intellectually but with feeling. We have to know that we don't want to do that. That is part of this evolutionary leap. I remember realizing how--there is a point you get a grace period. When we know something is wrong, but it doesn't show, and we could get by, we could fake it, we could cover it over. We can tell our children are pained, but they look okay. They are not sick. They do what we tell them, and we let it go. It's in that grace time when you really know something is wrong, when you have the power to change it tremendously with very little effort or unpleasantness, and we're not socialized to respect that place and face it. We're basically socialized to hide and hope it will go away. It always comes back as a worse problem that's really a mess.

Like Arthur Young, Patricia thinks if we expect creativity, it will occur. Like Arthur and George Leonard, she stresses the need to accept mistakes. Patricia, like all the respondents, emphasized the idea that creativity combines insight and hard work.

PS: I was just thinking that the real essence or big thing that needs to happen to allow creativity is to say creativity is really already there. Creativity is the freedom to make mistakes, the freedom to do wrong, as anybody who is creative will tell you. In fact they do it so automatically, they sometimes don't even notice. Try this, that didn't work, great. Try that, that didn't work, great. Each time you try something that doesn't work, you get a little extra insight because you found out what didn't work. You are led in the direction of what will work. Our culture is so attached to being right, it's really astounding to me. We fake, we go numb, we will be bored in order to let ourselves look alright. It's not so much even seeing this period; it's being willing to act in the minute you see something rather than waiting because of the fear of not looking alright or not wanting to rock the boat, because you will rock the boat. When you see something in that grace period, you are actually going to make things get messier because you are going to uncover something that is fluttering under the surface. It's hidden so you don't have to. The power is then you are not afraid to say, "Oh, what is it?" and let a big mess come up. Like ruining your travel plans or dinner plans. Or it might not let you do certain things, it might cost you money, it might mess your life up, but it doesn't really. It just changes it. I think that the essence of creativity in individuals, the thing you notice most, is that they find no problem at all in making mistakes and then will hop from one thing to another. When somebody says you can't do that, you just sort of chuckle and immediately start thinking of how you can do it. You don't believe you can't do it. If you don't do it because you couldn't do it, then you don't; but you don't stop assuming you could. That's creativity, because creativity is leaving the door open all the time; it lets you keep shifting; it lets you get certain blocks out of the way and later you use those very blocks to build a bridge. It is win/win thinking, and it takes courage and effort.

251

LM: I think Einstein, whom you admire, once said that creativity is 99% perspiration and 1% inspiration. Seems to fit a little bit.

PS: There is a lot of work. The example I often use about getting something beautiful--I often associate creativity with beauty and not necessarily only art but all forms of beauty, a wonderful realization is beautiful. I always say Michelangelo was creative. Sure he sculpted the David, but what is entailed in sculpting the David is a lot of chipping rock, and the capacity in him, the inspiration, the vision, was he could see it inside the rock. He still had to do the work of chipping the rock.

I find the most intelligent people are willing to sort of be vulnerable all the time. They are always in a place of not knowing, which is why they keep on growing. And the children these days are coming in more balanced. They seem unbalanced to us because we have a bias on the linear side. We actually kind of harm them, because we insist that they do something against their nature, that they think the way we do. And, of course, this thing of support you're talking about requires working with that nature. When you start thinking in spatial wholes, you're going to get geniuses of a whole other order, that the linear thinkers aren't going to be able to follow. And that's part of why there is so much resistance to change. A lot of learning disability is really a teaching disability. It's that the people who are teaching and are sort of in charge of education cannot conceive, sometimes literally cannot conceive, of the style of thinking and the mode of thinking that the young people are having, which is feeling and spatial wholes. Not that they shouldn't have linear capability too and can speak and do things linearly, but we make the linear unpleasant for them because we ignore that other part. So it feels assaulted and cold and dry and unmeaningful. They get a "disorder," or they get dyslexia. They get nervous, they transpose and they tune out from stress.

Like Patricia, the writer and aikido instructor George Leonard sees a naivete in creativity. He stressed creative energy and, like Patricia, the importance of not defining anything as a mistake. Later in the interview George demonstrated the idea of accepting mistakes as new information. He thinks Americans are creative because they are capable of living in ambiguity, and he thinks staying in the moment encourages the creative process. His highly creative moments are precipitated by his breaking into a sweat.

GL: You notice that the United States is probably the most creative country in the world. One reason is that we are willing to live with more ambiguity than other nations. In the Soviet Union, they are desperate for order. Anything that departs much from order makes them very nervous. It makes us all nervous. But if everything has to be order, then you start running tapes, and you don't see existence as it really is. If you see existence as it really is, every moment is infinitely creative.

One of the best ways to get in touch with your own creativity is to get into the present moment one way or the other. One of the things that happens in aikido is something called randori. Randori is multiple attack, where three or more people come at you full speed. So you throw and throw and throw. It's really like being attacked by many people. Generally it only lasts 20 or 30 seconds.

That's all you can stand. It's very intense. Somebody who is even in good shape is totally winded by that time. It's even more intense than boxing. You throw somebody, and as soon as you throw them, they get up and come at you again. So in the course of a good randori, let's say maybe 20 or 30 attacks. It's like being attacked by 30 people. There is simply not time to think about it. You simply have to stay in the present moment, or you are flat on your back. Those are the choices you have, or you are trapped or hit. It's marvelous because you get a little taste of what life could be and how life, in essence, perhaps is. You have to really be in the present. It is having no idea that you are going to do it that's exciting. So aikido does get you into many opportunities. You can see the difference between thinking about experience and becoming one with experience. You become totally one with the dance. You have heard that many times there is no distinction between the dance and the dancer, and that's a great moment. Another exciting thing, as a teacher I watched some brand-new student in white belt, and we're doing some regular techniques over and over again, and that's when you do specify the technique. And I like some beginner to make some awful mistake. I say, "My God, I see a technique." I've learned many new techniques from brand-new beginners who don't know how to do it and do it wrong. I think if you really understand that nothing is wrong, everything is part of the matrix in the flow of existence, then you can see possibility in everything that people call mistakes. Music is very similar to aikido. All creative acts are basically the same. In music, I have it all the time when I'm improvising. There is a tremendous difference, and I even got a physical indicator when I'm just thinking of the chord and thinking this series of notes would deliver this chord and kind of editing and thinking and so forth, and then the next moment, it's playing me--you've heard all that. Anyway as soon as that happens, I know because I break out into a sweat. I first start to sweat, and then I know I'm doing it right. You're one with the experience, and that's creativity.

The whole idea of the energy field that comes out, that you really are unique in all the universe. You are also universal. You might say you are the universe from a particular point of view. You put two people together in an intimate relationship, you've created another entity--a third entity--and it's the awareness of that third entity that a lot of people in their relationships miss. They don't realize that it is you, me, and us, and that us is not just something casual, it's something awesome. It's absolutely awesome to take two people and create this third entity. Something new, as I say in The End of Sex. The news spreads out like wildfire. This is big news. This is news with a capital N. A new entity has been created.

Tom Robbins, novelist and artist, thinks creative people tend to be creative in more than one area. His thoughts about creativity led him to describe two types of genius. One type is obsessive, and the other is expansive. As was stated in Chapter 4, he speculated that artists begin expressing themselves in their medium as children.

TR: I wrote when I was a child, and other writers that I know wrote when they were children. It's like Van Cliburn. A woman came up to Van Cliburn and said, "Oh Mr. Van Cliburn, my ..." (you know who I'm talking about--the pianist who won the

Tchaikovsky medal, the first American to win it)...she said, "My son could be a great concert pianist but I can't get him to practice." And he said, "Madam, if your son had what it takes to be a great concert pianist, you could not keep him from practicing."

LM: Could you name for me a few people you would classify as creative?

TR: Gary Snider, Robert Bly, Pablo Picasso, Fellini...most of the people I am naming do more than one thing, and to me those are the really creative people.

LM: How do you see yourself as like these people?

TR: Well, I think I'm perhaps a victim of the same congenital insanity.

LM: Which is? Elaborate.

TR: Well, there is a certain way of dealing with reality which entails creating your own reality. I think a truly creative person finds many outlets for it. There are two principal kinds of creative people, I think. There is one, let's take the examples of Suteine and Picasso. Suteine was a painter, and that was all he could do. He was totally obsessed with painting and he was born to paint and he wasn't good in anything else and had no interest in anything else, couldn't create in any other medium. Whereas Picasso could have been a great musician, a great playwright, choreographer. He dabbled in all those things. Just everything he touched, he brought his imagination and creativity to.

LM: Do you think that maybe the difference you are talking about is the difference between a specific talent and sort of creative lifestyle?

TR: No, I think one is obsessive and the other is a more life-encompassing, world-encompassing genius. This is not to say that Suteine was not a genius too, because frequently a genius has severe limitations, but I think there are two kinds of genius. One is large and expansive, and it overflows into every aspect of their lives. The other is very narrow and extremely obsessive, and those people are generally not very happy.

LM: How do you view intelligence and creativity?

TR: Well, I think intelligence enhances creativity. The person who is creative but dumb is limited. They can only go so far. Can creativity enhance intelligence? Boy, I haven't the foggiest idea. I would say that creativity enhances life, and I would say that maybe creativity enhances wisdom.

LM: Are you more intelligent or more creative?

TR: Both. [Laughter] No, I don't know. I think I am probably more creative than I am intelligent. There are certain areas in which I am not very smart. There are areas like mechanics where I am really dumb. I really don't have a very high IQ.

The following is educator and industrial designer Rowena Reed's response to my question on creativity, intelligence, and genius. Rowena thinks people need intelligence and creativity in order to produce artistic work, but although they are related, for Rowena creativity and intelligence are not the same thing.

RR: There is a big difference between talent and genius. Talent is a mild sensitivity to whatever relationships you are discussing. I think talent in music would be an extreme or unusual, better-than-average sensitivity in aural relationships. I would say talent in art is an unusual sensitivity in visual relationships. Of course, there are degrees of sensitivity. I do definitely believe that intelligence is very important to the expression of creative art. I would say so. I don't know much about music, but I would say the same thing is probably true. When you think of all the great musicians and composers, performers and conductors, if you hear them speak, you get an impression that they are pretty intelligent. They have it all together. They have all the relationships in their minds. If a student is equally intelligent and equally talented, it doesn't take him very long to find out after he is out of school and has gotten his education that he could make more money with his intelligence than with his talent--at least make it a lot faster. I don't know how that would have been 50 years ago, but now I don't have to tell you that money is a measurement of success. So the temptation is for that young person to get some kind of a job with a very good financial future.

LM: How do you see creativity and intelligence as being alike?

RR: Well, they are different, but I think they are like two sides of a coin. You need both of them. You need intelligence to make use of your creativity, if you have that kind of imagination.

LM: So you think that intelligence facilitates creativity?

RR: Yeah.

LM: Do you think it works the other way around as well? Do you think creativity facilitates intelligence?

RR: Of course. Creativity is a large part of intelligence. Intelligent people have to be original and imaginative.

Neils Diffrient, industral designer, thinks creativity requires some talent or other tool.

LM: I'm not looking for a Webster's definition here, but rather a personal way of describing creativity. How would you define creativity? You may approach that personally, or more objectively, however you want.

ND: I think it starts with being given a set of tools to work with, whether they're emotions or skills or urges, whatever. You've got to have something that acts as the medium in which you can exercise yourself. That I feel very strongly. In my case it was drawing. The second thing is, I guess, a kind of intelligence. You can't be too stupid, you know, so I'd think you would have to be intelligent to some degree, though I was never intellectual at all. The final thing is motivation.

For the poet, photographer, and dancer Norma McLain Stoop, discipline is the key to creativity and, indeed, to living well. Norma sees no connection between intelligence and creativity. She believes that once people learn self-discipline, they have the ability to be creative.

LM: Product is a very important part of creativity?

NS: I'm asking that. Is it even creativity if you do nothing with it? Is a diary creativity or only if you draw conclusions from what's happening? That's a very good question to ask somebody, by the way. If you can do one thing well, and it doesn't matter if it's floor scrubbing or what, you can do anything well. There is a reason for that. This is for creativity, and this is what a lot of creators ain't got. The important thing is discipline. If you know how to do one thing well, you had to learn the discipline to do that well; therefore, you can push that discipline into whatever you choose. This is what I'm living proof of. I'm never scared to try something new.

LM: How do you see creativity and intelligence as related?

NS: Not at all. There is no correlation at all. None at all. I think some of the dumbest people can be extremely creative.

LM: Do you see yourself as being more intelligent or creative?

NS: How can I put it? I'm unfortunately very cerebral.

LM: I have four words that I want to throw at you and see what you have to say about them. Those words are intelligence, creativity, talent, and genius.

NS: They are all words I don't like very much. Talent. Everybody has talent. Everybody could do just about everything that all the famous people do. But most people are afraid of success.

Success is much harder than failure. Therefore, most people do not employ their talents. Everybody has talent. Talent is no God-given thing. Intelligence. God, I don't even know what I'd call an intelligent person. An intelligent person to me is somebody who can hold a halfway decent conversation. In these days when everybody goes to college, I think more people are dumber than before. An example is after my lecture at a college, hands went up. I thought, "Isn't that nice?" What do you think they all wanted to know? They had the same question because as soon as I answered, hands went down. "Do you really know Frank Zappa?" Juniors at Temple University and that was all they could think of.

LM: It's a matter of discipline, you were saying?

NS: That's the whole thing. As a matter of fact, discipline is the whole key to living.

LM: Do you think perhaps that discipline is the key to moving from being an intelligent, creative, talented person to being a genius?

NS: I don't go for genius.

LM: What word would you use? Exceptional, outstanding, innovative?

NS: The best.

LM: Do you think that discipline is what makes the difference between the average and the best?

NS: Absolutely. Auden is one of the great 20th-century poets, and I think he was very creative. One of the reasons I think so is that I think poets are probably among the most important people in the world because they change the way people think. See, people think of people as being creative when they can just paint a good picture or write a good poem, and that isn't it at all. Picasso changed the way people looked at things. Poets, if they are any good, change the way people think, either the process or about things. That, I think, is the most important thing. I think if you are creative in a way that doesn't influence people, it really isn't of any importance.

The following excerpt is writer and psychologist Carl Rogers's response to my request that he compare himself with someone he considered creative. To exemplify creativity, he said a person must have a product, and that product must be novel and carry the unique stamp of the creator.

CR: Perhaps I'm like Dickens in being able to write. It always amazes me that other people don't write like I do. It seems to me the easiest way to write is from within, making the material personal, and yet that's very rare in professional fields. That way when you say I do this and I do that, or I think I found so and so, that's open to--then the reader is still open to hold his own opinion which can be different. It doesn't sound like the genuine truth. I think creativity is the ability to create something which is novel and which has the unique stamp of that person on it. It really is like fingerprints. Nobody else could have done it in quite the same way. I think there needs to be a product. For instance, you might have a very creative fantasy, but unless you translate it into something--a picture, writing, sculpture, or something, a new recipe for dinner, no one else has any idea whether it's creative or not. You can be very intelligent and not creative at all, and a person can be very creative and not highly intelligent.

LM: So you see creativity and intelligence as being two separate things?

CR: Two separate things, a definite relationship but not a high correlation.

LM: Do you think you are more creative or more intelligent?

CR: Pretty good at both. See the modesty?

In his description of creativity, writer and educator Paul Torrance told me about his manifesto for children, which contains guidelines for helping children develop creativity. He thinks the definition of intelligence should be changed to encompass creative thinking. For Paul, creativity requires going beyond the norm, the purely rational, and the logical.

PT: Well, I think if we had a reasonable definition of intelligence it would include creativity. But as they are now measured, there is some overlapping, but there are some differences, I think. To be intelligent, or to behave intelligently, one does have to be a little creative, and to be creative one does have to be a little intelligent. But I think creativity involves going beyond what is the norm, going beyond the purely rational and logical. So I see that as being the big difference in being able to transcend logic and memory.

LM: If you had one piece of advice to give to people who are rearing children or educating children, what would that be? And you can give more than one, if you would like.

PT: Well, I think what we have in the manifesto for children is to teach your children not to be afraid to fall in love with something and pursue it with intensity; to know and understand and to take pride in their strengths and practice those and explore it and enjoy your greatest strengths; and to free yourself of the expectations of others and walk away from the things that they try to impose on you, and free yourself to play your own games and to teach your own mentor to help; don't waste a lot of energy trying to be well rounded; do what you love and can do well and learn the skills of interdependence.

Paul's manifesto for children presents the essence of his discoveries about facilitating creativity in children. For adults, Paul supports, among other things, question asking, the freedom to make mistakes, and follow-through.

Like Paul and Norma, aikido instructor and teacher Wendy Palmer described discipline as an important ingredient in creativity. Like George, Arthur, and Patricia, she emphasized mistake-making as an important element of the creative process. She agrees with Frank that determination and courage are necessary attributes for the creative person. Wendy elaborated about the body's intelligence and its role in creativity. She sees unified focus as the most important element in creativity and stressed the creative process over the creative product. Wendy believes that anything is possible. She teaches her students how to focus kinesthetic experience in order to accomplish their vision or task.

WP: I feel like what's important now in creativity is being willing to go the distance to be good at something. In things that I've studied, especially the Eastern disciplines, they teach you that it's the path or the process, not the goal. So to me, the creativity of life is to really enjoy the process as it goes along and then not be so attached to the goals and not be so freaked out when it doesn't work out. If there is a barrier that doesn't work, I don't take that I'm a dumb person. It just didn't work. And if it does work, I don't take it that I'm a good person. It just happened to work. It's my firm belief that anything is possible. So I feel that part of being able to be creative is trying to imagine tremendous possibilities and then having the courage to continue with them. I feel for myself that, if I really work and apply myself, I will succeed. This is what I teach, too. If I'm able to get unified, the attention becomes like a laser. If your attention is like a laser, there is nothing that can't be done. And we see this by, you know, there are moments when grandmothers pick cars off the pavement, and this is completely focused attention.

The one thing that I love hearing about Einstein is that he got the idea for the equation, his great energy equation, from feeling his arms. I feel that most of my pushes toward a new vision, which would fall into the category of creativity, are a lot of really strong sensations that I get in my body rather than just separate concepts. It's like when I want to go to Hawaii and surf the waves, my body wants to do that. When I want to sing on stage with 20,000 people in the audience, my being wants to handle that. When I want to make a really beautiful jacket, there is a kinesthetic, a somatic experience with it. I believe that the greats had a somatic experience with their vision so they were able to implement. I'm not very good at adding 2 and 2, but to translate the kinesthetic vision through into manifestation is really my main interest. To be able to bring the vision to a kinesthetic experience. That happens with me naturally. What I'm able to do as a teacher is to lead people through techniques to the process of translating their vision into a kinesthetic experience. From there I teach them how to focus that kinesthetic experience so that they can accomplish their vision or task.

In the following segment, Wendy relates the intuitive knowledge and abilities she possessed as a young child. She thinks if we can learn to relax fully, we can open ourselves to our intrinsic self-organizing properties and enjoy maximum efficiency. Relaxation is important because when we are tense we generate stressful thoughts that interfere with the body's wisdom. She thinks our culture is out of balance because we over-emphasize our mental capacities. Wendy stressed the need to regain balance between our bodies, minds, and hearts. She thinks in doing so we will achieve a truer intelligence.

WP: I've always known things, and I really didn't know how I knew. I only knew that I knew. For instance, when I was young, even more than now, I could just go in when my father's stereo would break, I was 6 or 7 years old, I would go in and fix it. I had no idea how I was fixing it. I could fix almost anything. I'm still a pretty good fixer, but not as good as I was when I was a little bit purer with it. I think there are different interpretations of intelligence. For instance, I can hardly spell, and I can't do math. So from one point of view you would say, well, I'm not so intelligent as someone who had gotten straight A's. My real fascination in this work would be, the subtlety would be uncovering the true intelligence of the body. There is this tremendous intelligence in our bodies. We are programmed for success. So in my work, what I encourage people to do is to try to create an environment of openness and relaxation and unification, and the system will then self-organize for maximum efficiency. What gets in our way is our mind. It's a tricky concept, because in one way, you see the mind as the seat of intelligence, but from an intuitive point of view, the mind interrupts the tremendous intelligence that's in the body .

So-called higher intelligence seems to have made us more unhappy as a culture. I can't call that intelligence because it has made us unhappy. I'm sorry. To work more efficiently and more in harmony and more what I think is creative in its loving aspect, I think we have to start to shift away from the cognitive awareness and try to cultivate more of our sensing, our intuitive intelligence and creativity. It's already there. We don't have to train it to be intelligent. I have to qualify that because it is a paradox, but in my opinion, it's the reverse from what would be taught in a normal school. The difference between a more sophisticated culture and a more primitive culture.... The way I'm looking at things now, the primitive culture in a certain sense is more sophisticated. It's more in touch with the sophistication of the body, and the more sophisticated culture is really out of touch. It's not that I'm against mental intelligence, but I think it has been pulled out of proportion. I think I would divide it into three categories of mind, heart, and body. The head is the center, and it's a very nice center, but not if it's dragging the heart and the gut around with it. The idea for me is balance. The head and the gut and the heart should work together, listening to each other and changing rather than the mind trying to shut the heart up and ignore the gut.

A number of ideas about creativity were repeated by several respondents. Both Wendy Palmer and George Leonard stressed the physical aspects of creativity. Self-discipline and follow through were often described as essential. Openness, especially to mistakes and unusual perceptions, courage, and flexibility were described as necessary. Willingness, determination, and incentive were listed as key to the occurrence of creativity. An ability to be free of others' expectations, an ability to create one's own reality, and a trust in one's body were discussed. Several respondents named support for the individual as helpful, although Arthur Young disagreed. He said a person must be creative without support. Several respondents felt that expecting creativity would facilitate it. Everyone agreed that work is an essential ingredient in creativity.

The Unconscious Mind and Creativity

Dragon smoke, says poet Robert Bly (1975), was left behind as ancient Chinese poets rode by on the backs of dragons. The smoke is inspiration, and in poetry it means a leap between the conscious mind and the unconscious has been made. In good poems, several leaps between the conscious mind and the unconscious occur. Bly proposed that with the dualistic split between the mind and body and with Christianity's emphasis on the exaltation of the spirit, mortification of the flesh, and the suppression of animal instincts, especially sexual drives, the unconscious was seen as evil and was guarded against. Leaping poetry, which is the richest poetry, encompasses all forms of consciousness.

The next area of interest is the role of the unconscious in creativity. As reported in Chapter 2, several theorists attribute important aspects of the creative process to unconscious mechanisms. For that reason, and because I am aware of the effects of my own unconscious life, I was interested in how these 11 creative individuals conceptualized the unconscious mind.

Philosopher Arthur Young, the inventor of the Bell helicopter, defines the unconscious as the universe in potential. His idea of the unconscious mind as the universe in potential encompasses Carl Jung's theory of the collective unconscious. Arthur thinks the unconscious mind consists of those things we have not yet incorporated into our consciousness. He sees the unconscious, the superconscious, and the universe as basically the same, and he thinks the superconscious is the source of creativity. He proposed that we often have difficulty accessing unconscious creativity because the unconscious presents information and impulses in a manner difficult for the conscious mind to understand. Two of the necessary skills of the conscious mind are the discrimination of useful from useless imagery and the extrapolation of the meaning of sometimes vague or confusing messages.

> AY: Well, I think the unconscious is part of us, part of the world. I've always liked dreams, and I very much enjoyed Jungian analysis. Dreams are important in this school for self-development. You were taught to use dreams to help you move along, and I got, finally after about a year, what you call high dreams. That was very exciting. I happen to have an exact trine of Neptune to my sun, exact to the minute, and it makes for easy access to the unconscious. I get along with psychics very well, but I wouldn't call myself psychic. But then the question of what does the unconscious mean, I don't think it's your unconscious; I just think that it's the unknown,

that which is in the universe and you haven't yet made a part of your conscious field of view, so to speak. So in a sense, tapping the unconscious is like tapping the superconscious or the universe as to be. It's perhaps not externalized, but it's there. The unconscious must be like a vast city that we just don't know about. It's not just some dumping place of memories; it's the real universe as it is in potential or not in the physical. In that sense, if you really wanted to get at the source of creativity, that would be an important place to look, because that means there's a lot more than we know that's there to be tapped.

In the following quotation, Arthur told a story about a message from the unconscious that was misinterpreted.

AY: Now, it is like the difficulty with languages. When you translate something from one language to another, you change it a little. But with the unconscious it is even more difficult, because you're translating something that is not in words into words and concepts that you are familiar with. I'll give you an example. A couple or 3 years ago, before Carter was elected, I got this call from someone in Montana, a long distance call, from a very much alarmed person. He said he had had this psychic revelation. That Tutankhamen would rise from his tomb and take over the presidency. This was real to him, and he was very sure it would happen, and I must do something about it. I heard him out and so forth, and I got him to stop. What could I do about this? Well, I thought it was some distorted psychosis or something. Then, about 6 months later, I was in Washington at the time of the inauguration. They had this remarkable exhibit of Tutankhamen in his tomb. People were lined up for miles trying to see this thing. It was getting much more attention than the inauguration of the president. So I would say literally he was stealing the show from the president. No doubt, this person had had a precognitive vision of this stealing of the show and misinterpreted it as taking over the presidency. This shows how much you can distort the messages from the unconscious and how it takes a lot more, I mean, it's not just dumping it out; it's careful knowing what you are saying. That takes years and years of familiarity. So tapping the unconscious, which would be a source of creativity--you might say a child who is smearing paint around is tapping the unconscious to some extent, yes, but you would be more interested in someone who could do it with more skill and discrimination.

Much like Arthur views the unconscious as the source of creativity, Wendy Palmer described the unconscious as untapped creativity. Like Arthur, Wendy has developed the skills necessary to use unconscious imagery and feelings. She defines the unconscious as the seed of creativity. Wendy described the physical rushes she experiences just prior to creativity. These rushes seem similar to the goose flesh Norma experiences when she becomes excited about the things in which she believes strongly, and to George's breaking into a sweat just prior to an important insight or creative output.

WP: Well, I feel like the unconscious is the deep core of you. Sort of lava at a molten level. As it comes out to the surface, it sort of hardens or solidifies or becomes a clear vision and a kinesthetic, manifest experience. So the unconscious represents the pool of the molten lava of creativity that is untapped. It's the seed.

Sometimes when I wake up in the morning, I just feel these rushes of energy in my system, and I know something special is going to happen. Sometimes if I sit with it, I can know the area that it's going to happen in. I think those are signs that the energy of the unconscious begins to surface. Like I'll get rushes as if I'm nervous, except I'm not nervous, so it's like excitement in my system. What I've learned to do is not to be nervous, but to welcome it, and start to be interested in seeing if I can figure out what dimension or what quality of my life it is going to come forth in.

George Leonard, writer and musician, described our bodies as one way to access the unconscious mind. He thinks the body is an antenna that is tuned to the unconscious, and the more we receive from the unconscious, the more creative we will become. Like Arthur Young, he talked about the fact that we receive unconscious information indirectly, and he stressed the need to focus our awareness in order to make use of this information. Like fellow aikido instructor Wendy Palmer, he sees the body as the most important avenue to the unconscious mind.

GL: Well, there will always be more unconscious than there is conscious. My feeling is that we have this huge and wonderful antenna that's tuned in to the unconscious. If you can read this antenna and get the messages from it, you can certainly ... even though you are not bringing in that kind of awareness directly, you indirectly could be aware. That antenna is your body. The moment we are really in tune with our own bodies and the bodies of others, the more we can experience our so-called unconscious impulses. Therefore, be more aware of them and be a better person. Be a more creative person.

The humanistic psychologist and teacher Carl Rogers, did not attempt to tap his unconscious. He did not analyze his dreams or meditate. He thought more in terms of his nonconscious mind than his unconscious. I think that some of the functions Carl attributed to the nonconscious other respondents attributed to the unconscious, making the distinction difficult to understand. It seemed to me that Carl defined his unconscious as unaccessable and his nonconscious as accessable.

CR: I don't quite know how to answer that. I feel my unconscious is what lies behind my intuition, but I guess I'll make it a negative summary. I don't make use of dreams. Somehow I've tried to, and I don't get much out of dreams. On occasion, but certainly nothing very creative. I don't think I attempt particularly to tap my unconscious. I think more of my nonconscious mind. My nonconscious mind is so much more impressive than the brain. It's illustrated in the fact that in biofeedback, how do I raise the temperature of this finger? I don't know. I don't have any idea, but given the needle showing the temperature and being asked to make that rise, yes, I can make that rise. How do I do that? My nonconscious mind can do things my unconscious mind has no idea of, and I think I'm talking about something quite different from the unconscious. I think that the unconscious plays a part, but I don't feel ... I read some of Jung's stuff, and I realize he really captures the unconscious. That doesn't seem to be an important aspect of my life. So I would say, again, that I'm smarter than my conscious mind, but that isn't weighing any particular stress on the unconscious or on broader consciousness.

Playwright Frank Hogan believes that he receives guidance from a spiritual level and is given this guidance through dreams. He thinks the difference between himself and less creative people is that although others receive guidance through the unconscious, he is willing to accept this guidance and act on it. Many other creative individuals, including Niels Bohr, Robert Lewis Stevenson, John Keats, and Puccini reported receiving creative guidance through extraordinary experiences involving the unconscious mind (Harman & Rheingold, 1984). Gowan's (1977) findings support Frank's idea that listening to and acting upon this guidance is the key. Gowan writes, "When Michelangelo did the Sistine Chapel, he painted both the major and minor prophets. They can be told apart because, though there is a cherubim at the ears of all, only the major prophets are listening." Frank also gains insight during periods when he is slumbering between sleep and waking.

Frank described one instance in which he based an entire section of one of his plays on an image revealed to him in a dream. Like Arthur, Frank often experiences creative insights as originating outside of himself. Frank's idea of the need to take an insight and use it well is similar to Arthur's idea of discrimination. Arthur said discrimination is a necessary skill in creativity. Frank stressed the action following the insight, again pointing to the principle of hard work as an important aspect of the creative process.

> FH: I use dreams. As a matter of fact, there is a wild section in The Joshua People that comes totally out of a dream. I stashed it away in my head and didn't write it immediately. It's a marvelous section. But it came ... it was given to me. I think the creative thing, to some extent ... the creator is the medium, to take it from somewhere. ... The trick of it is to take it from wherever it is and to get it on a piece of paper or whatever you have to do. I think those people out

274

there, whoever they are, Maynard Keynes, at this point, had made his contact with me. I'm absolutely certain of that. I'll show you proof if you want.

LM: Are you talking about a higher level of some type?

FH: Yes, of a spiritual level, whatever you want to call it. These people, this power that is out there, everybody is not willing to accept them or accept what they're saying. And the number of people who really accept them, I think, is limited, the number of people who will accept it and act on it. I accept and act.

For the singer, editor, and poet Norma McLain Stoop, myth and memory combine and provide her with raw material for poetry. She, like other respondents, emphasized the importance of accepting mistakes. Norma believes the unconscious plays an important role in creativity. In the following segment of her interview, Norma experienced a rush of excitement similar to those described earlier by Wendy.

LM: What role do you think your unconscious mind plays in your work?

NS: I think it plays everything. I think it's everything.

LM: In what form do you get unconscious material?

NS: I get it mostly as myths. I told you I'm so terribly drowned in myths. Myths, forgive me, are also religion. All of that blends in with my childhood and all of the other things which I am so obsessed with, such as war, very obsessed with war--private and public war. See, I've been sick a lot. I was very sick for a while during World War II, and I would just sit and listen to the radio literally from morning to night and think.

LM: Do you remember dreams?

NS: No, my sister remembers dreams. I remember about two dreams a year.

LM: Do you have other images at all that flash in from what you would consider your unconscious? I'm wondering from what vehicle you get your unconscious information, how you get that information.

NS: It's everything. You see I'm too dumb to know how it comes. It just works out that way. I'm somebody who has an awful lot of, for having lived so long, a lot of words and music that I've heard. Music is extremely important to me. Words, music from the past and the present in my mind, and I have events in my mind that happened to me or my gods and heroes, which was all linked together to me. When I was little, they were in my, I mean, there was--I have a poem about it. The rows of cantaloupes, I would plant seeds right next to the rows of cantaloupes, and I was sure that soldiers in armor were going to pop up from them. You know what I mean? When I get excited? I always have goose bumps or electricity down my arms.

LM: Your whole face just changed.

NS: It's when I get excited. I believed it. What I believe in, I believe in so very much. I believe in the things that I believe in terrifically; but I know that the things that some of the greatest people in the world through the ages have believed in have turned out in other times to be proven very wrong. Therefore I know that I can be very wrong also. I find that .that is the most exciting thing. Being wrong is much more exciting than being right.

LM: Because you learn from that?

NS: You learn twice as much. It's yin and yang, sort of. I told you you learn from unhappiness more than from happiness, from deprivation more than from plenty. I love opposites. I think opposites are the same, sort of. They tend to flow into each other.

With the exception of Carl, all the respondents believe that their unconscious plays an important role in their creative process. Carl referred to the parts of his mind that are important to his creativity as his conscious mind and his nonconscious mind. The body, dreams, myth, and meditation were named by the coresearchers as ways to access unconscious material.

A number of respondents reported the belief that their unconscious processes are of primary importance to their creative output; however, some were more able to express how they access this material than were others. Some respondents, such as Rowena Reed and Tom Robbins, were concerned that scrutinizing the process too closely might be dangerous. At the time of the interviews I thought Tom was afraid that analyzing it too closely might take away the magic.

Most of the respondents think, as I do, that the unconscious plays a critical role in creativity. The difficulty is in accessing the rich material available in the unconscious mind. Creative individuals discover unique methods which are appropriate to them. Examples provided in the previous section are dream analysis--a method used by Arthur and Frank; the body--George and Wendy's favorite tool for liberating unconscious material; and for Norma, myth.

Art

The next topic discussed is art. I chose to address art because, through art, many people express their creativity. In the following pages the coresearchers respond to questions about art, art's role in society, and the importance of art to them.

Below I have quoted writer and inventor Arthur Young. Arthur is displeased with current art. He likes design and would enjoy seeing more emphasis on design in art. His father was a painter, and in his interview Arthur described how his father's critical faculty increased more rapidly than his painting ability, which continually motivated him to do better work. For Arthur, anything done well can become art.

LM: How do you define art?

AY: Well, of course the arts are painting, music, and so on, but I think you mean something more general in the sense that anything that's done well can be art. Well, I don't know what more I can say.

LM: Do you see art as having a role in society, as having importance?

AY: It doesn't seem to have much today. I wish there were more art shown on the design of things, like automobiles and so on. The Japanese are beating us in that game. In a sense, there is something about this question of whether there is more than one definition of rightness.   For a long time art went into the idea   of   art for its own sake, irrespective of resemblance to actuality, but I don't think I can say any more on the subject.

LM: Does art have a place in your life?

AY: Well, both my parents were painters, and I used to paint. My wife, Ruth, paints. I miss art. I don't see any on the TV, and modern paintings don't satisfy me.   The music passes ... that's the way it is mostly today.   But I was brought up in that atmosphere of self-criticism, and in that sense I think that's more pertinent to what you are talking about.   When you paint, you don't just put paint on the canvas and walk off. You're fussing and fussing to get it just right.   You paint over and over again. But you're always trying to, my father used to say that this thing was driving him on.   His critical faculties would increase more rapidly than his ability so that he never did satisfy the urge to paint something the way he wanted it to be because his critical faculty would be increased. This interaction of one's critical faculty and whatever you do, you keep trying to do it better.   I was very happy when they put my helicopter in the Museum of Modern Art.

LM: You mentioned your father never was satisfied with his painting.   Have you felt satisfied in your life with the work you've done?

AY: Well the trouble is if I am, I lose interest in it.   You are always moved on by the things you can't solve, not the things you solve.   That's natural.

Playwright Frank Hogan defines art as anything that goes beyond craftmanship. For Frank, art's main function is to educate. Like Tom Robbins, he thinks art adds spice and flavor to life.

LM: How do you define art?

FH: I think something that goes beyond craftsmanship.

LM: Do you see art as having a particular role in society? What is this role?

FH: Art's role in society. I'm not certain that society isn't getting too much involved in art, that they're not affecting art, negatively, in two ways. I think the idea of someone buying a painting for $2,500 from the artist--and jerking down to the lowest possible price--then re-selling the painting for $50,000 or a $100,000 with no residual money going to the artist, and then 50 or 100 years later, the painting bought by some museum for a million bucks--is pretty rotten. The whole idea of people acquiring art as a symbol of wealth and power while artists are starving.... And, too, I think, art may be becoming too academized, if there's such a word. I think theatre is not being helped, for example, by the number of universities which have theatre courses. I think they're establishing an old-boy network of theatre.

LM: How do you think society would be different if we didn't have art?

FH: Oh, it would be much more boring. It would certainly be boring. It would be duller, probably not as advanced.

LM: So one of art's roles is to spice things up a little bit?

FH: I think art is a great educator. I think it is the educator.

Patricia Sun, teacher and visionary, sees art as an external reflection of the unconscious. For her, art is difficult to define. She especially likes art that is beautiful, inspiring, and harmonious. Like Tom Robbins, she thinks art's primary purpose is aesthetic; however, Patricia thinks art can be functional as well as beautiful; it can stimulate people to think, to feel, and to expand their view of the world. Patricia also thinks art can tap the unconscious, for both the artist and the viewer.

LM: How do you define art?

PS: Again it has a lot to do with inspiration and, for me beauty. Of course it's hard to define inspiration and beauty. It's hard to define love. It's hard to define all the mystical qualities that inspire us. You always know them when you feel them. I remember once helping friends decorate their apartment. We went looking for paintings and everytime we saw a painting we liked, the salesperson would come over and tell us the life story of the painter. There would always be some interesting thing on how they did this or how they did that. I realized they weren't selling the painting; they were selling the artist. They would say how the artist is getting big and who bought their last painting. So art became an investment. Different people do like different things, and I very much like Japanese art and old masters, not modern art. I love beauty and harmony. There are words in Japanese for that kind of harmony. I can spot it in a minute. I can feel it. When I was younger, I used to have to resist the urge of rearranging people's furniture. Some modern art seems unpleasant to me, like the soup can stuff by Andy Warholl or Dada art, but it does reflect the sterility of out time and our fear of being original and inspired. So while I don't like it, it is an artistic result.

Much like Wendy Palmer, Patricia thinks art, myth, and drama tap the unconscious and provide a mirror of our psyches, so that we can see those parts of ourselves more clearly. Patricia views punk as a current example of how creative expression can wear out old fearful images.

LM: Rollo May, in one of his books, talks about art, and he talks about what I sometimes refer to as ugly art. I think it's sort of the soup can thing you are talking about. He talks about it in terms of the artist being the most sensitive person who sees a little into the future and reflects this in his art. He talks about the fact that the current art is as it is and what that might be reflecting. That might be considered a purpose in art, to sort of make us aware of this upcoming mental attitude toward things.

PS: Oh yes. It has some of the same function that myth does and good stories and good dramas, which is an art form also. Art is to tap the unconscious and to put it out, and ugly art does cause people to consider and think, whether you are embracing it or rebelling against it--either way, it causes people to think. So that's all true. I guess I was speaking of it from a more experiential end of doing it and also what I like to see.

I don't think it is an accident punk is in. And it has its good points. I'm not just saying that in a negative way. I think young people are attracted to punk because it helps wear out the older generation's boogeyman images on what we think they are by how they dress. That's quite a statement. It's creative, and it's artistic. I remember people, when it first started happening, parents coming to me real upset because they thought their teenagers were going mad, being ugly and demoniac. They weren't demoniac. They were just mirroring back the shadow of the parents, the way the parent envisioned the demoniac. They were saying, "We're your children, we're your babies, and we are not demoniac." So it kind of wears that out. I think it serves that purpose, even if it is unconscious.

LM: Do you see the role of art as being a social change agent or one of beauty?

PS: Both. And of course drama and television and movies, they are all art. That's making something up out of nothing. It inspires and causes people to think and feel and go numb, all of which is the function of art. It helps people become more conscious of what they are choosing unconsciously. It both inspires and hurts.

LM: I'm guessing that the reason you do what you do is to help people see things and maybe change society.

PS: Oh yes. Although I never say that, because that puts you at a terrible disadvantage for accomplishing what you are trying to accomplish. The closer you get to the real present, here and now, things that matter to people, the more link you have.

LM: How does the art of other people affect you?

PS: Some tremendously. Some not at all. Now I'll say a part I don't like. The kind I don't like, I don't see. It looks like litter to me. I just don't hardly see it. There's the kind I like, and then there is a lot of middle stuff which is pleasant, and then there's the kind I really dislike. And to me, it's the difference between noise, music, and magnificent music that totally moves you, and it's kind of at that same kind of level. The kind I like touches very special things inside of me, like perfection and beauty and inspiration. For instance, I think one of the most magnificent sculptures ever made is Michelangelo's Pieta. And I see it as a statue of a woman, and a woman holding her dead son. She is sitting extremely grounded. Her legs wide apart. Jesus' body is beautiful and dead. You can feel it is dead as you look at it, and it's laying across her legs. She is very grounded. She has an incredible look of compassion and sadness and love all completely melded together. She's very beautiful, and she is grounded. Like planted and strong. It is a symbol of containing the Resurrection in the place where it would be most hard to contain it, in the mother. It's very much a female energy thing. I love it. The skill is magnificent. I think it's really beautiful. I could look at it for days and see more and more.

LM: Do you use art, do you utilize art?

PS: I utilize it personally to replenish me, like nature. I mean when I see something that's

284

beautiful, it just makes me feel so good and alive and glad I am alive. I use it a little bit in my flyers, not a lot. I paint and sculpt.

The writer and psychologist Carl Rogers saw art as reflective of the inner spirit of the time and a personal expression of the artist. He said that art must create some sort of movement in the viewer.

LM: How would you define art?

CR: It's a very difficult thing. I think, and this is a personal definition, that art is made up of two elements. It is the expression, a very personal expression of the artist in some way, and it is also the reader or whatever being moved by the creative product. It seems to me that it is a reciprocal kind of thing that's hardly art unless it is both a creative personal expression and is received by someone as being a significant event. That is my personal definition.

LM: Do you see art as having a particular role in society?

CR: Yes, I think it expresses the inner spirit of the times. That's why a lot of modern art disturbs me, because if the world is as mixed up as that. ...

Like Patricia, novelist and artist Tom Robbins described art's primary purpose as aesthetic. Like Frank, he thinks it adds flavor to life. Below is Tom's definition of art.

TR: Art is the vehicle for the transportation of aesthetic values.

LM: How do you think art fits into society? What do you think is art's role in society?

TR: It provides what life does not.

LM: Do you see art as having a purpose beyond itself?

TR: It has many purposes beyond itself, but they are all secondary. Its primary purpose is strictly aesthetic, and if a painting or a book or motion picture, piece of music, is not primarily aesthetic then it fails as art. That's why ... it becomes social realisms that permeate the arts in the Soviet Union today ... the new arts not the old ballets. It is such a failure because its primary function is political.

In the following quotation, Tom expresses his idea that art deals with revelation rather than communication. In other words, art allows and even encourages personal interpretation. Tom appreciates art that is self-contained, and he likes for his readers to remain aware of his books as something apart from themselves while they are reading them. Tom is especially moved by beautiful sentences.

TR: Well, its ... art to my life is like garlic to spaghetti sauce ... without it, it's just stewed tomatoes. [Pause] The difference between art and communication is that a lot of people mistakenly think that art has something to do with communication, and it doesn't. Art deals with revelation, and the difference between revelation and communication is that communication is a one-to-one system in which there can be only one legitimate interpretation. If you are asleep in a hotel and someone yells "Fire!", you can only

286

interpret that one way and get out fast, or you will experience a tragedy; whereas in a work of art, there might be l3 different interpretations of equal value. That doesn't mean that all interpretations are correct. Some are just dumb. But there is more than one. And that is what distinguishes art from journalism.

LM: One of the things I've always appreciated about art is that I can interpret it so that it's meaningful to me personally.

TR: Yes, it reveals rather than communicates. Now I think Jackson Pollack is a realistic painter; whereas Andy Wyeth or Norman Rockwell are abstract painters. Andy Wyeth is abstract because he is painting two-dimensional reductions of a three-dimensional world. His paintings refer to something outside themselves. Whereas Jackson Pollack's don't. They are wholistic, intrinsic, self-contained. They refer only to themselves and not something outside themselves. Therefore they are real objectives, and Andrew Wyeth paintings are not. Well, this is what I'm trying to do in a more limited way because the nature of the medium is more limited that way. In writing it is to give the book itself more of a real quality as a real object instead of trying to seduce the reader or delude the reader into thinking that he or she is on Tara plantation with Scarlett O'Hara picking cotton. That they are actually ... I'm saying, "Look, you are reading a book, but it's OK, isn't it?" I mean, it's still valid and entertaining and exciting, and you don't have to be made to feel that you have escaped into the book. You can become aware of the book in your hand and the weight and the smell of the pages and the sound of it as you open and close it. It's a real thing, and that doesn't make it any less of a valid and entertaining experience.

LM: Do you use other people's art to stimulate your own art?

TR: Sometimes. If it's a dry day, I might want to read another writer just to get the juices flowing. There are particular kinds of writers who I read. They're ones who are real poetic, who write poetic imagery, and who write beautiful sentences. When I read beautiful sentences by other people, it makes me want to do it. It's that envy-love thing again.

LM: What about art other than writing? Would you go to a ballet or to an art museum or a gallery?

TR: Not for the purpose of being stimulated, no.

LM: So you stick pretty much to your own art.

TR: I'm stimulated pretty much by other things. Music and things, Bob Dylan, for example.

LM: You said the film too, that you use film.

TR: But, of course, when I'm in my studio in the morning ready to go to work, I can't go out and look at a film. I could, but it would be a waste of time. So what I would do is pick up a particular writer and read for 20 minutes.

Educator and designer Rowena Reed, described artists as the predictors of the future and art as the dramatizer of life.

RR: Art dramatizes life. Art does dramatize the visual relationships, and music the audio relationships.

LM: What do you see art's role in society as being?

RR: I think it is very important. If you go back and look at the history of art, then you find out the history of society. I think artists are always ahead of their time. They predict, and then society comes along l0 or 20 years later.

LM: Do you see art as operating as a social change agent for society or as a reflection of future society or both?

RR: I guess both, and it depends on what kind of art. Commercial art usually follows fine art by at least l0 years and takes the values, the organization, the relationships they worked out in fine art and more or less bastardize them and make them simpler, quicker, and more financially rewarding.

LM: Do you ever use other people's art to facilitate your own expression?

RR: Not directly.

Below is writer and educator Paul Torrances' definition of art. For Paul, art encompasses perfection, elaboration, elegance, and intuition, and is produced by people striving for excellence and quality.

PT: Well, I think ... let's see, art is the perfection, the elaboration, and the elegance that goes beyond what you could achieve by.... Art involves intuition that goes beyond the dimensions of ... striving for an excellence. Some people see it as being fancy, but I see it more in terms of quality and excellence.

When asked to define art, Norma responded with one word, "excellence." In her own art she likes to amuse and puzzle people.

LM: Art is excellence?

NS: Anything becomes art if it is done to the top degree it can be done.

LM: How do you see your work as fitting into society?

NS: I amuse people. I puzzle people with a lot of my poems. Those are two things I love to do--amuse and puzzle. Believe me, Kid, there ain't been a good poet that didn't want to amuse. That is something the U.S. is very silly about. They think light verse or lyrics to songs are unimportant. They are terribly important.

The following excerpt is from the interview with George Leonard. He thinks that the reader of a book gets more from the book than the writer intended or expected.

GL: I'm totally convinced that the reader of a book knows much more about a book, a really intense reader knows much more about the book than the author. I think I could prove that to you, because an author never has the experience of reading his book for the first time. With Education and Ecstasy, I had a striking experience. Joe was a good old boy, good journalist, just a great guy.

He got a copy of_Education and Ecstasy_ and just flipped out. He gave it to all his friends. They read it, and he got more advanced copies from the publisher. So there was a little plot there I didn't even know about. So I called Joe, I was coming to Atlanta, and he said, "Oh, my God, you're coming to Atlanta. You've got to come out to dinner. Everybody is reading your book. We've got to talk to you. Wow, this is happening." I went to dinner at his house. We sat around the table, and they all started talking about the book. My mouth is hanging open. I realized they see much more in it than I had seen. They know better than I do, because it had been awhile since I had read it, and I've never read it the way they've read it. The author never gets to do that. They were talking and talking, and I said maybe somebody will ask me something, but they didn't ask me anything. Then they are talking, and slowly I get up from the table and walk away. There was a piano. I stopped by the piano. For the next hour, I played piano. I played jazz, and they were talking about Education and Ecstasy, and I'm playing the piano. I realized that was how useful I could be to them, by playing the piano. Because the reader knows better than the writer. That's absolutely important. I think that's true with all works of art.

For Wendy Palmer, art has two main functions. One is to provide a wider range of emotional experience. The other is to project parts of our psyches into the external world in order for us to be able to re-experience them artistically. Like Wendy, Patricia Sun thinks these two functions of art are relevant.

WP: Art's role in society. I guess I have to go back to the Greeks, and the main principle of Greek theatre was to allow people to experience some of the emotions, the more radical emotions of pain and suffering and happiness and those things without having to do it in their own homes. TV gives my children the opportunity to experience qualities, emotions, differences, similarities in something that has some space outside of themselves. So they have a chance to see the world from that point of view. I think it represents aspects of our internal life, art does. It gives us an opportunity to see it and put it out there and look at these aspects of our internal life in particular ways. It's very important. I think my daughter is an artist, and she's not good at math, and she's not good at those things, but I feel she has a real artisticness about her. I feel there is a richness in her life because of that. And fortunately she's in a place where she can see different art.

LM: Do you use art in any way? Do you make use of other people's work? Does it have any particular meaning for you personally?

WP: Well, some of the art that I keep in my house, I enjoy, because it creates particular moods. It mirrors ambience inside myself that I want to cultivate. With some of the clients that I see, I encourage them to draw or paint their experience, their feelings, because it's a chance for them, especially the ones that are very caught up, to distance themselves from the inner space and to look at it, which is the purpose of art--to get it out there and look at it. I love the impressionists. In terms of painting art, I've enjoyed the energy of the impressionists and looking at the paintings. I've always loved all of Michelangelo's sculptures and the aliveness and the warmness of the marble. I love marble. A lot of the modern art leaves me pretty cold, and that's fine.

LM: Do you ever find yourself stuck and use other people's art to get unstuck?

WP: Yes, I do. I think it's probably more explicit, often reading certain little phrases or books helps to unstick me, but occasionally dance can do it.

LM: What role do you see your art playing in society?

WP: I think that one of the reasons there is a feeling of frustration and built-up level of stress in society is that people aren't getting satisfied. They are getting their material needs, but they aren't getting enough satisfaction. I think the one thing that aikido as an art does is satisfy people.

Wendy sometimes uses other people's art to facilitate her own creativity. Like Patricia, she is not fond of much modern art. Like Arthur, Wendy thinks that people today are not getting their aesthetic needs met.

In these interviews art has been described as the revealer and dramatizer of life. It was defined by the respondents as anything done well, anything that goes beyond craftsmanship, as perfection, elaboration, elegance, and excellence. It was described as being primarily aesthetic by some and primarily functional by others.

Besides adding beauty, harmony, and spice to life, art was seen as meeting significant social and psychological needs. Some of the functions of art named were: providing an external reflection of unconscious material; stimulating thoughts and feelings; reflecting the inner spirit of the times; and predicting the future. Also it was reported that art is necessarily a personal expression of the artist and must facilitate movement of some kind in the audience.

Creativity's Golden Ages

Another question of interest had to do with the reasons for and the effects of so-called golden ages. Throughout history there have been times of heightened creative output. I wondered how the coresearchers would respond to this phenomena. Wendy believes these times to be a phase of a natural cycle.

LM: What about history? It seems there have been spells of creativity, the Golden Ages, the Renaissance, and then dead times. Do you have any way of explaining that?

WP: I think I spoke about it briefly because it's on a larger scale when we talked about the pulsing effect of creativity and how it comes forth. The pulsing effect of planting a seed and waiting until it comes forth. I can, in any situation, whether it's a personal life, a personal monthly cycle, looking at decades, there are ebbs and flows and pulses just like the tides. There is an open or extending kind of an opening into, and then there is a more retreating/receiving. It's sort of a flow of things--ebb out and then return back and ebb out and return back. I feel it works through larger cycles through thousands of years, as well as cycles within years or the cycles within a month. There are these times when we are ebbing out and more creative, and there are receptive times, fruition times. Dark times lead to the next renaissance of spiritual awakening. I had never seen in my life anybody or any period where they sustained positive creativity. It always comes in cycles and pulses and ebbs and flows. So I think those creative times in history are part of a larger grouping of cycles.

LM: Do you think if you had not come along that some other person would have fulfilled your functions?

WP: That's kind of a funny way to pose a question. Most of the questions for me I relate to some kind of a map, and that one just doesn't fit into any of my maps. I mean, what a way to think. God. If I hadn't come along--Well, I definitely believe in the larger pattern of things. I'm sure the larger pattern would be fulfilled regardless. It seems quite obvious that I happen to be in the larger pattern of things. No question about it, the universe continues its evolutionary movement with or without the individual.

Norma thinks golden ages occur because money is available in a particular area. Like Wendy, she sees golden ages as parts of a cycle and thinks the truly important times are those preceding a golden age.

NS: Well, right to start with, all those times are geographical, not just dates. In other words, the whole world did not blossom during the Renaissance. As far as I'm concerned, the Medieval days were the great days. They were the days when the ferment was terrific. It isn't when the things are happening that are the great times. The great times are the times before that when the barrels are fermenting. In another 100 years, that is going to be the explosion.

LM: What you said about geography, you are saying that not only were the times specific but the places were also specific?

NS: I don't consider the Renaissance was the whole world. The Renaissance was particularly in Italy.

LM: What facilitated that happening in Italy at that time? Why did that happen then and there?

NS: I think the whole reason there was a Renaissance--oh God. See, you made me think. The whole reason there was a Renaissance was the countries in which the Renaissance came out happened to have a lot of money at those times so that the princes were able to finance the work.

Industrial designer Niels Diffrient's idea is that a cultural richness exists at the time of a golden age. He does not think golden ages occur by accident, but rather a social medium exists that facilitates an artistic or cultural advance. This social medium may be connected to the collective unconscious. He thinks an intensity of interest in a particular field supports the occurrence of a golden age.

ND: I've thought about it a lot. I have some mundane answers. I think that it's a matter of accident. But all of these people seemed to have existed in a period of time when they could concentrate on what they had in an uninterrupted way, and there was a social medium in which they could grow. I have a kind of theory right now that the reason there aren't any geniuses in my kind of activity is that the culture is very poor. It's a poor time in which to do what I'm doing. There doesn't seem to be any real substance in the culture related to design. Now, why there should have been a Frank Lloyd Wright, who is another genius, I'm not quite sure--with the exception that I know around the turn of the century, there was a kind of homogeneity of culture and an intensity of interest--call it the collective unconscious--but it was support.

LM: You used the term collective unconscious. Do you think there is an unconscious connection between people in a given culture and that they might unconsciously, without even knowing each other, support each other somehow through that.

ND: Yeah, I think so. I'm not fully aware of how it works or why it works, but there's got to be something of that sort. I don't know how extensive it is. I don't know if it's broad, over the entire culture, or if it's just between one and one, person to person, or what.

Rowena Reed and others spoke of the cyclical nature of dark and golden ages, with the dark ages providing the fermentation for the following burst of creativity.

RR: I don't know. It's quite true. I know what you are saying. I guess a number of factors must come together like a kind of flowering and then sort of burst and then relax, like waves gathering themselves up together again until there is a period of great intensity.

LM: You find there is not much happening right now?

RR: I think that the young artists are not taking it seriously enough. They are thinking of it as a means of advancement and public relations.

LM: They are dedicated to themselves rather than their art?

RR: I think so.

LM: When you were talking about the flowing, are you saying the dark ages are maybe a fertilizing time?

RR: Yes, and then it came to a head. Then there was a relaxed time after that and gathered itself up into another good time. I think the early 20th century was such a time when they were all working in Paris. The contemporary movement ... that was a great time.

LM: Right now is what?

RR: I think this is a relaxed time.

LM: When do you think we'll have our next burst of creativity?

RR: I don't know. It's hard to tell. How do you know that there will be any? I think we are living in a terrible age. I'm worried a great deal about a holocaust. I think people are crazy. I think they are behaving ridiculously. I'm sorry, but I think Mr. Reagan is crazy.

LM: Had you not been born, do you think someone else would have done what you have done?

RR: I suppose so. I think they would have been bound to.

LM: Do you believe that, if anyone who has made a great discovery or a great contribution had not been born, some other person would have? Had Einstein not been born, would someone else have come up with his theory?

RR: Yes, I think some scientist would have come to the same conclusion.

Carl Rogers thought creativity might be contagious and that the catching nature of creativity enables the occurence of golden ages. He also said that golden ages grow from social need.

LM: It seems like there are a whole bunch of real smart, creative people, and then there's a period where not much happens, and then there is another clustering. How might you explain that?

CR: I think it is contagious. And then they do seem to be ... when the sky is dark, the stars begin to shine--one of Charles Beard's summary statements giving history in a nutshell. It does seem when society has some kind of social need, people arise to meet that need.

Frank agreed with Norma. He said that golden ages of creativity occur when society has money for support.

FH: I think Maynard explains it. Financial.

LM: When there's money available, there's creativity?

FH: Roger Fry quotes Maynard as believing he can show just how much inflation of currency is necessary to produce an outburst of artistic creation. Maynard says that if Shakespeare had been born 50 years earlier, England couldn't have afforded him.

LM: Do you think that if you had not been born, someone else would have done the things you've done?

FH: No. Not exactly, no.

LM: Do you think that if Shakespeare had not been born, someone else would have ...?

FH: Oh, not absolutely. Would have had the same effect.

LM: If Einstein had not been born, would someone else have...?

FH: Yeah, but I think you're in a different field. I think you're into science here. Yes, I think that. Yeah, I think in science, yes, but in art, no. I think it's too individual.

LM: So if Picasso had not been born, probably no one would have conceptualized art in the way he did and expressed it the way he did?

FH: Not exactly the way he did. Though it was ready to break out. Someone was going to do it. My feeling is that you're not going to get another Shakespeare.You wouldn't have gotten one. Picasso ... I think that somebody would have come along that would have been somewhat like this. I think there are variations which are new. I think nothing is basically new. New is an advertising word, isn't it? A hype. A gimmick. But creativity means originality, and originality means going back to the original.

Like Wendy, Norma, and Rowena, Patricia described the important work of the various dark ages as preparation for the following golden ages.

PS: I believe we live in a duality plane and things run in cycles. That doesn't mean that creativity is gone during the cycle where we don't see it. I mean it is a part of the process for the next level of creativity. How to make use of that when that happens, rather than fight the river, is part of how I see making change. One of the times that we considered kind of uncreative was the Dark Ages. I think the Dark Ages was very potent and set the stage, really, for the Renaissance. That the mystical feeding as well as the misperception that went on during the Dark Ages gave birth to the Renaissance. I mean, it isn't an accident that the great cathedrals were built mystically. These unique buildings with no explanation as to how they came into being sort of sprouted up all over around the same time.

I remember, I don't know if you want to put this in here, but I remember once when I was in Italy. I went to a cathedral in Florence, and I had a lot of feeling about it as I got near it. We were going to go in the side door. We were filming for the BBC, so the people were all kept out, and there was just the film crew. I had an urge to go around to the front and walk in at the bottom part of the cross. There was a dome over the center, cross shape. As I walked in, I had this feeling of wanting to be centered, and there were arches and how perspective works as you walk; it's like after each succeeding arch, there is a point, and it would lift. As it would lift, you could start to see the bottom of this dome and the skylight at the top. At first it's the earth, it's green; and then there is Jesus sitting on a throne; and then there is this line that comes straight from the top of his head, straight up, to a symbol of the Holy Spirit, a dove, that says, "Here is man." It gets lighter and brighter. It's painted lighter as you go up; the skylight makes it get lighter, and as you are walking and see these arches, it's like the top of your head lifts off. There is this incredible physical feeling of the top of your head lifting off. I just had a premonition about it or something.

Anyway, I felt it, and I thought it was wonderful. I told the guy that was the director, and he tried it, and he said, "Oh, my goodness," and was so excited. So then the Italian Docents that caretake and show you around came in. The director said, "Tell them about it." I said, "I'm sure they know." I said, "This was built into this. This is not an accident." He said, "No, tell them." As I'm telling them and they are listening and they went back and they tried it and they are all excited. They come up to me, and they said, "How did you know that?" They really wanted to know how I knew that. I started to say, "Well you know the thing that's beautiful about these buildings is that they were built by people who let them be built, not people who designed them, but who let them be designed." It is that which made them so special, so wonderful, and their eyes got like saucers. They looked like this to each other, and he said, "Wait a minute, wait a minute," and came back with a letter written by the architect to the workers who built the Cathedral which said, "I have not designed this building. Let the spirit that designed it move through you as you build it."

The previous anecdote expresses how people can open themselves to what Niels called the collective unconscious of the time. Patricia, Arthur, and others spoke of allowing inspiritation and creativity to come through them. That allowing is what Patricia referred to when she said that the people did not build these buildings, they let them be built.

Many respondents agree that creativity occurs in cycles that encompass times of output and times of inner growth. These cycles may be shorter and personal or may be longer, like the dark and golden ages of history. The respondents generally attributed as much importance to the dark times as to the golden times.

Golden ages were attributed to several related phenomena. Respondents reported that golden ages occur when money is available, when a social need exists, when there is intensity of interest, and when the collective unconscious of the time supports particular concepts or images. Creativity was described as contagious.

Summary

Not the radiating image,
Nor the hidden idea,
Nor the rhythmical harmony,
Nor love create.

Idea, rhythm, image, air of fecund love,
Merge into one form
From which the verse, the flower,
The world come out.

Niccolo Tommaseo

This chapter presented the respondents' ideas about creativity, intelligence, the unconscious, art, and golden ages of creativity. Each coreseacher brought a personal perspective to these subjects, and understanding these aspects of creativity is elemental to understanding creativity in its broader movements. In addition to the presentation of these idiosyncratic responses, some generalizations have been made.

Historically, creativity has occurred in cycles that encompass times of output, or golden ages, and times of inner growth that appear to be lacking in progress, or dark ages. Generally, the respondents attached as much importance to dark as to golden ages. Golden ages were attributed to several related phenomena; money, social needs, interest, as well as the movement of the creative energy of the collective unconscious. Our era was described by the respondents as a dark time. An individual's personal creative output also seems to occur in cycles of golden and dark times, and the respondents are able to act as synthesizers harmonizing the thesis and the antithesis or their creative movement.

Because creativity often is expressed in artistic mediums, I was especially interested in what the respondents think about art and its function in society and our lives. One function of art is to provide an external reflection of the collective unconscious, sometimes providing safety for us as we experience some of the darker aspects of ourselves. It often reflects the inner spirit of the times. Art's reflective and predictive qualities, its function as a stimulator of thoughts and feelings, and its purpose as the provider of a safe projection of our shadow may explain some of the darker, more violent art being produced and sought today. More traditionally attractive art graces our lives with beauty and harmony. Both types educate and meet relavant psychological and social needs.

With the exception of psychologist Carl Rogers, everyone believes that their unconscious mind plays a determining part

304

in their creativity. Different individuals employ varying methods by which to access unconscious material. Examples given are dreams, meditation, yoga, myth, and trust in one's body.

Self-discipline, follow through, openness to the making of mistakes and unusual perceptions, courage, and flexibility often were named as aspects of creativity by the respondents. Willingness, determination, and incentive were listed as key ingredients in creative thinking. The ability to be free of other's expectations and the ability to create one's reality through hard work are necessary attributes of the prolificly creative.

CHAPTER 8

THE CREATIVE PROCESS

Combining an understanding of the creative processes of these 11 individuals with data about their lives, histories, and personalities leads to conclusions about creativity. Chapter 8 presents the creative process as it is subjectively experienced by the respondents. The questions posed in this chapter were included because they provided a framework through which the coresearchers could describe their creative processes.

The primary areas of investigation included in this chapter are: (a) objective and subjective experiences of the creative process; (b) attitudes about creativity; (c) affective style of creativity; and (d) similarities and uniqueness in creative individuals. The research question addressed is: How do these people experience the onset of the creative moment? Through an act of will? Through external stimulation? Through spontaneous impulse? How do they describe the creative moment? How do creative people report the experience of their creativity?

Typical Working Day

One way of looking at the creative process is by examining how creative people spend their time. I was especially interested in how these people work, and because I wished to gain understanding of their daily lives, I asked the respondents to describe a typical working day. Following is poet Norma McLain Stoop's response.

NS: I can't say very typical because they change. When I get up in the morning--I never get up until 10:00--I fix my breakfast, and usually I type. I pay bills, go to the office. On the days I go to the office, I go around 1 or 1:30 and proofread and copyedit for anywhere from 3 to 5 hours. But, I can't go to the office everyday, because often I go to movie screenings at 2:30. I usually take somebody and we have supper afterward. Sometimes I go to a discotheque after that, sometimes not. If I don't go to a movie screening in the evening, I usually go to the ballet. There is usually a reception after it, sometimes black tie. Then I'm out late, and then I'm really on.

LM: A night person.

NS: No. It's work. If I'm going to a movie, even though I am reviewing it, it's not work. But if I'm going to a ballet, and a reception after, that is work, because I have to be on. I've got to say intelligent things.

Playwright Frank Hogan believes that the subject of his work determines his schedule, for example the characters in his play <u>Finn MacKool</u> were morning people. He always stops working before he has exhausted the material he is ready to write.

FH: On a typical working day I get up about 6:00, 6:15. Well, it probably starts earlier than that. I have a tendency to wake up in the morning somewhere around 1:00, 2:00, 3:00 and stay awake for a couple of hours, during which I think about Maynard and whatever else is going on. I get up about 6:00. I turn on the Christian religious station over in Jersey, and there's a man on there who's doing a 5 year tour of the Bible. I listen to him every morning. I run in the house for 20 minutes first thing, and then I have breakfast, and I shave and shower, and I walk up to 72nd Street and buy a <u>Times</u>, rain or shine, snow, regardless, and come back...six blocks up and six blocks back, twelve blocks. And I come back and fix myself a cup of tea and a piece of toast and sit right where you're sitting and do the <u>Times</u>, clipping as I go on my favorite subjects. Some I send out with letters, that sort of thing. It is now 9:00, quarter past 9:00, and I fix another cup of tea and write my letter to Ethel. Then it depends. I will either do some research I have to do, or I will check spelling or something, kind of fix up the day before. I may stop, if I'm writing something at the piano, and do that for awhile. I may go out and mail letters, or do a little shopping. I come back and may do a little writing then. Then I have lunch and do my biofeedback for a while. It is about quarter past 2:00, and I began writing in earnest now. If it's a good day, I'll write until half past 5:00, 6:00. I find that projects control the time of day they are going to work. My basic belief is that the subject controls what you do. The characters in the play <u>Finn MacKool</u> were morning people. They wrote in the morning.

LM: So they have a life of their own.

FH: Oh, absolutely, yes. They run the thing, and you'd better behave. Be available all the time to them. Then I try to stop for the day before I've run out of what I'm ready to write. That way you know where to start the next day, you have momentum. Sometimes after I stop writing I go out again, shopping or I'll take a walk. Then I come home, fix

309

an old fashioned, have dinner, take a tray and glass of wine into the bedroom, prop myself up in bed, and watch the MacNeil-Lehrer report. I may make or get a telephone call or two and go to bed by 10:00.

Teacher and industrial designer Rowena Reed begins her day with breakfast. Rowena is in her eighties, and her health is not as good as it used to be.

RR: I eat breakfast--a lot of people don't.

LM: What time do you usually get up?

RR: If I had my way I would get up early and go to bed early. I really have to have 9 hours sleep. If I don't, I'm really sick, and I can't be creative or anything else. During the past year I haven't been able to do that. One of the reasons is because my classes start at 1:00, and I have to be fresh at that time. I get up about 7:00. I used to always have a bath and dress before I had breakfast, but I find it's not good for my hypoglycemia, I sometimes get up and eat first, then I get dressed. I have a mild attack of hypoglycemia, and I may rest for a few minutes. Then I'm ready for work. I work in the studio. I have a little office behind that door. I won't show it to you because it's pretty untidy.

LM: You work in the mornings?

RR: Yes. Not every morning. I haven't been able to do it all the time, because I have this problem with my eyes. On the days I go to school I don't write. I look over what my students are doing, and plan what I'm going to say in the afternoon.

Writer and artist Tom Robbins describes his day. He has found that his schedule is a little different during the writing of each book.

LM: So non-work days, you couldn't typify. But a work day?

TR: On a work day I get up about 9:00, get dressed, wash my face, go the the post office. That's ceremony. Come home and have something to eat, like peanut butter and rice crackers, and try to get to my desk by 10:00. Then I take a lunch break. I used to work from 10:00 to 4:00. I found on this book stopping by 2:00 with a lunch break--at that point I was exhausted. So I'd take a nap, and after the nap, on 3 nights a week I go play volleyball. And the other nights I would either go get my son, Fleetwood, pick him up after school, which I do frequently, do something with him, or mess around with girls. Go to the movies. I like to read. I am interested in the evolution of consciousness, and would like to do more reading and experimenting in that area, but I'm usually too wiped out after a day of writing. If I'm home alone, I listen to the radio and tapes a lot. I've become a real radio fan here in the age of TV. There's this station in Canada in particular that has some wonderful programs.

Visionary and psychotherapist Patricia Sun had difficulty describing a typical working day.

PS: Oh dear, I don't think I have too typical a day. Everyday is a little different. I get up early, I get up late. Mostly I get up early. I tend to wake up when the sun comes up and sometimes a little before that. I like to lay in bed in the morning and remember my dreams and think when it's quiet. Of course, a lot of the time I am traveling, going places, so I'm always doing something different to catch planes, to meet schedules, being in different kinds of environments. I'm very flexible, and that's handy considering how I live. There was a time when I really wanted to work in my garden, when I wasn't traveling, and I still like to do that.

In her working day, Norma has more face-to-face interaction with other people than most of the respondents. Frank reported a method of writing he has developed that has helped him. He always stops each day before he has exhausted his material, so that the next day beginning is easy. Most of the respondents have devised work schedules, and follow them.

It is interesting to note that most of the respondents reported a number of ways in which they care for themselves each day, such as feeding, exercising, grooming, resting, and meditating, but few discussed caring for others. Tom, Wendy, and Paul were exceptions. The greatest portion of Paul's day is spent caring for his wife; however, before the onset of her illness he did not have this responsibility. Tom reported that caring for his son is an important part of his day. Wendy, who like Paul, is not quoted in this section, is the youngest respondent, and spends time each day caring for her 2 school aged children. I think that the advanced age of the respondents may be a contributing factor in this phenomenon. Many of them spent more time caring for others earlier in their lives.

Another interesting observation is that most of the respondents commented about some way in which they receive input during their days. Norma goes to movie screenings and ballets. Frank reads the Times and watches the MacNeil-Lehrer report. Tom socializes with his volleyball team, attends movies, listens to radio shows, and reads. Stimulation and input is important enough to the respondents for them to provide for it in their daily routines.

Serendipity and Synchronicity

Although they are elusive qualities, it is generally accepted that serendipity and synchronicity are aspects of the creative process. Aikido instructor Wendy Palmer related these occurrences to the sixties. She thinks synchronicity occurred more often in the sixties because people expected it and were more trusting.

LM: Have serendipity or synchronicity played a particularly large role in your life?

WP: Yeah, during the sixties--that was what a lot of the sixties was about. The vibes. Pick up the vibes. I had a vibe that you were going to be here, right? I had a vibe I would see you. Now 90% of all interaction was through that kind of mode. One of the nice hangovers of the sixties is there is still some of that happening. One of the strong points of the sixties was that people believed it was going to happen. [Pause] Yes, but not as much as it used to.

Writer George Leonard stressed the connectedness of all things. He thinks that synchronicity occurs far more often than is generally thought.

GL: Yeah. I think first of all that everything is probably synchronicity. I think if you get into that space, you see everything is connected. It's called positive paranoia, positive schizophrenia. You can even see that everything is absolutely connected: your being here, my being here, what you're saying. Wanting this interview has given me a lot of ideas about doing a piece on creativity for Esquire. Let's make the assumption, this is strictly for the sake of argument, that everything is totally synchronous. Everything is connected, everything is meaningful. Every license tag you see has specific meaning to your life. Just say that. In some philosophical systems, that could be the case. I agree with you--that then the variable is, are you aware of it? More creative people are generally more aware of it.

Like George, educator Paul Torrance emphasized the importance of focusing awareness on synchronal events. He thinks serendipity is important to creativity, and people who desire to be more creative need to learn to recognize and use it when it occurs.

PT: Well yes, I think chance, serendipity, and so forth are very important, but you have to be able to recognize them when they happen. And make use of them. I think that's the same thing that happens in discovery and invention. These discoveries were probably discovered by hundreds of individuals before, but they didn't grasp the significance of it and didn't make use of it.

Inventor of the Bell helicopter and philosopher Arthur Young practices moving beyond linear thinking for the purpose of encouraging synchronicity. His experience is often of something working through him. He emphasized the need to listen to the inner voice.

LM: Another area I want to address is the role serendipity and synchronicity play in your life and work.

AY: That's much too difficult a question. I mean that's fate. Almost all the important things have not happened because of my efforts. I have just been a witness to them. It is as though something is working through me.

LM: You have an awareness of those things occurring.

AY: Oh yes. Very definitely a fact. One of the spookiest things is that I find myself doing things that make no sense until later. A psychometrist I worked with had an exercise. He thought he could teach people to do these things. It was to buy tickets for the best show, go to the theatre, tear up the tickets and go home. Make yourself independent of rational reason. No one with any sense would tear up the tickets and go home. But you have to be independent of common sense if you are going to listen to that inner voice. I pull out a coin to see if it's heads or tails to see if I'll do something. Anything to be independent of my reason.

Tom experiences synchronicity in his work.

TR: All the time. I have an example. I was writing about beets, and I was writing about immortality, and in my research I picked up a book....This is not a book I expected to be a part of my research; it's called the No Aging Diet, but I just wanted...you know, it was just on the periphery, and I just thought I'd look at it. It's the "eat beets and grow younger diet," and to my surprise there is something in here about beets and rejuvenation.

Like Tom, Norma experiences synchronicity in her writing.

NS: Very much so. I would say that's probably how I got my--yeah, one of the reasons I'm as well known as I am today was that. OK. The first piece I wrote for <u>After Dark</u> was a piece on <u>Oh Calcutta!</u>, and it so happened that it was one of the first times in history a national magazine had frontal male nudity in it. A very good photographer took the photographs. I wrote the story. Needless to say, the reason the story became famous was not because of my story, but because of those photographs. Now, it was the first story I had ever written in my life. First of all, I have an article that's going to be talked about for years because it was a trailblazer in male nudity. Secondly, for my first article, I'm on the "Today Show." Isn't that magic? Isn't that exactly what you're talking about?

Carl experienced serendipity often.

CR: I'll start looking at something, and I'll come across an article in the newspaper that opens up some whole new thing I didn't know about, or friends sending stuff, or stumbling on an article I hadn't expected to look at. I feel serendipity plays a big part.

Like George, Patricia thinks synchronicity happens all the time. Like Paul and Arthur, she emphasized focusing one's awareness on synchronicity. Patricia said that the people who think they don't have synchronicity in their lives do have it, but they don't see it. She also thinks the more one notices synchronicity, the more it will be experienced. She attributes this occurrence to a universal law that like attracts like. Both Patricia and Norma described synchronicity as having a magical quality.

316

PS: Well, synchronicity happens all the time. Of course there is coincidence, and at another level there really is not. There is a flow and order in the universe, and when you tap into your receptivity and your awareness, you encounter many phenomena, everything from how astrology works to certain aspects of physics. I think the most powerful way to receive it is to enjoy it, to use it, and expect it to come again. If they don't see it, they don't think they have it. And another thing happens. When you accept it and move into the style of thinking that's big enough to hold it, it actually draws more to you. It's because you become a magnet for the second emotional law in the universe--you attract what you put out. If you put out fear, you get fearful things. If you put out love, you get loving things. If you put out curiosity--like I was saying, I have a thing I want to solve or know, and I asked for it. Now I had already been given it, but I didn't recognize it because a part of me wasn't accepting it. So when I prayed more intently to get it, I had synchronicity start popping all around me. It had almost a magical quality.

The respondents reported experiencing serendipity and synchronicity as a part of their creative processes. Several stressed encouraging synchronicity and most expressed value in focusing on it. Evidently, serendipity and synchronicity are two pieces in the puzzle of creativity.

Inspiration

Inspiration, like serendipity and synchronicity, is an element with an elusive quality that is important in the creative process. Many coresearchers, including Tom Robbins, Carl Rogers, Paul Torrance, Wendy Palmer, Patricia Sun, Frank Hogan, and Niels Diffrient, reported insights coming during other activities, such as shaving, walking, having a drink, and just before, just after, or during sleep. Tom Robbins likes to surround the creative act with excitement and mystery; George Leonard with playfulness and a sense of fun. Frank Hogan gets his creative juices flowing by writing letters, reading the paper and taking a walk. Inspiration has been a force in Frank's life. What Frank describes as inspiration in the following quotation sounds a great deal like synchronicity.

LM: What has the role of inspiration been for you?

FH: Very important. I think inspiration, guidance, hope. But what happens in creativity, I think, is that...you've got a subject, and that can come from almost anywhere, and once you establish the fact that you are writing about a given idea--I'm talking about a long project--then it is absolutely amazing how much that subject is going on in the world. It's around you everywhere. And all of a sudden the whole world is full of John Maynard Keynes.

Patricia relates inspiration to God's love. For her, inspiration is a touchstone. It provides the courage and drive she needs to actualize her creativity. Inspiration makes Patricia happy.

LM: What role does inspiration play for you?

PS: I don't really see inspiration as a role. A role to me is a kind of category you put something in to get feedback and have a different perspective on it. I see inspiration really like the Holy Spirit. I see inspiration almost like what the word means, to inspire, to breath in, to take in life. It's very yin: it's very much like being penetrated by God. When I see the sky is blue, you know there are different theories about the meanings of colors, and light blue is supposed to mean God's love, and I always chuckle when I see a big blue sky, and I say, "God loves us all," and we don't even pay attention. Inspiration is the touchstone that gives you the drive and courage to do the perspiration part. The perspiration part is actualizing here. That's how Einstein meant it. I love to inspire people. I love to be inspired. I love to see someone else inspire someone else. Everything about that makes me happy.

Rowena Reed was uncomfortable discussing inspiration. She described inspiration as a state of mind, illumination or enthusiasm.

RR: Inspiration is a state of mind that one achieves. A state of enthusiasm for... a state of illumination for a certain project or work. If you get enthusiastic about it, then you are inspired to work. ... It isn't good to talk too much about these personal emotions. There is something about it; if you stir it up too much, you muddy the waters.

For Paul, inspired work is superior to uninspired work.

LM: Has inspiration played a big role in your life and in your work?

PT: Yes, I guess with most of the things that I've done there has been some inspiration. I think it occurs all the time. You do things with a purpose, whatever that purpose is.

LM: Do you have insight that inspires imagery, or is it more moving through daily work?

PT: Well, some of both. I think the best things and the most productive things, the most powerful things come like "that," and I think that then the books practically write themselves. And I think they are generally the better ones.

Tom emphasized the work involved and deemphasized the inspiration. Because he is a professional, he does what is necessary to generate his own inspiration. Spontaneity is paradoxical in his work, because he can not make himself spontaneous, yet he can create a framework through which spontaneity often occurs.

TR: Well, when you are a professional, you don't sit around and wait for inspiration. Inspiration is for amateurs. I go to my desk everyday, 5 days a week, and I figure my muse will find me. Maybe she doesn't come, but she doesn't have to go checking the bars for me. You generate your own inspiration. But you can't be completely spontaneous, and yet spontaneous things occur within that framework all the time.

Niels finds inspiration almost everywhere.

ND: I get inspired at every turn. Anything I do, everyone I talk to, everywhere I go, I just seem to be spotting a new area of interest.

Like Tom, Norma stressed the work. She dislikes the term inspiration.

> NS: I have so much to tell you about what I think of inspiration. No professional writer works on inspiration because the word has come to mean something completely different from what it is. You may say I have inspiration because I am about to go to bed, and I am interrupted by an idea that comes to mind. When I was a very successful freelance poet, I sat down in my study at 8:00 every evening and wrote and typed until 11:00. This is not what you call inspiration. I would sit down and say, "I am going to write a poem for <u>Christian Science Monitor</u>," and I would write the kind of poem they might publish. I would say,"I am going to write a sonnet," having no idea what it would be about. As soon as I said, "I am now going to write a sonnet," a sonnet grew on my paper. Now that ain't inspiration. That's sitting on your rear end and just working, doing.

It appears that inspiration occurs in the lives of most of the respondents, even though they deemphasized it and emphasized the work. I had expected that a strategically placed failure at a vulnerable time in one of their lives would have moulded failure, the inspiration to dry up and never return. But that has not happened, all their rough times have been smoothed, and have often been viewed by the respondents as growth producing. It is of course possible that other people have had such an experiences and have not continued to work, and therefore would not be appropriate respondents for this study.

Some information about the creative process has been presented in the previous quotations. The questions addressed how the respondents spend their time on working days, and how their creativity is influenced by serendipity, synchronicity, and inspiration. Another way by which I had hoped to gain information about the creative process was by asking the respondents to describe their experiences during an outstanding creative accomplishment.

Respondents' Creative Processes

Modern language may be deficient, or the creative process may be rare or mystical to such an extent that words are a difficult medium to peg the experience, if in fact it will lend itself to being pegged. Earlier, novelist Tom Robbins said that his most outstanding accomplishments were, in his opinion, his beautiful sentences. I asked him to describe the experience of writing beautiful sentences in hopes of discovering his perception of his creative process. Tom uses a number of sensual metaphors to describe creative writing.

> TR: Well, there was no one around. I'm talking in terms of a sentence. I was alone in what I call my studio writing them, and it usually evolved...it very seldom came out full blown. I would write this sentence, and it wouldn't quite work. Or it might have been a perfectly good sentence grammatically, and in terms of the sense that it made, but it was kind of flat, and I would change a word here and a word there. It might have taken me a half hour.

> LM: So writing these sentences is hard work?

> TR: Yes, most of the time. But once in awhile they will just arrive full blown.

LM: Does it happen when you're writing or when you are doing something else?

TR: Both. It used to happen a lot when I was shaving.

LM: Is it a willful process...your creativity? Can you decide to go do something creative and go do it?

TR: Oh yeah, I do that constantly. But I cannot decide that today I'm going to do first-rate work. Or better work than I did yesterday. I don't have a whole lot of control over that. I just sit there and work hard and do my best, and sometimes it's better than others. It's like a lover...sometimes they are better than others. It is hard work, and it's lonely and frustrating work, but I also think that it is fun and exciting. I haven't found many writers who will admit that. Most of them seem to lead pretty miserable lives. Maybe they think it's necessary for their creativity to live a miserable life, but I think that is a terribly wrong approach. But to go out and sit at a desk for 6 hours everyday requires a certain amount of motivation so I try to surround the act of writing with drama and mystery, which makes it far easier for me to do it. I think of it as being slightly subversive. It's far easier to go and sit there hunched over this desk, which is hard physical work, harder than digging ditches.

LM: You sort of started answering my next question, which is--how do you bring on creativity? I'm thinking that drama has a lot to do with it. Setting the scene, getting the props, having the excitement...

323

TR: In my case, never letting myself know too far ahead what I'm going to do. Always keeping an element of surprise there. Like I never work from an outline. When I begin a book, I haven't the slightest idea how it's going to end or even where it's going to be in the middle. I have a vague overall sense of a plexus of effects that I want to create, and somewhere in my subconscious I have a fair amount of knowledge of plots or characters, but I don't bring it all up and look at it. I kind of squeeze it up like toothpaste, a little bit at a time, and connect a few dots everyday. I let most of it lie there and marinate in my imagination. And sometimes what comes up is--real frequently--a surprise to me and often a delight. Whereas if I knew in advance everything that was going to happen, then it would really start to seem like work.

Creative writing is like taking a shower in a motel. You have to fiddle with the faucets a lot to get just the right temperature and flow of water, and you're there luxuriating in it, and it's feeling really good, and everything is perfect; then somebody flushes the toilet in the next unit, and the whole thing is thrown off.

LM: What about your creativity do you find especially satisfying?

TR: I feel really happy when I write what I consider a beautiful sentence. I like beautiful sentences. I like to read them by other people. Sentences that inspire a mixture of envy and love, and I like to write them frequently. But when you get one that really works,...that's what it really is all about for me. That's what I'm here for--beautiful sentences.

LM: What do you feel for your beautiful sentences?

TR: Well, Alexander Pushkin was out of Moscow, and he was in St. Petersburg and detained there. He hadn't seen this work in a year and had forgotten a lot of it, and so when he got back to his studio, he sat down in a chair and began to read his galleys. It was almost like reading someone else's work after that long. He began reading, and as he read, he got more and more excited and finally he leaped up out of the chair and threw the galley proofs on the floor, and he said, "Pushkin, oh you Pushkin! Oh you Pushkin! Oh you son-of-a-bitch!" And that's the way I feel when I get one of those rare sentences. "Oh Tom, oh you Tom. Oh you son-of-a-bitch!"

Although Tom sometimes conceptualizes a complete work, he usually begins and then works toward the finished product in small steps. Several times during his interview Tom described his writing in terms related to craftsmanship. Motivation is necessary for him to go to his desk day after day and write, and Tom finds he is more motivated and writes better when he surrounds his work with mystery and drama.

Incubation, the stage of creativity that is most elusive, is especially important to Tom. He allows and trusts that his unconscious will do its part while his conscious mind is working on its part. He said he likes to "squeeze his writing up a little at the time, like toothpaste." When he succeeds in producing a beautiful sentence Tom experiences elation and joy; however, after he completes a novel he often feels exhausted and depressed.

Psychologist Carl Rogers reported finding himself doing little to prepare for writing. He was cautious about becoming too willful when beginning a new project. He said he was more successful with projects that developed obliquely. Although Carl was losing his sight, he still found it to be the sense through which he learned best.

LM: When you are undertaking a project and you are going to need to be creative in order to pull it off, can that be a willful process? Can you make that happen?

CR: I think the two big flops that I described both came about because I had that attitude. It was going to be a brand-new research and had to be creative; it was going to be good. I think that I have been much better off when things have developed obliquely. For example, <u>On Becoming a Person</u>, which is my most widely published and widely read book, that is a collection of papers. I had a good friend who helped me with them, a salesperson; I showed it to him. He said collections of papers do not sell very well. That was enough to discourage me for 2 or 3 years. By that time I had some more papers. And I thought I wanted to put them together. I put them all together, changing some things, and so on. I gave it a title of "A Therapist's View of Psychotherapy." I don't have much respect for publishers, but that was one time they did me a good turn. The publisher said a better title is <u>On Becoming a Person</u>. And I'm sure if it had come out under my title, it would still be...coming out under his title, it was very vital. I would say that was an oblique thing. I didn't think it was a very big deal, but it was an expression of myself. What happened is what happened.

LM: When you are undertaking a project, do you have any sort of ritual, or anything you do to prepare yourself?

CR: No. There are a lot of things that I don't do. I don't have a ritual; I don't meditate; I don't prepare myself. I seem to be sort of a down-to-earth person who just gets started on something interesting, and maybe something will happen.

LM: From which of your senses do you think you learn the best? Sight, touch, smell, taste....

CR: I think without a doubt--sight.

LM: When you think creatively, do you use any one sense more than another?

CR: I don't quite know as to the creative moment, but what immediately follows is usually an unspoken verbalization. I have to put words together in my mind to fit the experience. It would be sight because sometimes I see it in the form I'm going to write it in.

LM: It is very interesting in that you were talking about learning best through reading and seeing. I learn better through hearing. When I'm thinking things out, I think them in words. You put written words together. I put spoken words together.

CR: It still is true when I'm writing anything significant, I write it longhand.

LM: Can you remember back to the time when you were first formulating your theory? Can you remember how you felt then, what you experienced?

CR: Yeah. I was a visiting professor, free of committees, free of many phone calls, away from

327

the home base, very few interruptions. I listened to hours and hours of recorded interviews trying to figure out what didn't seem to go well. I gradually wrote down some of the things that I thought. Then while vacationing in Mexico, I remember working out a very tight logical expression of those conditions. I remember when I first presented a paper to a sophisticated audience at the University of Michigan. The psychology department at that time was quite heavily influenced by psychoanalysis. It just didn't fit in with psychoanalytic theory at all. I can't give you the details, Linda; I would have to think more in present terms. I think when ideas begin to incubate, a new idea begins to sort of float around. It has happened when I'm walking on the beach or having a nightcap before going to bed. It would be that way, and I've learned to--it would happen before going to bed. Another thing that I have noticed, and it is not necessarily creative thinking, but if I'm in a conference and we are discussing issues, going to the bathroom is the most profitable thing I do.

I think the most creative things are not tedious at all. I would say there is an excitement about it. It's an easy flow. A thing begins to put itself together. I've done some painting too, and one thing about painting which puzzles me a little, even though I've never painted very much--I can just lose myself in that process completely. It's quite rare that I can lose myself completely to that degree in writing. Sometimes writing goes very smoothly, but I know enough to stop for meals or something like that; whereas with painting, I am not aware of the passage of time. One thing I've enjoyed is photography. That's quite different.

I haven't done much picture-taking for a long time. After you get into the picture-taking frame of mind...flowers in that doorway would be good, you begin to see all kinds of possibilities. You have to sort of get into the groove. The same thing is true of painting, I think. You have nothing to paint. But then if you have done some painting, all kinds of things to paint are everywhere.

It is interesting to note that while Tom uses mystery and drama to facilitate his writing, Carl did not use anything particular to prepare himself to write, but rather began and hoped something interesting would happen. Tom also goes to his desk and begins with the hope of something happening. The behavior of simply beginning is similar, the emotional climate is different.

Carl could do creative work while experiencing a great many outside demands and distractions; however, he described his most creative time as free of interruptions and demands. Earlier he reported that his ability to quickly shift his focus was one of his most outstanding qualities.

As was also true for Tom, Carl found his ideas came during periods of time when he was not working, after they had been incubating. Often his best ideas came to him just before going to bed. Carl said that when he was attending a conference, going to the bathroom was often the most productive thing he did.

Much like Tom, Carl experienced creativity as exciting. When he was at the peak of his creative production, he found himself flowing easily. When he painted, Carl often lost himself completely, an experience that was absent when he wrote. He found that once he began painting or taking photographs, that is, once he was into a painting or picture-taking frame of mind, he saw an increasing number of possibilities.

329

For Rowena Reed and Niels Diffrient, both industrial designers, creativity occurs in intense spells. Rowena feels physically stimulated when she is producing creative work.

LM: When you are being creative, when you are working, how does your body feel?

RR: Good. In fact, I can go beyond my strength often, and then I'll feel exhausted. I don't know whether I could do anything physically out of the ordinary, but I could work longer when I'm stimulated, keep longer hours. Normally, I'm kind of a short worker, then rest, but I can work longer at a stretch if I'm stimulated.

LM: Can you think of any physical sensations? When you are working, do you feel any other physical sensations besides that your endurance seems to be expanded?

RR: That's a good part of it. I'm not conscious of my body as a handicap or something that gets tired. If I'm really working hard, I forget all that.

LM: So it becomes natural, it flows, it's easy.

RR: If I'm tired, I don't realize it until after I stop.

LM: Do you find you express yourself creatively visually, and you also learn best visually?

RR: I like to look at a thing when I'm trying to learn. I don't want somebody to read to me. I want to see a page myself.

LM: What about your kinesthetic sense? You were talking about using clay, so I wondered if your sense of touch is very sensitive?

RR: Oh yes, I think so. If I had time, I would like to use my body more; I like dancing very much and I always did. More exercise and that kind of thing, and swimming, but not very heavy sports. Then of course I would stimulate myself because I like to read a lot. I love to go to the museums and exhibits--all those things. We all have ways of stimulating ourselves. I didn't have any problem as long as I was feeling well. But I really spent a good deal of time keeping myself feeling all right. Do you?

LM: I do.

RR: I'm the kind of person who works in very intense spells, and then I'll collapse, kind of build up a little more steam. Like a cat--like they say a cat is very quiet before he jumps.

LM: Is there anything you do to help yourself be more creative when you need to perform some kind of creative function? Any ritual, anything you can do to help yourself be creative?

RR: I don't know. I should say I always felt I had enough within me to be creative, but the best way to get it out was to be completely rested, and I wouldn't have any trouble.

LM: During very creative times do you have flashes of insight?

RR: Oh sure.

LM: Do you notice yourself behaving any differently in a way that would facilitate that happening, to keep it coming?

RR: Well I guess I would try to cut everything else out of my life. Cut away all but the essentials. I know I missed a good deal of other things by doing that. But it was all right. I was easier to get along with, but I was more selfish like Picasso in my day-to-day contacts with other people. I just wouldn't bother.

LM: Did your sleep habits change any?

RR: I think probably during the period of greatest intensity of teaching, I was stimulated because I drank coffee. I've stopped several times. I'm controlling it pretty well now. Coffee is not good for my eyes; it's not good for my hypoglycemia; it's not good for anything. You know what I think it is? I think it's like taking money out of the bank. If I drink several cups of coffee in a day, I just feel great all day long, even into the evening, and the next day I pay for it.

LM: How do you feel when you are working well? Do you feel exhilarated and happy?

RR: Don't you? I get tired of talking about myself. I'm not that interesting.

LM: Do you forget to eat?

RR: No, I could never forget to eat because I have to eat. But I lose myself, and I will work long hours. At least I did. I can't work quite as long hours as I used to, but I used to work 10 hours a day for 5 days a week. There really is a discipline to visual relationships. It isn't just all intuition, going into a trance, and letting it come out. I like to compare it with music. You wouldn't listen to a concert player if he hadn't studied music, if he just played by ear. Even for jazz nowadays, you have to have musical knowledge.

Like Carl, Rowena is able to concentrate fully on her creative task. One way in which she does so is to limit her life, particularly her social life, so that her focus is unified. Because she is in her eighties, and because she suffers with hypoglycemia, she has to dedicate a good deal of energy to caring for herself. As was true throughout her interview, Rowena experienced some discomfort and boredom in discussing herself. Although I would describe her as a thoughtful, reflective person, she seemed to me to be extroverted in her manner of structuring reality.

Niels Diffrient described experiencing a relaxed responsiveness during his creative process. He also thinks some of his best works are the results of accidents. He has faith in these accidents, and indeed, he described his life as a series of accidents. He described his sensation during creative output as smooth in the same way athletics well played can be experienced as flowing.

LM: You were talking about the way it feels, the satisfaction. Could you elaborate a little bit about how you feel physically and emotionally at that creative moment? What the sensation feels like?

ND: Well, I'm completely at ease with myself. It's sort of what I call smooth. Everything is working.

LM: You feel relaxed?

ND: Oh yeah. Relaxed and yet...not like lazy...Again, I compare it to athletics. You can be very responsive in playing a game, but not in the least tense. You can be relaxed, and yet using all your muscles properly and doing everything just right.

LM: So you're energized and relaxed at the same time.

ND: That's right. It's physical, total...total body. Your whole body feels like your brain, all in one. Of course, with me, I have to use my body. I'm either moving around making a model or a drawing or something like that. And it's all being applied toward an unknown goal, but yet known. I mean, I don't know what it's going to be, but I have a sense of it. And as I move along, I have a feeling that I'm doing it right. And in the end, I find out it could have been better. And then I go on. But while I'm doing it, I can get pretty excited about things falling into place.

LM: During that time, are you more aware or less aware of your body?

ND: Well, it varies. Bodily awareness in the sense that I'm using it and relying on it. I don't know why I rely on athletic comparisons; but if you're doing something athletic, you can be totally aware of your body, and yet not aware of it, if you know what I mean.

LM: So it's a more wholistic experience?

ND: Absolutely.

LM: Do you forget to eat?

ND: You can. But I find that I can sustain the intense part of this only in spells of four, five, six hours. Then I have to kind of get out and walk around, or something.

LM: So you're working on a project, and you reach that stall point where nothing's happening, and you take a break, and take a walk, have something to eat, whatever; and at some time during that break, you have an awareness about what the problem is, why you stalled, you have some new information?

ND: It can happen that way, or in other ways. I can come back to it without any inspiration and struggle with it a while. And it won't solve itself. And you struggle and struggle. Sometimes it goes on for days. And then one day it'll happen. Other times, like you say, I could take a break and come back to it and solve it right away. Sometimes I run out of information. Sometimes it's not right because I sense the machine is not going together properly, and I don't know enough to solve it. I have to get the right data together. I have to get the right information. I have to be dealing with the right company, a lot of things.

LM: This thing you've been referring to is very elusive--this part where you're stuck, and you go away for an hour or 3 days or a week, and then it starts again. Do you have anything that you could say about the "it?"

ND: Well, yes and no. I know something's going on. Technically I suppose it's the subconscious doing its job. I've read a lot of things--Freud, Jung, and other sources--they in their own way try to describe it. But I have no evidence that it's as they say, other than the fact that it actually happens. I guess I have faith that it'll get solved or that I will find inspiration, whatever. It's never failed. It may not always be the best, because, though I'm creative, I've never thought of myself as a genius. I don't think my work is always the best I can do. Sometimes I just don't get it done as well as I think it could conceivably be done, but because of the world I work in, there's an end to things. It has to end. As it probably should anyway, so I can move on to something else.

LM: Faith. Several times you've said things like, "The answer will come" or "It will answer itself." It sounds like you have an experience of the product or the concept sort of having its own life, its own direction, outside of you. Is that an accurate description?

ND: That has validity, yeah. It's not as though it's a mystical thing. It's just that there is a rightness to the assembly of physical elements, and that rightness exists. I have a feeling that things are going together properly, either by accident, or because I arranged them that way, or because somebody else gave me good criticism or whatever. I can tell, to some degree, when they're going together properly. And I rely on these accidents. My life is an accident, so I have to rely on accidents. It's been the best way for me to get along. Sometimes when I'm working, I live a kind of ongoing agony. I don't sleep well. I go into fits of depression, all related to work. Fortunately, my wife works too; so she knows, and she puts up with it. But if I lived with anybody else, they'd probably divorce me. My first wife did. Engineers I work with credit me with being a natural-born engineer. And when I do mechanisms, I work them out intuitively. I draw every part in them, I give them to the machine shop, and they make the part and put it together, and it works. I'm always sort of astounded. I don't know where that comes from.

LM: How did you decide to do this chair?

ND: How did I come up with the Jefferson Chair?
You know, it seems that I've never started any
project from a rational analysis of conditions in
arriving at a solved problem. It just seems one
thing or another combines. I know I had been
designing chairs for some time, and I had been
intrigued with the idea of a reclining chair. I had
also been dissatisfied with some of them, existing
ones that I own, designed by others. And I had
started sketching various ways....I liked the idea of
being able to lie down and work. I do a lot of my
reading in bed. Something about the relaxation of
not having to lift a muscle gets me deeper in
things. And this whole thing had been intriguing
me.

Then one day I had a chat with Bobby Catwalliter
[who at the time was with SunarHauserman, the
company that manufactored the chair]. He said,
"You know, I'm so sick of having to crawl in bed to
read and be comfortable. I wish you'd design
something I could sit in sometimes where I could
read." Well, that kind of stirred me up a bit. And
that was about the time that Bobby had come in to
do some work with me for a seminar, and I really
got serious about it. I sat down one day and put
together, in outline form, all the principles that I
knew about a reclining chair and actually drew
one. It turned out to be the first model I made. I
did it all in one day, showed it to Bobby, and he
said, "Well, yeah, go ahead, try it out." And I made
the model, and it worked pretty well. And then we
corrected that, we learned a lot of things; and it
was about that time that I began to realize
that the purpose here was not only to sit

comfortably, but to be able to do something while you're sitting there, or lying down, I should say. So then I decided, well, why shouldn't it be a whole group of things that help you work while you're in this chair? You could read, maybe write, maybe type, maybe do some other things. So it just came to me one day that I should try that out, see if it actually works.

So I went out and bought a cheap little bedside table, which everybody knows about, and I pulled it up next to the chair, and I thought that, you know, it had enough realistic potential, but it was such a poorly designed thing. I could see lots of potential to do a well-conceived piece of support equipment. And one thing led to another, and I just ended up designing all this paraphernalia.

At one point I realized the chair was going to be big and complicated and probably expensive, and I was not satisfied with the design, so I tried redesigning it and didn't get anywhere. One of the designs I even built a full-size model of, and I was unsatisfied with it. I thought to myself--and this was a year or so after I had left [resigned] the office [and began working on my own]--I just sort of chastised myself and said, "You've been an executive so long you don't even know how to design anymore." I really forced myself to sit in my room for as many days as it took, and I would keep busy, I would not stop when I didn't think I was going anywhere, and I wouldn't stop until I thought I had something good. I did nothing but draw or build models, anything I could think of to force this issue. It's one of the rare times I've ever done that.

338

And eventually something began to come out. In the drawings, I could see that I was evolving something. One drawing led to the next, and so on. I sort of slowly tried it out on this one occasion. Now, of course, there were always pauses in between--I had to sleep overnight, and I'd come at it with a fresh approach. But this was one of the first times that I really forced the issue and dragged it out and got, I think, some fairly novel developments.

Then I began refining. And I didn't want to lose the value of the idea, because I knew it had merit. But it could have been a flash in the pan if it wasn't brought to a really highly refined stage. That was the most important part of the effort--that forced period, and I think it was 3 days, that I just reeled off the paper. I must have used dozens of yards of paper. Everytime it would go wrong, I'd throw it away and start again. I kept a few of them. Now, I would draw full-size, you see, and drawing these things full-size for days is a lot of work. And I would work 14 to 16 hours a day. But that was the turning point that made it something of quality.

Then the final thing was the engineering. I had not engineered anything of any significance. I had always worked with other engineers. But I felt what I wanted to do would be lost if I had to transfer it to an engineer, so I proceeded to engineer it myself. I wasn't a novice at it; I've done a lot of this kind of thing. But I invented all the mechanisms and everything. [It took] months of work. So I stuck with it all the way through and eventually evolved it into what I thought was a very good design and probably one of my best.

LM: How much time are you talking about, from start to end?

ND: That depends on...it's not ended yet.

LM: Until you said, "Okay, let's manufacture it."

ND: Three years. I tend to forget myself a lot, and my absentmindness grows--I'm somewhere else basically. In another way, though, I'm a lot freer because my mind has a simple focus. The period I'm in now is terribly difficult for me because I'm doing nothing but sustaining-type work. I'm dealing with problems. I'm correcting errors. I'm pushing other people, trying to see that the thing gets made. I suffer during these periods. And it runs on for 3 or 4 years of agony. First of all, I fear that my child will be stillborn all the time, that it won't work, that it'll fail for one reason or another.

LM: Do you like the pressure of working at the last minute?

ND: It's a funny feeling. Part of it is because I'm afraid if I do it, it will fail. So I wait. The other part is that I guess I am waiting for inspiration. I don't know. The other part is that I'm basically lazy. I'd rather not do something; I'd rather put it off. I can't tell you. That's the one part I can't figure out. Now, I'll get up and go when I have to, but I have to have a clear and present reason to act. That's what I mean about sawing off the limb. I know things have got to get done, so I will slowly set up circumstances in which I've got to do it.

LM: Is there something you do to prepare yourself for creative work?

ND: I have to clean up around me, have to make sure my fingernails are clean, every little thing. I don't know why that is, but when I sit down to work, I want the situation to be such that I feel I can really get into it and not be interrupted if possible. When I was heavily into the design of this furniture, I would get down here by 7:00 most days so that I'd have 2 or 3 hours completely without interruption. And then I worked every weekend, because that was the best time. And I felt best when I knew I wouldn't be interrupted for 2 whole days. My work is so complex and involves so many interactive forces, that I have to work up a kind of pure mood, building up from the bottom a state of mind. In other words, I put all the paint on my pallet, and then I'm ready to paint. And then I can begin to generate. And I work up into a kind of a fever.

LM: Do you use other people's work for stimulation. Not necessarily your own field--some other art form?

ND: Yeah, and I don't do enough of that. I've learned a lesson, actually, in the last few years because of the concentrated effort that it's taken to do the full scope of the kind of work I'm doing--I've cut out an awful lot of things in my life. I've not gotten out into the world very much. And I think I feel the drain. And I think I've also missed some opportunities to shake myself up. I do a lot of sort of mundane things which I hate doing in a sense; but sometimes when I stall, I'll just go drag out the back issues of <u>Design</u>

Magazine and flip through it at random, just to kind of shake up the fix. I don't like doing that, in a way, because it's too close to what I'm involved in. But it is the only thing I have at my elbow. Whenever I feel stymied, if I could just go take a tour of the museums or whatever, it would be better, but I don't have the time.

Niels, like Carl, Rowena, and Tom, said he does his best work when he is uninterrupted. Niels makes special effort, like going to his studio several hours before anyone else, to have time free of interruption. Before beginning work, he makes order in his work environment, because disorder distracts him.

While working, Niels experiences himself wholistically, as if his body were his mind. Like Tom, when he begins a project, he has an intuition of what it will be, but he does not know fully. He allows the project to evolve. During highly creative times, he feels a rightness to the assembly of objects; he knows they are fitting properly.

He described his working as intense, and said he can maintain this intensity for four, five, or six hour intervals. Sometimes a solution comes to him quickly, sometimes it comes easily after a break--during which he receives inspiration from what he guesses is his unconscious, and sometimes he must struggle for a solution. He said that often when he is working on a project he lives in ongoing agony. The pattern of creative surges followed by release, followed by building pressure and then another surge of creativity was described by a number of respondents.

As did a number of respondents, Niels reported that revision is a critical aspect of his work. When Niels works, he begins with an idea that will fill a need, and then spends as much as several years elaborating on and revising that idea. In the preceding quotation Niels recalled the inception of the

Jefferson Chair, and told me that he spent the subsequent three years developing the prototype. The Jefferson Chair is an award-winning chair, and has received more publicity than any other chair has ever received.

Educator Paul Torrance, like Carl Rogers, sees the difficulty in willing creativity. He listed behaviors that can facilitate creativity. Paul thinks that in order to be creative it is helpful to become deeply absorbed in the project, to be willing to experiment with different approaches, and to be aware of creativity when it occurs.

LM: For you, is creativity a willful process? Can you say to yourself, "Well, Paul, I'm going to do something creative now" and go and do it?

PT: Well, it's not all that simple. I think that I know there are things that I can do to increase the chances that I'll produce something creative. It's not a pure will thing; you have to let it happen. But if you don't do certain things, it won't happen.

LM: What kinds of things can you do to help it happen?

PT: First of all, you have to become very deeply absorbed in whatever you are trying to do creatively. You have to immerse yourself into it. You have to be willing to experiment with different approaches and be aware of when it comes. Of course, when you get deeply involved, then one thing leads to another, and you start thinking of ideas and quality and class that you hadn't thought of, and it sort of speaks to you. It works in several ways. I suppose that typically you get into a new area or a new problem, and then you read about it, and you collect data and so forth, and suddenly it begins to fall into place. Sometimes, just as you are going off to sleep or while you're shaving in the morning--that's been a fairly frequent thing--you experience putting things into motion. Another thing is when I'm reading and have been working on a problem--something in the reading suggests a new idea.

Much like Niels makes order and Tom sits at his typewriter, Paul said that although he cannot will creativity, he can do certain things to encourage its occurrence. Much like Rowena, Paul stressed the essential quality of absorbing himself in his project. One way in which he absorbs himself is by collecting data about similar ideas. Paul also reported, as did most of the respondents, that he often has his best ideas when he is doing other things, such as shaving, after he has begun a project and focused his energy upon solving a particular problem.

Aikido instructor Wendy Palmer allows the inspiration to flow through her. She and Norma can feel the excitement of creativity in their bodies. In the following, Wendy described the period during which she was becoming successful in aikido. Wendy had said that her children were her most outstanding accomplishment.

> LM: Okay, your second most outstanding accomplishment?

> WP: I guess achieving in aikido, getting a second degree black belt in aikido. Along with that, being a woman and being a cofounder of an aikido school and teacher.

> LM: Describe what that time in your life was like.

WP: It was after separating from my first husband and really feeling that the next thing out there for me--there was a really strong intuitive sense, and I wasn't very clear what it was--but I knew I was being compelled toward something. It was also at a time, during the sixties for instance, I even didn't have to make sense of everything. The feeling was enough. I went to a number of different things--sufi dancing, this and that. One night, I went to aikido class with some friends of mine, and I remember sitting there. I don't think I even participated the first time, observing the teacher and the students and looking at it, and it was like something very deeply familiar to me. It reminded me of everything I loved in horseback riding. It was as if I had seen the gestures before. It was like a deja-vu when I saw it, and I knew that I would do this for a long time. I knew it would become a path for me. I said something to my friends when I went home, and they laughed and said, "Sure."

I became a very faithful student and went to every class I could for a couple of years. It was extremely compelling although only a couple of months after I had started, I remember being so frustrated at what I call running into myself, that I remember crying all the way to the school, and in the dressing room, during class, in the dressing room again, and all the way home. While I was on the mat crying, people would say, "Are you sure you want to do this?" I'd be going "Yes, I want to do it." Because I realized that it was myself that I was coming up against. That's what aikido does--it puts you against yourself. It was like I had hit this wall. I wanted to be outside. I wanted whatever it was to change, and I would be better.

That was a very powerful time in my life. I remember people around me being amazed about my level of obsession. There were a bunch of us into it. Many of us had small children and we all shared the baby-sitting--men and women--and we'd go together. We'd talk about it in the kitchen; we'd go to the park and practice. We talked about it all the time. It really felt right. This had given us tremendous possibilities in our life. It was a way to relate to each other and a way to work on ourselves. I was very hopeful in that time that this was something extremely special. I felt as if I had a rebirth, a renaissance. I felt that when I was a child. I was very wild and willing to do anything. When I married and had a child, I had contracted some; so this was--learning to fall was like capturing my childhood again, and the energy of the child went in that, the excitement and the fearlessness of it. So it was a very exciting, fast-moving time. I felt like we were going through strong changes very fast.

About 2 years later, I was asked to teach, which kind of surprised me because I wasn't very highly ranked. I had a blue belt. I started teaching and got my brown belt. I had 40 students. I couldn't understand it because there was a very high ranking black belt man in the area who was trying to get to teach, and here I was doing it. But for some reason, I had a flair and a capacity. I did that for 2 years. George [Leonard] and Richard [my ex-husband] occasionally would come in and help me--if I was out of town or sick or something, they would teach a class for me. The government closed adult education, and I said to my students, "Now you go study with my teacher in the city." They said, "No, we want to study with you." I said,

"I think you are crazy," but they said, "No, your teacher scares us, and the city is too far to go." So I went to my teacher and said "What do I do?" He said, "Well, I'll set you up with a dojo. You have to find a place, and you can be connected to our dojo here." So I went to George and Richard and talked with them to see if they wanted to do it with me, because I really didn't want to do it by myself. It seemed like really a big step to be a woman with a martial art's dojo without any partners. So they were both willing to do it, which was nice, because both of them had things going on in their lives. We all knew we were young and green at the time. It's been a journey since then. The same as when you get your black belt test--you have just arrived at the bottom of the mountain, and now you can really truly start to be a true beginner, because you are in a situation where you can begin.

I really enjoy sharing what I know, and also I enjoy learning, which I can from almost anybody, because the beginners especially are the most challenging people to learn from--they are not refined in the art yet. Mostly when I teach, I feel like what I do is channel. Unlike George or Richard, either of my two partners, I do not have a capacity to plan what I'm going to do. It's like this wonderful kind of spirit starts to come through me, and pretty soon I find that as long as I stay in the framework of the environment of working with the principles and my own center and I stay true to those basics, that whatever comes up--I find that I can deal with each thing consecutively without having to make any decision about what I'm going to do. It just arises, and it just comes forth. The nice thing about aikido is that at the moments

347

when that inspiration is not flowing very clearly, you can go right back to the form or technique, be very straightforward. Then when the inspiration is flowing, you can just let it come through. I get most of my impressions, intuitive impressions, through sensations in the body. In other words, I can feel "as-if" with the other person. There are times when I'm not really creative, and it's important to practice, to keep the tubes lubed, so when a creative urge comes through, you can just go. You don't have rusted pipes. It's important to paint so that when the inspiration for a canvas comes, you are accustomed to painting--it's not like you have to remember.

When Wendy first observed aikido, she felt as if it were deeply familiar to her. She became a faithful student. In the beginning, Wendy studied and practiced with others. George sometimes experiences creativity as a shared process.

Wendy described her absorption with aikido as an obsession. It provided her with a way to relate to others as well as a way to grow personally. This time in her life was very special to her. Wendy felt as if, through aikido, she had recaptured the excitement and fearlessness of childhood.

In both her teaching and practicing of aikido, Wendy feels as if creativity passes through her. She said that as long as she remains open and centered, the right thing flows through and she does not have to make any decisions. Wendy emphasized the need to "keep the tubes lubed." In other words, Wendy thinks that one must practice one's art even when there is no inspiration. Wendy can practice form and technique, and then she is prepared when the inspiration does come.

Poet Norma McLain Stoop expressed feelings of excitement occurring when she writes. When she is very excited, she feels goose bumps, like electricity, running down her arms.

LM: Are you aware of your body at all when you are writing?

NS: I'm aware of excitement.

LM: Do you feel energized?

NS: I feel that I've got to stay with it. That no matter how excited I get, I've got to stay on the beam, and I would say that if I have any physical feelings, it's through the back of my shoulders and my arms as I'm talking about it. When I get very excited, I get a feeling like goose bumps, only it's more like an electric current down my arms.

LM: Have you ever noticed that particularly good ideas for poetry come to you in any kind of pattern? Do they come to you at particular times of the day?

NS: They tend to come late at night, just before I go to bed.

LM: When you are tired?

NS: Yes. Not necessarily when I'm tired. I get keyed up--I'm a night person. I do work, like paying bills and so forth and typing, better in the morning, but I would say that I can write at any time of day. I can write very much to order. I always have written to order. If you used one word, I would really bash you, and that's "inspiration."

Norma was less willing to examine her creative process closely, somewhat like Rowena and Tom. Like many other respondents, she reported that she has some of her best ideas when she is doing mundane activities, especially just before going to bed. Norma also reported an ability to concentrate, but unlike the others, she does not experience inspiration. Norma described herself as being able to write to order, and throughout the interview, she emphasized that she writes strictly for a market.

Like Wendy, visionary Patricia Sun values the process of allowing new perceptions. She finds her creativity following a shift in consciousness or perspective. I asked Patricia to describe her creative process. Her description included mystical or psychic experiences, and a quality much like the "as if" experience described by Wendy, and Niels' feeling of relaxed awareness.

> PS: That's what I try to teach actually, and it's very hard to describe. There is a kind of internal letting go, which is a form of being inside the other person's shoes. Or if it's a mechanical problem and equipment isn't working, it's like there is some part of me snaps out above it all and then sees other perspectives that the me in front of it doesn't see. So there is like a gate lift, and I call that the intuitive mind.

> LM: You find that you are able to view this from a sort of overview....

> PS: I get a hint, or I get a direction, or I get a new view. Then that lets me interact with the world differently in the next moment, because from that place I put out a different energy, different questions, different thoughts. I start looking at different things, and then I find that problems get

unraveled in this letting go place, too. It's not only an overview, because it's so over; it's not anything real specific and that's the part that is so hard to describe.

LM: So your prejudices just sort of go away?

PS: Oh yes. Exactly.

LM: And you're open to what's there.

PS: Exactly. And you're open to whatever pops into your head, which is key. I always have been very intuitive or mechanically inclined, one, because I visualize how mechanics work and then intuit what might make it shift or change and work. One time I had a very fascinating experience, which I almost hesitate to tell you. I'll tell you anyway, and we'll see how it comes out. I had a car, an old Fiat station wagon, and the gears were just about gone. I knew it was just about gone, but we were using it anyway, because we had to. I didn't have any money, and I had to go do this one more trip. I went down the hill, but I couldn't get up the hill. I called my husband to come and follow behind, and it couldn't go up any kind of an incline. I live on top of hills. So the idea was he was going to follow behind me, and then we'd park it. I'd get it as close to our home as possible. When he was behind me, I had a funny shift in consciousness. It's a thought that logically is so ridiculous that we wouldn't let ourselves really vividly think it. But I got the thought. In my mind's eye, I imagined a silver cord tied around the bumper and a giant hand in the sky pulling the car up the hill. I thought, "Oh well, I'll try that." And it worked. I went up the hill 45 miles an hour. My husband was shocked. He said,

"What did you do?" I said, "You'll never believe this." When we got it up there, there was nothing left to the gears. They were totally gone, but it got me up to where I was going.

LM: That's a case of getting beyond the way we normally see things.

PS: Exactly. I don't say that we can causally do that at will, but I do think you can be open, and when it comes, you can use it. There is a difference in that. It's not from a linear side; it's from the spatial, intuitive side. Once I went to a symposium on parapsychology at Berkeley. As part of the symposium, and there were many hundreds of people there in the audience, they did hundreds of ESP tests of all different sorts. I got every single one right. It was funny how I got them right. Again, I got this funny feeling beforehand; it's a kind of clear fog, which seems contradictory. There was a clearness and a smoothness to it, but it had a nebulousness at the same time. I felt like I got a whole smattering of ways you can use intuition. Sometimes we'd have to choose a, b, c, or d ,and one would light up in my mind. You know, you would see it light up. Another time we would have paper in front of us, and one answer would feel sticky. One time they had artwork on slides, and they were showing it on the screen, and what we were supposed to do was--before they put the slide up--you were supposed to guess what you thought the slide would look like. So you just pick out of your head colors, shapes, whatever and write down on the piece of paper before they put the slide up. I had been doing very well, and they put a slide in but didn't put it up, and I had written down I saw a white mountain and three horsemen on horses. Then he said does anybody see any orange? I thought, "No, I don't see any orange." So he put the slide in, and there was this white mountain with three horsemen going up the hill. He said, "This is the wrong slide; it isn't supposed to be here." This doesn't happen to me all the time. This only happens when it happens. I don't particularly have control over it. The closest thing to control is caring greatly. I find that authenticness and genuine caring brings it more than anything else. I don't think that's an accident. I think it's because you let all your systems work as one. There is a genuine caring and a need to know. It is the clear openness of the need. I don't mean intellectual neediness, like, "Oh, I need a Cadillac, or I need this perfect man in my life." It is an in-the-moment, an almost organically full openness.

LM: Can you will creativity? Can you get up in the morning and know you've got a problem to solve and say "Well, I must get creative to solve this problem"?

PS: I don't think I have ever in my life said I have to get creative here. I think that happens automatically through the need.

LM: So it's the need that generates the behavior.

PS: Oh yes. I remember my mother once said that necessity is the mother of invention. I mean, it's an old saying, but it's true.

LM: One of those cliches that works.

PS: That's right.

LM: When you think creatively, do you think in one sense?

PS: Imagery, mostly imagery with feeling. But even the imagery that happens in your mind's eye, I mean, like dreaming, obviously in technicolor, and there's lots of movement, but I smell and feel and taste in dreams. Taste and smell are not as frequent, but when they happen, they are very strong and very meaningful and very old.

LM: When you experience this imagery, it is imagery in the way of vision? Do you see people and objects? Is it written?

PS: Oh no. Sometimes written things come in to emphasize a point, but they kind of rise in over the picture and glow in words.

Like Paul and Niels, Patricia is creative in response to need. Also like Paul, Tom, Wendy, and others, she cannot will creativity; however, there are certain things she can do to facilitate its occurrence. She said the most important thing she does is care deeply. When she cares, she experiences an internal letting go that enables her intuitive mind to function more fully. When she is open, Patricia gets a hint or a direction that leads her to a solution. When Patricia thinks creatively, she thinks primarily in imagery, which is usually visual, but sometimes is multisensory. Her motivation for creative thinking is a perpetual need to know.

Below is philosopher Arthur Young's description of the time during which he was building the Bell helicopter. His project began with his dissatisfaction with Einstein's theory of relativity. Arthur chose to build the helicopter because he thought it would take longer to build than most things.

LM: Could you talk to me a little bit about when you invented the Bell helicopter? Why you did it, and what your life was like? How you felt at the time?

AY: Well, see I wanted to do philosophy. I was not satisfied with relativity, and at that time I left college; my brother died. This was quite a shock--not the brother I told you about--another one. I realized that time had surprised us. In relativity, you treat time just as if it were space, i.e., you formulate it so you essentially predict it. It seemed to me that relativity deprived time of its essence, which was that it brought surprises. Time was something that you couldn't predict. So that changed my theory, the theory I was trying to put together, to become a theory of process instead of a theory of structure. Relativity is essentially structural in that you use formulas to describe everything, i.e., it's in four dimensions, but it includes time as if it were a dimension. But if time is bringing changes, then you can't expect to do that. It's a process of something that changes as it goes along. I couldn't figure out much more. I realized that I needed to learn how things really are in nature. That would be good practice for philosophy. Someone said my philosophy was a philosophy made by an engineer. My rejoinder was, well, I started with a helicopter, but it was a helicopter made by a philosopher. After I found it wouldn't fly the way I thought it would, and so on, I'd have to describe 10 years of work, because by the time I went to Bell, I had worked out the principles and had a model I could fly out the door and back again. I took that to Bell and demonstrated it, and they liked it, so we made an arrangement. Then I was to have the facilities to make a big one. It was just like going into a department store and saying "make an automobile." There would be a lot of people rushing around willingly, but they don't have the things you need, so I had to make them.

LM: Why did you decide to make a helicopter?

AY: It seemed to me it would take longer than other things, and I needed time. I had an experience with radio things that I'd thought I'd invented; I would read about them in next month's magazine. One of my crew came asking for a job. He unrolled these sheaths of drawings of helicopters and I said ,"Whatever got you to draw these helicopters?" He had been a jail warden and used to think about escape from jail. Well, it would take longer than most things and give me a chance to catch up. Anyway, I spent about l2 years developing the principles and took it to Bell and then about 3 years getting what they call the production prototype. It took about a year to get the first one flying, but then it took 2 or 3 more years to get the bugs out so it could be manufactured. By that time I had trained more people, and the helicopter could take over as a product instead of the airplanes which Bell had been making for the Russians during the war. This required a complete change of philosophy for the company. That was the subject of the <u>Bell Notes</u>. I had to learn how to cope with the organization. It was really more difficult than making helicopters. I had to change the mental approach of all these people who had seniority. They didn't like to have to learn something else again. At any rate, that taught me a lot about people. I've always liked mechanical things, but I learned more from that ordeal. Then I got into yoga and Zen philosophy and Hindu philosopy and ESP. That required a totally different worldview.

LM: Did you begin having experiences with things like ESP and develop your interests because of those experiences?

AY: When I decided to take up the helicopter, I thought it would take years to learn how things were in nature, and then I could get back to my philosophy. But the helicopter experience took longer than that, and I got very exasperated with these problems of management and took up yoga. Well, then the yoga got me into different mental states, having future dreams and things that were totally mind blowing. But they also gave me more incentive, or more clues you might say, toward philosophy. Since science neglected all these things, this was an even greater challenge. There were a lot of advantages I had by trying to include consciousness and ESP. I would say to myself that I had to dig deeper into the various subjects that I had thought about before. I mean to talk about the nature of space and time in a relativity sense, you can argue about measuring rulers shrinking and things like that, but it's all pretty hypothetical. Or things going at the speed of light. But if you recognize that there is such a thing as ESP in which you're transcending time, then this is a clue to cosmology which you couldn't get with any amount of measuring rods. I would say the seeds of the theory come from that recognition of having to dig deeper than science does.

For Arthur, building the Bell helicopter was not as difficult as learning to work within the corporate structure.

357

He discovered that in order to build the helicopter, he had to learn how to cope with the organization and persuade people with seniority to learn something new. For him, doing so was an ordeal. It was during this time he began practicing yoga to deal with the stress. The yoga led him to Zen philosophy and ESP. Incorporating these new experiences into a theory of the universe became his greatest challenge. This theory is presented in his book, <u>The Geometry of Meaning.</u>

Frank describes his creative process. Like Arthur, Patricia, and Wendy, Frank reported that mysticism plays a substantial role in his creativity.

LM: If you had to choose a particular work that you've done that you would consider your best, your most outstanding, which would it be?

FH: I have a very...well, first of all, as a 70th birthday present for a very good friend of mine, Mrs. Oscar Huffman of Albuquerque...she knew that I had written a song for Hildegarde called "Over 50, So What?"...and Ethel, Mrs. Huffman, said to me when she was 2 or 3 years away from her 70th birthday, "I would like you to write a song for my 70th birthday." As the time came close, I had no song, and I knew I had to do it. I tried various things, and then I realized her life was too diverse, accomplishful, to be one song, so I wrote a series of songs called, "Songs for the Seventies," which are very good. The piece runs about 10 minutes, and there are probably 15 songs. I think that is one of the best things I've done. In some ways, and I hesitate to say this, it is the smallest, but in many ways, it is big.

LM: You think the quality is very high.

FH: The quality is great. It is just what it is supposed to be. It was a birthday present.

LM: So you knew you had to do it. How did the beginning occur for you? Use whatever terms you'd like.

FH: Ethel Huffman's birthday is August l5th. I would think of starting in about March. It was not a constant thing. I was working on other things. Then there came a point where this had to move to first priority. I knew a good deal about her life. I knew it had to be very special. I got my basic idea from something she had said to me the night she came into town. Her husband had just died, and she had come to see a reading my play Finn MacKool, and we had dinner afterwards. She was staying in the Lombardy, and as we were going down the corridor into the dining room, she said, "You know, Frank, I want to get out of Santa Fe. I want to live in San Francisco. I don't want to become a Santa Fe widow, because I am a woman fulfilled." That became the key.

LM: When you were writing that, was your life different than it is other times?

FH: I was leading a quite normal...kind of writing it all the time. The line about the movie star and Oscar, her husband, I remember, I was shopping at the vegetable market up on Broadway when that line came. The idea of the lullaby in it is based on a lullaby my mother made up. I took some of the music from things I had already written and did new lyrics to them.

LM: What about your current work?

FH: All that stuff over there, that's all Maynard Keynes. Everything in the room is Keynes. What my nephew Bill sent yesterday, that was a piece on Maynard Keynes that he found in a business paper. I've got somebody in London getting me information.

LM: So you absorb yourself completely.

FH: But nobody has tackled Keynes this way. They tell you that he married this Russian ballerina. Well, great. But they never get into the reasons why a homosexual marries a ballerina. And there are some damned good reasons for it, including the fact that you don't run around--a guy who is running the finances of the world--as a homosexual. You don't come to the Savannah Conference as a homosexual without a wife upstairs in the room, or a girlfriend, or something that says, "I'm like everybody else." Certainly, you don't do it. And he was bright enough to know that. They don't write the person of Keynes. They write Keynes as an economic theory. I want to write him as a person.

LM: So you began the project with a desire to show him in a different kind of light?

FH: As a human being, absolutely.

LM: Can you say, "I'm going to go write ten pages of this play today" and then go sit down and make that happen, make yourself be creative?

FH: I can't.

LM: Can you facilitate that process in some way, help it along?

FH: Yes. When I used to go to the baths, that would work. A couple of nights after that happened, when I came home, the communication with Maynard was incredible. Absolutely incredible.

LM: Would that be the reason you'd go to the baths?

FH: Well, let's not kid around. I went for sex. But I knew it would help my work. Another project I was writing, a very personal play, the "my family autobiography." Interestingly enough, my brother is not in it.

LM: Interestingly enough. [Laughter]

FH: Consciously, a conscious decision not to write him. My mother, father, two sisters. But it's abstract. Can't You Think Of It Either? is the title of it. I had a good idea in my head about what I was writing, obviously. I saw what I was writing. I knew the twists and turns and the abstraction of it. And I think it was a very...kind of routine time. I would get up in the morning as I do everyday, go up and get the Times, come back and read it, write a letter to Ethel Huffman, whom I wrote the songs for. She has got a collection of some 3,300 letters I've written to her. All that stuff is going to the University of Wyoming. But this particular period, I had discovered that I could go right through the day...I would stop about 5:00, fix myself a drink, go up to the roof, stand up there for about an hour, have a drink and think about what I was going to write the next day, always stopping short of where I finished. It was a very, very tricky format I was using. I sustained it for the entire time of the writing.

LM: In a way you were preparing yourself for the next day.

FH: Which I do regularly.

LM: Are there any other ways you prepare yourself?

FH: I wake up in the night, and I think about it. I seldom do not think about something I'm writing on. It is very seldom that Maynard is out of my mind. Or some of the people I'm trying to pull together. My rule is that I never sit at the typewriter unless I know what I'm going to write. I also, as I said, write a letter everyday; every working day, I write a letter to Ethel.

LM: To the same person every day.

FH: Yeah. And I write other letters. I'm a letter writer. I write. I love to write letters. I like to get letters. But Ethel is the one...in those letters, and there are about 3,300 of them, and it's about a l0-or-ll year record, more than l0 years.

LM: Is the writing of the letters a preparation for the other writing?

FH: Yes. My fingers find out where the keys are. She understands that I am a writer, not a typist. It gets that part of it done, and it gets my head going and my fingers going at the same time.

LM: That's very interesting to me personally because--I've never had this insight before, but I do the same thing. I write a lot of letters, and I find myself, if I'm stuck particularly in my work,

362

I go write a letter. And I've never put it together before, that the reason is it's still writing, it greases the wheels.

FH: That's the same thing I do. And also, it's a kind of diary, really, about what I'm writing, because I talk to her a great deal about it. See, I talk to her, I don't write to her. I talk to her a good deal about what's happened the day before and what great discovery I've made about Maynard. I find that I have to make the discovery about five times before I realize that I've really discovered it. Then it's all right to write it. When it's going well, Linda, there is absolutely nothing in the world like it. Nothing in the world like it when you're taken over by this...thing. When it's really going well and you're not worried about the typewriter, there is nothing. The other day someone called me, and I stopped to answer the telephone. I had done a piece of writing, not long...I have become a rewriter, really, and I love it. I love the idea of going back and reworking a thing. Not overworking it, but going back and finding the layers that go down, the depth that you can get into a paragraph, which is coming now in the Maynard stuff. I have so much material that I can go back over what I wrote 6 months ago, and I can say, "Oh yes...." The telephone rang, and 2 hours had passed, and I had no idea what time it was. I thought it was half past two, and it was half past four.

LM: You've talked about having this special connection with the person you're writing about...can you talk about that any more--just how you get connected, what that experience is like, how you feel when it's occurring?

FH: At first I used to be frightened. I am not anymore. What I think I have is the ability to accept it. Sometimes I shut it off. I have a file there which I call "Dreams and Prophesies," which have to do with Maynard. They're amazing, absolutely amazing what's in there. They are a combination of dreams and this before-sleep thing. A light is the key to it. Eyes closed. Relaxed. And this light appears, very tiny light. White. Often at the beginning of it there are what I describe as light birds--flights of light birds--colored, which are red, blue, gold. They fly in and make patterns, kind of like putting down a curtain or raising a curtain, starting something--but always from left to right. Then I start focusing on the light. Sometimes I'll put my eyes way in back of my head, so far back that they hurt when I'm trying to follow the flight. And the light will change, expand. Sometimes it'll be like a square, like a television screen almost, and something will happen in that. It resembles a television screen in that it is...the background is basically gray, but a lively gray, not dull. And sometimes this light will climb up over what looks like mountains, and the mountains will kind of come in and surround. One night, this screen was this gray, lively gray, and in bright white light against it was the giant word--in a script lettering--"Yes." And the light birds come back again. And whatever is going to happen kind of in between their appearances. Sometimes my perspective is different. Sometimes I'm up high looking down into an arena-like place.

One time in the light there was the message, "People will come to you, write their name out of the window, off the water, seeing places I've been." What fascinated me about it was the word "write." What did it mean? Which meaning did the word have--write, right/correct, rite? People will come to you, write their name--but name is singular! I ran into a similar occurrence recently. Sunday morning I read the Bible, and in the Bible reading I came across this same thing where you have a plural subject...well, a plural pronoun really, and a singular object. It's in Revelations I:l3, I think. Like I said, I used to be frightened of this. They're not as active at this point as they were back earlier in the Maynard project. I think he must feel secure at this point.

LM: Do you believe it's this man's spirit that comes to talk with you?

FH: I don't know what it is. I interpret it as being some kind of connection with him, which I understand is not too unusual. I have a man whom I call my in-house economist because I don't know anything about money. I showed him part of the script, and he said, "Oh, you're doing the same thing that I do with two people." He said he had two people. He told me who they were--one was Balzac, and I don't remember the other one. That's the only other person I know who has this same relationship with whatever it is. But I don't understand it.

LM: There are two ways that I think of immediately to explain that, and I'm not saying that it couldn't be both at the same time, or it might be something else. It could be part of your own unconscious.

FH: Absolutely.

LM: Or it could be something of the spirit world. Or it could be both, or it could be neither.

FH: I agree totally. I am not claiming anything other than what happens. I don't understand it. And I don't know that I want to understand it. It might destroy it if I understood it.

LM: The artists always say that. In these interviews, the theorists and the scientists all talk about creativity, but the artists say, "Oh, no, I don't want to talk about it." It's interesting. Like it'll go away.

FH: Well, I think there is that element in it. I think you have to trust it. And trust as I learned from [my psychoanalyst] Max Geller, is a very special thing. It's not like love. I can love you, but you don't have to love me. Not so with trust. Trust must be a mutual, two-way thing because if I can't trust you, you can't trust me. That may be part of an unspoken agreement between the spirit or whatever power whether it be in your head or in space. Carson McCullers said it differently, and I've written a love song based on her saying, "All young things need privacy...." And they do!

Like a number of the respondents, Frank works on a number of projects simultaneously, and he becomes absorbed in his work. As was true for Paul, Patricia, and others, Frank cannot will creativity; however, he can facilitate the likelihood of its occurrence. In the past, Frank has experienced a surge of creative energy after the sexual release he has found at the baths.

Frank described some of the ways in which he facilitates his writing. Two of his morning activities are especially helpful. He reads the <u>New York Times</u>, and he writes a letter to his friend, Ethel Huffman. Both activities help him begin thinking in a verbal modality, and the letter writing provides him with a way to begin, to prepare for his work.

In the evenings, Frank always stops before he completes a particular task, so he will have an easy start and a prescribed direction in which to go the following day. He also relaxes for a few moments alone, and reflects on that day's work, and plans the next day's writing.

It is interesting that Frank and Tom, both creative writers, approach the activity differently. Tom's preparation for the next day's activities is less planned and more intuitive. Tom sits at his typewriter each day. Frank does not sit at his unless he knows the material he is going to write.

Absorption and revision are common themes and are also expressed by Frank. He described himself as a rewriter, saying he loves reworking his material. Like Rowena, Tom, and Norma, all artists, Frank fears that too close an examination of his creativity might diminish or destroy it. Spirituality, mysticism, and dreams, are paramount to Frank's creativity. He attributed many insights and ideas to his spiritual life.

Writer George Leonard has used brainstorming and other techniques to facilitate creativity. Playfulness in creativity is important to him. In the following quotation, George described the writing of a play. This writing became a production of sorts, with a silent audience playing a role.

> GL: I said to my friend, "Why don't you and I write a musical and write it on <u>The Emperor's New Clothes?</u>" It's a great story of all times, and I said, "Let's do it this way." We were both staying at the Hotel Elysee, where we always stayed when we went to New York. I said, "We're going to

allocate only 1 hour on two different occasions to do this. The first one hour we're going to brainstorm the theme for the musical. We are going to brainstorm the treatment. We're going to have an absolute limit of 1 hour; therefore we're going to go in this crazy overdrive: an altered state of consciousness. We're going to ask everybody who wants to watch a genius at work to come." So we told a lot of people to come watch us, and I said, "Bring champagne." Hedgepath had his guitar--he's just a madman.

So we had all these researchers and people from Look all hanging from the roof, and they watched us work. We were being crazy. So the way we brainstormed was by getting little slips of paper and just any idea that came up (you know how that works), we'd write it down. Anybody who said, "Wait a minute," or even looked funny got one warning. The second time he had to leave the room for 5 minutes. The third time he was banned forever from the brainstorming session. But we didn't want the other people to talk; it was just going to be the two of us. So we got a bunch of people. We sat around on the floor.

Within 1 hour we had worked up a basic idea for the music, and Hedgepath had come up with the wonderful idea that we were going to have this mythical king, kind of like Tolkien, and the kingdom was populated with different classes of people who were never allowed to touch each other. There were Ergs and Trolls and Garms and Nardleys. The Garms are the police force, and the Nardleys are the ministers, and the Ergs are the workers, and the Trolls are the fun people who don't like to wear clothes, but dance all day and night. So we thought that up, and so then we waited 1 day, and the next session was only going to last 1 hour. In that session we were going to write the title and the basic ideas for 20 songs. So we did that. Then I flew back out to the West Coast.

Hedgepath had a story, and he came to San Francisco. I said, "You're going to come to my house, and we're going to take 5 days, and in those 5 days we're going to write l0 songs." Sure, ok. So he flew out. Well, my ex-wife decided to go to Yosemite with the kids. I was in a state of euphoria. So he came out. I had a big old house at that time in the hills and he stayed in one wing of it....We took the songs, ideas, the 20 songs, and started writing. Basically he'd like me to write the music first. Sometimes he would write the words first. He wrote most of the words; I wrote some of the words. My wife and two kids were gone, and we had that whole huge house. People came by and watched us work every night. Mike Murphy came. He met his wife that night. They left together. Both came to watch us carry on and raise hell. So we wrote l0 songs in 5 days. That's another thing to do with creativity. First of all, to be silly, be willing to be a fool. That's one thing to learn--is to be a fool. Set yourself impossible schedules, break up the context of your normal life.

LM: Do you see your aikido as being creative?

GL: In aikido, you can see down to the heart and soul and the essence of creativity. Aikido is all creativity. Through aikido I learned everything you would want to know about creativity--the moves of aikido and the way that it's always done in response to an attack; therefore you can't plan ahead. You get the whole out of the essence of the creative act. Creativity is inevitable, and the only way we are not creative is when we somehow block it by beginning to listen to repetitive tapes in our culture. But if we are willing to get totally in the present moment, we will automatically and inevitably come in contact with truly novel material. Every human being is ultimately, everyone is born a creative human being. I would also just like to say that there is a hell of a lot more creativity going on than most people realize.

George thinks every human being is born creative. He stressed the need for fun in creativity, and he described his feeling during creative output as euphoric. During these times he obtains an altered state of consciousness. Several respondents, including Wendy, Patricia, and Frank reported that the altered states they achieve facilitate their creative processes. The brainstorming sessions seem to provide George with the kind of drama Tom enjoys, although the manner in which Tom and George achieve drama is significantly different. Both George and Arthur suggested changing the context of one's normal life in order to facilitate creativity.

Endings

Endings are a part of the creative process and are a part that trouble many people. Norma, Tom, Niels, Rowena, Paul, Frank, and Wendy responded in the following ways to the questions about ending. Norma ends a poem when she has a good last line.

LM: How do you know when a work is finished? When do you quit?

NS: I know that. That's so easy. You just know it. You've got a good last line. There are three things you've got to have in a poem, and it's just about the same in an article. You've got to have a good title, because without a good title no one will read it. You've got to have a good first line and a good last line. When you've got a good last line, that's the end of the poem or article.

Tom has a sense of a work being finished. While he is writing he feels good. In the past he has suffered extreme physical and psychological stress after he has completed a book, because he experiences all the tension he had not allowed to affect him while he was writing.

LM: Do you always have a sense of being finished, or do you ever just quit because you are sick of it?

TR: Oh no, I would never do that. In fact I feel pretty good. I am a little tired, but I feel ok until it is done, and then I go into postpartum psychosis. In the past, I have kind of fallen apart physically for a few weeks when they were done because of all the tension and stress I hadn't allowed to affect me, because I knew I had to go on. Then when it's done, it just all catches up with you at once. But I was aware of this...you hope you can learn a little bit from experience...and I was able pretty much to avoid it this time because I knew it could happen.

Niels stops work on a project when it is close to balance.

LM: How do you decide you are finished?

ND: When you're close enough to balance that it holds together.

Rowena stops when she thinks she has done the best she can do.

LM: How do you know when a work is finished? How do you know when to quit?

RR: When you have carried it as far as your knowledge and experience will take you. You feel it is the best you can do in that particular situation, that particular combination of relationships, that particular work you have carried as far as you can. You say, "All right, I don't feel like working on that anymore." At least I know when I have reached my limit. I can't do it any better at this time. Maybe I could do the same thing better 10 years from now, but if I have done the best I could, then it's time to stop.

Much like Rowena, Paul takes a work as far as he can and then stops.

LM: When you are writing, how do you know when you are finished?

PT: Well, sometimes you get to page 20. [Laughter]

LM: You know, you can rewrite and rewrite, but do you have a way to know when you are done?

PT: I always take it as far as I can.

Frank experiences what he called symptoms when he finishes. He equates it to the physical feeling of falling out of love.

LM: How do you know when you are finished? When do you quit working on a piece?

FH: Ethel Huffman's husband, Huck, once said to me, "It takes two people to do a painting. One to paint it, and one to tell him when to stop." It is very good if you have somebody to do that. But short of that, there's lot's of symptoms. It comes with a physical feeling. Kind of like falling out of love. The tension leaves your stomach. Your thighs ache. In the days before AIDS, it was a time for celebration--a trip to Everard's. You miss the feeling you've grown used to. It's so obvious, the feeling...there's no mistaking it. You kind of shake your head in disbelief. Lost. And wonder, "Is this me? Did I really do that?" You know instinctively when it's done. These things all take on their own life, regardless of what it is. They have their own life. What you do at this point is you release it and say, "You're free. Go!"

For Wendy, knowing when to stop is an art in itself. For her, it is an aesthetic experience.

LM: How do you know when something you are working on is finished?

WP: That's an interesting issue and one I don't have a clear answer for. Knowing when to stop is aesthetic. I think it is an art, an art in itself. Understanding beginnings is an art, and then endings. What does it mean to end?

Ending was reported to be an internal experience. It seemed to be difficult for the respondents to describe. Most of the respondents knew when to end in one of two ways. Some, like Paul and Rowena, stop when they have gone as far as they can. Others, like Tom, experience internal feelings that they recognize as accompanying the completion of a project. Frank has fulfilled his project when his imaginary characters cease to rear in his consciousness or when, metaphorically speaking, they become comfortable enough in their positions in his imagination to stop impinging on Frank's's consciousness to do something with them. This is his unique way of knowing that he has finished his project to its necessary conclusion.

Summary

He who binds to himself a joy,
Does the wing-ed life destroy,
He who kisses the joy as it flies
Lives in eternities sun-rise.

William Blake

It is vital that we remain aware of both components of the creative process. From one perspective, we see clearly that we can not force creativity; creativity must be allowed. Simultaneously, and from a different perspective, we know that we must manufacture creative products through the sweat of our brows. Here we have creativity's paradox, and here lives the metaphor of a well tended garden.

The garden, when properly attended, is fertile, damp, and free from the affects of pests and weeds. It is receptive, prepared. Work has been done. The stage is set. We must continue to toil so that when the creative impulse arrives we can take action, beginning the next step of hard work. Creativity is a gift that is present to us all. The scope of our vision, our willingness to receive the gift, and our dedication to the project transform seed into flower, even while knowing that the outcome does not fall entirely under our control. With creativity we can not cause; however, we can facilitate.

This chapter presents the responses to the questions about the coresearchers' experiences of the creative process. The act of immersion into their subject matter or project is not confined to set boundaries. Several of the coresearchers, including Tom Robbins, Frank Hogan, Paul Torrance, Norma McLain Stoop, Carl Rogers, and Niels Diffrient, said that their creative insights often come when they are engaged in daily routines, like shaving or walking. Ideas often arise around sleep, at times when the conscious mind or will is relieved of demands. Everyone described absorption in the project and focused awareness as essential elements in creative thinking.

All of the coresearchers have formalities which aid their work by giving it structure or form, facilitating it toward completion. Novelist Tom Robbins surrounds his writing with excitement and mystery, George Leonard with playfulness and a sense of fun. Compulsive respondents tend to formalize their complusions, thereby getting them out of the way, allowing the entry of creative action. Frank Hogan does his professional writing after writing letters and reading the newspaper. Industrial designer Niels Diffrient makes order in his studio before he begins work.

Unlike writers Tom Robbins, George Leonard, or Frank Hogan, psychologist Carl Rogers did not do a great deal to prepare himself, again demonstrating the individualized nature of the creative process. He noted that there were a number of things he did not do, such as meditate or reflect on his dreams. Frank often is inspired by his dreams. Carl was careful not to become too willful about creativity, whereas George uses techniques such as brainstorming in the presence of an audience to facilitate creativity. Both Tom and George are firm about including work and play in the creative process.

For industrial designers Rowena Reed and Niels Diffrient, creativity comes in intense spells. Niels stressed a relaxed bodily responsiveness during his creative process. He also thinks some of his best works are the result of accidental events. He has faith in these accidents, and he describes his life as a series of accidents. Educator Paul Torrance does not think creativity can be willed, but does think it can be facilitated. Aikido master Wendy Palmer allows the inspiration to flow through her. She, poet Norma McLain Stoop, writer George Leonard, and fellow designer Niels Diffrient described feeling the physical excitement of creativity. Norma's description of the sensations in her arms during creative excitement was similar to Wendy's remembrance of a description of Einstein's. Visionary Patricia Sun values the process of allowing new ways of perceiving. She finds her creativity follows a shift in consciousness. Philosopher Arthur Young stressed not letting information hinder creative thinking. At one point in the interview, he remarked about Sikorsky's helicopter having the bumblebee as its emblem, because aerodynamically, the bumblebee can not fly; however, the bumble bee thinks it can, and flies.

The following chapter presents the conclusions of this study. The research questions first introduced in Chapter 1 will be answered. Other general conclusions will be drawn, and recommendations for future research will be made.

CHAPTER 9

CONCLUSIONS AND RECOMMENDATIONS

Enter by the narrow gate; for the gate is wide, and the way is broad that leads to destruction, and many are those who enter it.

For the gate is small, and the way is narrow that leads to life, and few are those who find it.

Jesus, Matthew 7:13-14

The purpose of this volume was to gain understanding and information about the personalities and creative processes of people who exhibit exceptional creativity. Eleven respondents who were described by their peers as exhibiting excellence in their creative fields were selected to participate in this research. In addition to being outstanding in their fields, all 11 were poly-creative.

To represent the diversity of a spectrum of creative thinkers and to avoid the biases choosing people from only one area might have introduced, I chose respondents who worked in a variety of areas. The following is a list of the respondents and their primary professions: Tom Robbins, novelist; Paul Torrance, educational psychologist; Carl Rogers, counseling psychologist; Arthur Young, physicist and inventor; George Leonard, writer; Patricia Sun, visionary and psychotherapist; Wendy Palmer, aikido instructor; Niels Diffrient, industrial designer; Frank Hogan, playwright; Norma McLain Stoop, poet; and Rowena Reed, industrial designer.

The data were gathered in face-to-face interviews using a multiple case study format (Bogdan & Biklen, 1982). An open-ended interview guide gave minimal structure to the interviews. The interviews, totaling about 40 hours, were taped on an audio tape recorder and transcribed. The transcriptions and other personal communications with the respondents comprised the data, which were analyzed qualitatively, using inductive and deductive analysis (Glaser & Strauss, 1967). Approximately 1/10 of the interview transcriptions are included in this volume as direct quotations.

Research Questions

Results of the analysis have led to the formulation of preliminary answers to the original research questions. In this section I have stated each of the research questions and summarized what I found. When applicable, I have presented support for the findings of previous research.

1. What is the creative person's concept of creativity?

To answer this question, I asked the respondents for a personal definition of creativity. Physicist, inventor, writer, and philosopher Arthur Young's definition encompassed the ideas of a number of the respondents. He emphasized the two determining principles in creativity: the spark, and the development of the creative idea or insight. He compared these to the sperm and the egg in biological creativity. Arthur thinks the creative spark comes to the person from an outside source, such as the collective unconscious, and he believes hard work and faithfulness to the insight are required to develop the idea into a material reality. He thinks everyone is creating all of the time, and the difference between normal, unnoticed creativity and exceptional creativity is determined by the depth of the creator's personal vision.

Visionary, psychologist, and teacher Patricia Sun agreed with Arthur Young that creative people are more open to allowing insight to come through them than are less creative people. Both stressed the receptive function of the creative person. Both Arthur and Patricia contend that mistake making is a valuable activity in the creative process. For Patricia, creativity and the evolution of the species are closely related. She defined creativity as love and openness. Arthur defined it as self-discovery.

Arthur Young defined the unconscious as the universe in potential. He thinks the unconscious consists of those things we have not yet incorporated into our consciousness. He defines the unconscious, the superconscious, and the universe as basically the same thing, and he thinks it is the source of all creativity. Two necessary skills for the creative person are the ability to discriminate useful from useless imagery and the ability to extrapolate meaning from vague or confusing messages.

Arthur used the metaphor of a well-tended garden to illustrate his belief that although we cannot make ourselves creative, we can make ourselves more open to creativity, thereby enhancing the likeliness of its occurring. He thinks that giving oneself permission to know the answer opens the door to creativity. Patricia, like all of the respondents, maintained the idea that creativity combines insight and hard work.

Novelist and artist Tom Robbins thinks that creative people tend to be creative in more than one area. He described two types of genius. One type is obsessive, and the other is expansive. He described the working styles of Suteini and Picasso, both painters, as exemplary of his idea.

Educational psychologist, creativity expert, and teacher Paul Torrance thinks that intelligence should be redefined to encompass creative thinking. For Paul, creativity requires going beyond the norm, the rational, and the logical. In order to facilitate creative thinking in adults, Paul, like Arthur, supports question asking, the freedom to make mistakes, and follow-through.

Writer, editor, humanistic psychologist, and aikido instructor George Leonard, like Patricia Sun, spoke of the naive quality of creative individuals. George stressed creative energy and the importance of not defining anything as a mistake. He thinks the Americans are more creative than the Soviets because we are more willing to live in ambiguity, which is essential to the creative process. Premature closure limits the possibilities and inhibits creative thinking. George also said that the ability to stay in the moment is an essential element of the creative personality.

For poet, editor, and photographer Norma McLain Stoop, discipline is the key to creativity. She believes that once people learn self-discipline, they have the ability to be creative. Like other respondents, Norma emphasized the importance of accepting mistakes, and she acknowledged that her unconscious plays a role in her creativity.

Aikido instructor and teacher Wendy Palmer described the unconscious as untapped creativity. Wendy, George, and Arthur talked about how we receive unconscious information, and the need to focus our awareness to make use of this information. George, like Wendy, views the body as our most direct venue to the unconscious. Industrial designer, writer, and teacher Niels Diffrient experiences a freedom in his movement when he is in the creative flow.

Playwright and biographer Frank Hogan stressed courage, willingness, and determination as essential to bringing an idea into realization. Frank defined creativity as revolution. Frank believes he receives guidance from a spiritual level. He thinks the difference between the more and less creative person is that the more creative person is willing to accept guidance and act on it. Like Arthur Young, Frank emphasized the two elements of creativity, the insight and the action. Also like Arthur, he experiences creative insights as originating outside himself.

The responses of all the coresearchers, with the exception of psychologist, theorist, writer, and teacher Carl Rogers, support the psychoanalytic view that the unconscious plays a critical part in the creative process (Arieti, 1976; Barron, 1968; Freud, 1901, 1908, 1910, 1924, 1947; Jung, 1959). Unlike Arthur, George, Wendy, Patricia, Paul, and Frank, Carl did not do anything to tap his unconscious. He thought more in terms of his nonconscious mind. He said that for creativity to have occurred, there must be a product, and that product must be novel and carry the unique stamp of the creator.

Focused attention was continually presented by the coresearchers as a vital ingredient in creativity. Wendy Palmer named focused attention as the most important element in the creative process. Patricia Sun thinks that if we expect creativity, it will be more likely to occur. George, Arthur, Wendy, and Patricia stressed mistake making as a critical element in creative thinking. Patricia agrees with Frank Hogan that courage and determination are necessary attributes for the creative person. Wendy believes anything is possible. She thinks if we can learn to relax fully, we can open ourselves to intrinsic self-organizing properties and enjoy maximal creativity.

Throughout the interviews self-discipline and follow-through were described as essential to creative thinking. Openness to mistakes and unusual perceptions, courage, and flexibility were described by respondents as

381

necessary ingredients in creativity. Willingness, determination, and incentive were listed as key to the occurrence of creativity. An ability to be free of others' expectations, an ability to create one's own reality, and a trust in one's body were discussed. Several respondents feel that expecting creativity will facilitate it. Everyone agreed that work is an essential ingredient in creativity. Everyone except Carl Rogers thinks their unconscious plays a vital role in their creative process.

2. What personality characteristics enable creative people to persist with their creative endeavors?

I assumed that particular personality characteristics enable creative people to persist in pursuit of excellence. Some of these are personal, applying to only one or two respondents, and others are more general. A general characteristic that applied to all the respondents is endurance. Endurance is the quality that has been most instrumental in Niels Diffrient's continued creativity. Examples of more personal characteristics are Niels's abilities to philosophize, generalize, and use reason and knowledge both visually and verbally.

Tom Robbins has found that he needs to protect himself from other people to remain creative and fresh, because success has brought with it an influx of people who either want to use him or hurt him. He described himself as "a very private person." His need to protect himself has made him more reclusive. Tom described himself as a Hermes type, because he dislikes groups and never wants to be just a member of a team. He does not think of himself as particularly egotistical and has been concerned that his lack of ego might interfere with his success as a writer. He thinks his Hermes personality may be facilitative to his enduring creativity.

Rowena Reed, much like Tom, avoids excessive introspection because she thinks it could interfere with her creative process. The traits she thinks empower her creativity are her thoroughness and liking to get to the bottom of things. Rowena said she would have been bored had she not spent her life actualizing her potential.

Paul Torrance is persistent. He described himself as devoted to his work, which for him is recreation. Paul has dedicated his life to actualizing a vision.

Norma McLain Stoop thinks her self-discipline and her willingness, indeed, her desire, to make choices are the personality characteristics that enable her to persist with her creative endeavors. Both Norma and Carl Rogers stressed discipline. He thought his persistence and determination enabled him to succeed. Much like Tom, two qualities to which Carl attributed his success were that he was a loner and did not take himself too seriously. All of the coresearchers displayed a sense of humor.

Rowena Reed, Tom Robbins, and Arthur Young did not want to become overly introspective about their creative process. Arthur described himself as inquiring into the nature of existence. Arthur and Patricia Sun see themselves as curious. Patricia listed her outstanding qualities as curiosity, kindness, and courage. Patricia described herself as able to be thoughtful and determined when the task at hand is worthy of her effort. She reported that others often describe her as strong, thoughtful, and determined. Patricia named genuineness as the quality that led to her success.

George Leonard sees his playful nature and his creativity as essential aspects of his character. He is disciplined and hard working. He also thinks he may be a little arrogant, and that arrogance may facilitate his continued creativity.

George's arrogance and Tom's Hermes attributes are similar. It appears that some aloofness helps them maintain their creative output.

Another motivation for continued creative output is the desire for recognition and the desire to be viewed by others as special or unique. Norma McLain Stoop and Frank Hogan, both writers, expressed a strong desire for recognition and uniqueness. Tom Robbins, also a writer, expressed a desire to be appreciated for his uniqueness. Tom wants his work to be recognized, but does not desire personal fame.

Rebelliousness may be a personality factor conducive to creativity. Wendy Palmer described herself as highly antiauthoritarian. Patricia Sun and Tom Robbins use existing rules as long as they work and invent new ones when they do not. Niels Diffrient experiences no use for authority and, much like Tom, described it as a senseless, uncreative force.

The knowledge each participant has that death is inevitable may be a contributing factor in enduring creativity. Paul Torrance thinks we may want to leave something behind to provide a type of immortality. Frank Hogan, like Paul, is glad a major university is collecting his works. Tom thinks people are creative to prove they exist, because through creative work we leave behind some of our identity and uniqueness.

The respondents expressed various levels of individualism, ranging from a statement of individuality to overt rebelliousness. Independence and the ability for divergent thinking are attributes possessed by the respondents. Courage is another important personality characteristic demonstrated by the members of this group. Each respondent is hard working and determined.

Adjectives like persistence and endurance were mentioned again and again in these interviews. In response to the question about his most outstanding quality, Paul, for example, replied, "...just being able to hang in there." Carl described himself as focused and disciplined with a whim of steel, and Niels named endurance as his most outstanding quality. Many of the coresearchers, for example Paul, Carl, and Patricia, demonstrate persistence in their creative output because they want to effect social change. Each is dedicated to a vision, although they may be dedicated to varying visions.

My data support previous findings naming drive, resourcefulness, and dedication (Taylor,1964) as motivational to creativity. The characteristics perseverance, imagination, knowledge, and self-confidence (Rossman, 1931) and sincerity and a need for solitude (Hirst, 1931) were characteristics of many of the respondents in this research. Of the characteristics listed by Torrance (1962), energeticness, persistence, altruism, assertiveness, versatility, an attraction to the mysterious, unconventionality, independence, oddities of habit, sensitivity, and an ability to accept the making of mistakes were present. I also found support for the theory that creative males are more feminine and creative females more masculine than their less creative peers (Jung, 1928; MacKinnon, 1975; Taylor, 1964; Torrance, 1962), because many of the male respondents had feminine interests and many of the female respondents had male interests.

As was suggested by Guilford (1950), most of the respondents demonstrated a sensitivity to problems. This research generated support for the hypothesis that creative people are receptive to creative ideas, have the propensity to immerse themselves in their subject matter, have detached devotion, see the right questions, and use errors (Henle, 1962). Many of the respondents were found to have greater personal scope, to be independent in their judgments, to be more self-assertive, to be more observant, to see things both similarly to others and differently from others, to be independent thinkers who are motivated by their talents and values and are able to hold various ideas at once. They also were found to be able to live more complexly in what they view as a more complex universe, to possess enough ego-strength to regress and return to normalcy, and they are creative as a function of freedom (Barron, 1963).

In a study of originality (MacKinnon, 1975), original people were found to be more serious, organized, rational, civilized, reliable, quiet, and responsible; whereas unoriginal people were found to be more emotional, restless, stubborn, and defensive. This study shows that creative people demonstrate the characteristics found by MacKinnon as descriptive of original people. Also supported by this study are the findings of Schimek (1954) that creative people are verbally fluent, curious, self-disciplined, and self-reliant and they have rich inner lives, and a willingness to admit fears and unconventional taste; they are autonomous and value intellectual independence. Supported are Gough's (1975) discoveries that original people demonstrate intellectual competence, inquiringness as a habit of mind, cognitive flexibility, esthetic sensitivity, and a sense of destiny. The data gathered in this dissertatioin also support Getzels and Jackson's (1962) hypothesis that creative people are problem finders.

This research has led me to conclude that creative people work because of an internal drive to do so. They are committed to their work and responsible to the public. Their primary motivation for continuing to work is the sense of fulfillment they receive as a result of expressing themselves through the work. A theme common through all the interviews is one expressed by Norma: that by not fragmenting herself she is more likely to be successful.

3. In what ways have creative people been influenced by relationships?

Relationships with other people affect all our lives. Relationships are named by psychotherapists as the life area more people wish to examine in a therapeutic environment than any other, which indicates the powerful force they possess.

When beginning this research, I assumed that relationships with others have some effect on creativity. My interest was to discover what that effect might be. As has been the case throughout this research, patterns in the effects of relationships on creative individuals are paradoxical. One pattern running strongly throughout the interviews is a pattern of individuality. It appears that the more creative people are, the more individualistic they are. The respondents perceived of themselves as having a variety of relationships and experiences, and they have attached different meanings to them. Some common perceptions of relationships also exist.

One life stage in which relationships are especially salient is childhood. For that reason all the participants were asked to describe their childhoods. A number of the respondents described themselves as shy children. Most of them spent a good deal of their childhoods alone.

Paul Torrance lived on an isolated farm and spent little time with any children other than his sister. Wendy Palmer had one girlfriend with whom she rode horseback, but she described herself as mostly being alone and in her own world. Carl Rogers had a strong sense of being different from other children, and he socialized primarily within his own family. He portrayed his childhood life as an inner life and himself as shy. Frank Hogan also felt different from other children, depicted himself as shy, and did not have friends or participate in games. Patricia Sun remembers being quite different from other children. She described her childhood as sinister.

Industrial designer and educator Rowena Reed, on the other hand, had a number of friends and belonged to clubs and organizations. Although Tom Robbins described himself as shy and never enjoyed groups of people, he spent a good deal of time with friends. Rowena Reed, George Leonard, and Arthur Young described their childhoods as happy and did not see themselves as unusual in their social relationships.

A type of childhood relationship that might affect creative development is the relationship between a child and a parent. I was struck that Rowena Reed and Niels Diffrient, both industrial designers, received a similar, subtle reinforcement for their creative endeavors. Both Niels and Rowena's parents liked the things they made.

Paul Torrance reported being frustrated because he, as a boy, was expected to learn from his father. He described his father as a poor teacher, and for that reason Paul constantly had to discover and invent ways to achieve a task. Although an adversity, he may have developed superior problem-solving skills as a result.

Wendy Palmer had a highly unusual relationship with her mother, and she credits this relationship as a principal cause of her creativity. Her mother suffered with multiple sclerosis. Wendy never saw her mother walk, and from the time Wendy was 12, her mother could not speak. As was true for Paul, what seemed at the time to be great hardship was a gift, because she developed her sensitivity and creativity to communicate with her mother.

Being separate and different was a goal of Carl Rogers's mother for her family. Carl thought he was strongly affected by her separatist ideology. Both he and Rowena told me they were well cared for by their parents although their parents were not demonstratively affectionate. Carl said his parents showed him and his siblings much attention by reading to them and taking them on trips.

All 11 respondents experienced psychologically distant relationships with their parents. This distance sometimes existed in a warm supportive environment and sometimes in a difficult one. This distance may have fostered independence, followed by creative thinking. In addition to this distance, all 11 respondents reported experiencing their childhoods as unusual. It may be that the experience of feeling unusual was actually an experience of individuality, and someone with a more objective viewpoint would have considered them less unusual than they considered themselves. I have spoken with other people who recalled feeling unusual or different as children. These respondents share that experience. In addition to feeling as if they were unusual children and experiencing psychological distance from their parents, all the respondents remembered their childhoods as unusual. Some respondents reported extremely happy childhoods; others reported difficult or painful ones.

With the exceptions of Niels Diffrient and Arthur Young, the respondents perceived of themselves as experiencing some adversity during childhood. With the possible exception of Patricia Sun, none of the respondents were abused or neglected as children. I expect most children experience adversity of some sort, and the crucial factor might be how these children coped.

Frank Hogan, Paul Torrance, and Norma McLain Stoop reported that they suffered an extended illness in childhood, and the illness promoted their creativity. Norma said her parents brought her books to read during that year, and that the memory of those books continues to be instrumental to her creativity. They volunteered that information when describing their childhoods. I did not ask them if they had been sick as children. Tom Robbins, Carl Rogers, Wendy Palmer, Norma McLain Stoop, Rowena Reed, George Leonard, and Arthur Young reported some childhood experience as inspirational or creatively facilitative.

Frank Hogan remembers his parents fighting with each other. Several of his accounts lead me to the conclusion that as a child he believed that his parents cared more for his brother Bill than they did for him. This perception caused Frank to strive to be different than Bill, and I think it was partly responsible for his drive to be creative and successful. Although he did not define his childhood as unhappy, the childhood he described to me was far from peaceful.

Unlike Frank, both Tom Robbins and George Leonard described happy childhoods. Tom described both his parents as creative and said his mother treated him with love and reverence. George's family supported his endeavors and were lenient. I think it is interesting that both George and Tom approach creativity with a sense of joy and playfulness. The light-heartedness of their creativity may be a result of the support they received from their parents as children.

Like Rowena's, George's, and Tom's, Arthur Young's childhood was happy. He recalled one instance when his father intentionally tried to facilitate his creativity and initiative. His father forbade him to have a ham radio in hopes that he would acquire one as an act of independence. This occurrence may be why Arthur believes that supporting creativity is not necessarily a good way to encourage its development.

Much like Frank, Norma defined her childhood as happy, but described it as difficult. Her parents demanded she be "the best" and expected her to perform for their guests. She had a competitive relationship with her mother. Her parents were wealthy, and Norma had governesses who introduced her to ideas and activities that facilitated her creativity. She thinks her parents' demands are the reason she is creative and successful. She said that as a child she was like her parents' "little performing dog."

Patricia Sun's parents were quite young when she was born. She described her childhood as painful. She did, however, believe her parents loved her. Several times during the interview Patricia quoted her mother, saying that what her mother had told her had in some way been helpful or true. The following is a quote about her parents from her interview.

> I asked why I had been treated so badly? Why were people crazy? Why did they harm me? Why did they go unconscious? Why did they lie? Why did they go blank? Why did they project on one another? ... I didn't understand that, and I did feel very sad as to why that was happening to me. But also a part of the answer I got was so that I would be smart, so that I would be wise and figure it out. It's been priceless for me, because I don't think there is any other way. If I had had an easier childhood, a happier one, a less uncomfortable one, I think it's very possible I would have just gotten into the world on a normal level....

As is demonstrated by the preceding descriptions, creative people experience a variety of childhood environments and relationships. Certain commonalities in the data lead me to conclude that childhood relationships influence developing creativity. One such commonality occurred in the childhood experiences of Rowena and Niels. Both received subtle reinforcement for their artistic endeavors, and both became highly successful industrial designers. Another striking resemblance exists between the love and support Tom and George received and the joyful, playful approach they take to creative production. I also was struck by the hardships faced by Wendy and Patricia and by how they have grown to view adversity as opportunity.

The data support the theory that creative people often experience bashfulness and a need for solitude (Hirst, 1931). The interviews with Rowena, Niels, George, Tom, Arthur, Carl, and Norma suggest that in childhood creative people often enjoy some special skill and are rewarded for possessing it, and several interviews indicate that creative people often experience distance in their relationships with their parents (MacKinnon, 1975). Barron's (1975) discovery that writers' childhoods are reported as unhappy, that they felt isolated and were extremely sensitive, was supported by Frank's interview, but not by Tom's, Arthur's, Carl's, or George's. Helson's (1965) similar findings about creative women were also supported by some interviews, but not by others.

These discrepancies can be interpreted as a need for further research, or, as I think is the case, as support for my hypothesis that creative people, as a group, display too much variety and richness of experience to draw many all-encompassing conclusions. Although creativity can be addressed as a process, creators must be understood as members of a group and as individuals.

The data gathered for this research point to two conclusions about childhood relationships and creativity. One is that the nature and quality of childrens' relationships with others helps shape their creative development. Another conclusion is that no specific type of childhood relationship is a requirement for the development of exceptional creativity.

In addition to childhood relationships, I asked about another type of relationship, that of a mentor, because it has been found that having a mentor does enhance creativity (Torrance, 1984). Aikido instructor Wendy Palmer, psychologist Carl Rogers, educational psychologist Paul Torrance, mystic Patricia Sun, novelist Tom Robbins, playwright Frank Hogan, and industrial designer Niels Diffrient did not have mentors. Poet Norma McLain Stoop did have a mentor, but in singing, a career she did not pursue. Industrial designer Rowena Reed and writer George Leonard had mentors. Inventor Arthur Young experienced several mentor-like relationships. Several people who did not have mentors, like Niels, Carl, and Paul, did have relationships with people they considered teachers. My findings do not support Torrance's.

I was surprised by how few of the respondents reported relationships that were currently helpful to them as creative individuals. I expected each of the respondents to have special relationships with people who inspire, challenge, and in other ways facilitate their creativity. Frank reported having a sexual relationship as a young man that was supportive of his creativity. The closest response to my expectation for current relationships was Niels's statement that his wife, because she is a successful working artist, understands his moods and needs and does not interfere with his work. Wendy and George were also notable exceptions, although not in the way I expected. Both reported learning from others, especially in aikido. To facilitate his creative thinking process, George sometimes employs brainstorming techniques and works in the presence of an audience.

More often the respondents described solitude as helpful and relationships as detrimental to their creativity. Norma did not work for 32 years because her husband did not want her to. When I asked Tom what had hampered his creative work, he responded that people had.

> I was hampered by just about everybody. By teachers, by most of the women I've been involved with. Not deliberately, but by making demands you just can't make on a creative person and expect them to be creative. They can't turn you into Ozzie Nelson and still expect you to be Henry Miller.

Perhaps the lack of adult relationships supporting creativity is an American phenomenon. Americans as a group value independence, autonomy, and individuality. I expected the respondents to have special relationships that provided them with an opportunity to grow in their creativity, perhaps

393

because of my awareness of such relationships. The relationships of Henry Miller and Anais Nin, Simone de Beauvoir and Jean-Paul Sartre, and the relationships of groups of artists and of writers who lived and worked in close proximity in Paris throughout modern history lend support to the concept that interaction with other creative people enhances creative output.

Another explanation is that creative people tend to require the stimulation and support of groups early in their professional development and then later, after they formalize their individual styles and ideas, seek solitude. Often important artists in new schools of thought begin working and living in an artist's colony and, as they grow in their art, leave, and work on their own. Two examples of such colonies in this country were the artists surrounding Buckminster Fuller and Joseph Alber in Black Mountain, North Carolina in the mid-1940s and those surrounding Jackson Pollack in Greenwich Village in the 1950s. Several of the 11 individuals I interviewed followed this pattern. Wendy Palmer's interaction with a group of friends who all were studying aikido when she first began attending classes, Niels Different's and Rowena Reed's attending art school and working for large design firms before working on their own, and Carl Rogers's and Paul Torrance's graduate school careers might be examples of support for this hypothesis.

4. What do creative people report as aids and obstacles to their creative endeavors?

Creative people experience different occurrences as helpful and hurtful to their creative expression. Throughout these interviews I found myself continually surprised by the respondents' descriptions of those things they judged as aids or obstacles to their creative endeavors. Several coresearchers reported that childhood experiences, including hardships, adversity, and support had been facilitative or stifling to their creative development.

Designer Niels Diffrient's exceptionality was noticed early in his life; however, he reported his perception that little was done to encourage its development. His father did provide him with materials with which to work, and his artistic pursuits were not discouraged. His father providing these materials, combined with his parents' showing his construction and drawings to neighbors, may have provided him with subtle reinforcement to continue his experimentation and growth. Niels described himself as equally good artistically and mechanically. His talent and self-understanding have probably contributed to his success.

Both Niels and Paul grew up on farms in the South and demonstrated creativity at an early age. Neither perceived of themselves as receiving any special guidance because of this attribute. Niels and Paul, like all of the respondents, began creative output early in their lives. Both men received an education because they did not follow in their families' paths for them. Niels, to his father's dismay at the time, did not use the trade school scholarship offered him by the Ford Motor Company. Paul, because of his learning disability, could not farm.

While growing up Paul faced the hardships of being poor and isolated, and lacking the ability to succeed as a farmer. He, like Norma and Frank, suffered a long illness as a child. He views some of these hardships as aids and others as obstacles to his developing creativity. As a child, Paul's learning disability segregated him. He thinks it may have aided his creativity because it made him comfortable being a minority of one. Paul said that "to be creative, there are times you have to be a minority of one. ...If it is too uncomfortable, you're not going to do it. I have attained enough comfort to take that kind of risk."

Psychologist Carl Rogers's creativity may have been aided by his upbringing. He remembers being shown care and attention by his parents. They read to him and took him on frequent trips. Carl may have internalized one of his mother's family prayers, "Come out ye from among them and be ye separate."

Aikido instructor Wendy Palmer also faced hardship as a child. She attributes her creativity partly to this early hardship. Wendy was the younger of two sisters; however, she accepted the role of caretaker of a terminally ill parent. She expressed the belief that she developed her creativity in response to her relationship with her ill mother.

As was true for Carl and Paul, designer Rowena Reed's family cared for her, but were not demonstratively affectionate. Although she did not want a traditional education, her father insisted she attend college before going to art school. She thinks both her college and art school educations facilitated her creativity. As was true for Niels, Rowena received subtle reinforcement from her parents. Rowena described both her parents as creative, especially her father, and thinks she may have inherited some of his drive.

Two aspects of playwright Frank Hogan's early life seemed to have influenced his development: his Catholic upbringing and his subsequent rebellion to it, and his powerful sibling rivalry with his older brother Bill. Frank's belief that his parents cared more for his brother Bill than they did for him and his desire for recognition by his family motivated him to be successful and creative. His homosexuality was a strong influence in adolescence and on into adulthood. Frank thinks good sex directly facilitates creativity. As a young man he found a great deal of support for his creativity in a sexual relationship. One reason recognition is important to Frank is that it was not in his family's plan for him. Frank described his mother as creative. Frank's greatest adversity was, in his opinion, not having a mentor. Frank, Carl, and Tom were reared in restrictive religious environments. All three rebelled against it.

Writer Tom Robbins's family was Southern Baptist. Tom began writing as a child. He described both of his parents as somewhat creative. He thinks that much of his childhood fostered his creativity. Speaking of his childhood creativity he said, "My parents certainly encouraged it. They gave me a lot of support both financially and emotionally. My mother wanted me to be a writer." Tom has found relationships to be obstacles to his creativity, as is discussed in the section of this chapter that addresses the effect of relationships on creativity. Carl and Tom both reported that being a loner aids creativity. Tom thinks his most outstanding quality, and one he began developing in childhood, is his imagination and that it is paramount to his creativity.

Inventor Arthur Young grew up in an affluent, creative environment. His father was an artist. Several respondents, like Tom, named parental support as facilitative of creativity. Arthur disagreed. When he was a boy his father opposed his having a ham radio in hopes that he would have one as an act of independence. He did, and Arthur thinks that resistance is an aid to creativity. Later in life Arthur once again transformed adversity into opportunity. When he was building his helicopter, he found working with management extremely stressful. To cope, he began meditating and practicing yoga. The results of these practices were the greatest breakthroughs into higher levels of creativity he had ever experienced.

Writer George Leonard's childhood was extremely happy. He was a success in a creative field at the age of 17, conducting Atlanta's second largest swing band. His family supported his endeavors and were lenient. George sees playfulness as the greatest gift he received from his family. George's cousin was his mentor, and he found having a mentor at an early age an aid to his creativity. He believes his childhood fostered his high level of creativity.

For visionary Patricia Sun, God has always been the recognized source of creativity. She had a difficult childhood, and she believes its being so was necessary to her creative development. Patricia believes our society hampers natural psychic abilities, which, if more fully operational, would enhance creativity. Both Patricia and Tom said authoritarianism suppresses creativity. School suppressed her creativity, and like Paul, George, and Frank, Patricia thinks our educational systems prevent children from developing their natural creativity. She thinks that with changes schools could foster children's creative abilities.

Paul, Frank, and poet Norma McLain Stoop suffered long illnesses in childhood. Norma attributes expanded creativity to the time she spent infirmed. Her childhood was spent in an affluent and demanding environment. Her parents demanded she be "the best." Norma thinks this requirement for high standards is the foremost reason for her creativity. Like George, she was educated in a nontraditional manner, and like George she thinks a nontraditional education aids the development of creativity. Norma thinks opposition is necessary for people to gain clarity about which things are important to them. As an adult, she enjoys a challenge.

Throughout his life Carl Rogers met adversity and won. He thought that some types of adversity can aid creative thinking. The following quote is an example he gave of a time he turned an adversity into an aid to his creativity. "For example, I went through a really horrible period with a patient, and I realized after that [time] and after some therapy, that my doing therapy was much improved, my creativity was much enhanced. Even though at the time...I was going through a lot of hell."

Another aid to creativity is the creative production of others. Most of the respondents see art as helpful to creativity because it adds beauty, harmony, and spice to life; however, art was not reported to be as critical an aid to creativity as I had expected. Patricia thinks art can aid creativity in that it can be functional as well as beautiful, stimulating people to think and feel, and that art can tap the unconscious for both the artist and the viewer. Most of the coresearchers reported enjoying art, but they did not use art to facilitate their creativity to a significant degree.

Several respondents reported self-care as aiding their creativity. Such care was sometimes described as feeding, exercising, grooming, reading, or meditating. Another interesting observation is that most of the respondents commented about some way in which they receive input. Norma goes to movie screenings and the ballet. Frank reads the New York Times and watches the MacNeil-Lehrer report. Tom socializes with his volleyball team, attends movies, listens to radio shows, and reads. Stimulation and input is important enough to these people for them to provide for it in their daily routines.

Another theme expressed by several respondents, especially Patricia, Wendy, and Arthur, is that adversity can be used as opportunity. Norma and Arthur think opposition can act as an aid for creativity. Rowena thinks her work has been hampered by her good disposition and conventional ways. She thinks nice behavior can be an obstacle to creativity. It is important to remain aware that the adversity that aids creativity is natural, not imposed adversity.

I wondered if money would be perceived by creative people as an aid or obstacle to creativity. Only Norma said her work is greatly affected by money, because she said she always writes for a market. Tom works harder when he is being paid well. He prefers to work under less pressure. He writes best when he surrounds the act with secrecy and drama. George views himself as lazy, and with the exception of two books, he usually writes when he has need of money. Niels finds money to be an aid to his creativity because it gives him freedom from the restrictions of working for other people.

I also wondered if creative people find criticism helpful or harmful to their creative output. Frank said criticism affects him personally but not professionally. Tom referred to critics as a school of piranha. Over the years Wendy has grown accustomed to criticism, and it affects her less and less. Paul's feelings differ depending on the amount and quality of information about his work his critics have. Occasionally he will change his point of view and go beyond where he otherwise would have; however, he usually experiences it as an obstacle to creativity. Both Tom and Frank find criticism hurtful. The other respondents were not greatly affected by criticism. It was rare for anyone to find criticism helpful. The impression the respondents gave is that feedback does not affect their work. Only Paul reported that criticism can be helpful to his creativity, and for him it is a rare occurrence. Occasionally, positive criticism was experienced as entertaining or uplifting. Negative criticism may, as it does with Frank, motivate people to remain true to themselves, and in that way may aid creativity.

Most creative people recognize the need to allow ideas to incubate. As is true for Tom, Carl found his ideas came at periods of time when he was not working. He said that when attending a conference, going to the bathroom was often the most productive thing he did.

Although disagreement exists among the respondents about the obstacles to creativity, this research supports the theory that obstacles do exist. Most of the respondents think authority inhibits creativity. Criticism was generally viewed as harmful. The demands of other people and restrictive educational practices also were described as suppressive to creative thinking.

Because of the individuality of the respondents, there is variety and disagreement about what occurrences act as aids to creativity. The findings of this book lend support to the theory that certain circumstances are generally facilitative to the development of creative thinking. Subtle parental encouragement, reinforcement, and support in a somewhat psychologically distant environment aids in a child's developing creativity. Education, especially nontraditional education, including exposure to the world through experiences such as travel, encourage creativity. If children face and overcome hardships such as a long illness, the illness of a parent, a learning disability, a powerful sibling rivalry, or a restrictive religious environment, creativity may be enhanced. Another possible reinforcing agent for creativity is a role model. For adults, time alone, self-care, input, a desire for recognition, and a combination of support and opposition aid in creative endeavors.

5. <u>How do these people experience the onset of the creative moment? Through an act of will? Through external stimulation? Through spontaneous impulse? How do they describe the creative moment? How do they report the experience of their creativity?</u>

This question addresses the creative process. I was interested in how creative people describe the experience of creativity. I wanted to learn about their subjective encounters with the creative process.

For the majority of the respondents, insight was a significant component of the creative process. Many of the coresearchers, including Paul Torrance, Tom Robbins, Carl Rogers, Wendy Palmer, Patricia Sun, Frank Hogan, and Niels Diffrient reported insights coming during other activities, when their consciousness was directed elsewhere, such as shaving or walking, and particularly at times when their conscious minds or wills were at rest, such as just before, just after, or during sleep.

Although inspiration was reported to be a vital element in the creative process, most of the respondents emphasized the work and deemphasized the inspiration. Because he is a professional, Tom Robbins does what is necessary to generate his own inspiration. Spontaneity is paradoxical in his work, because he cannot make himself spontaneous, yet he can create a framework through which spontaneity often occurs. Paul Torrance thinks inspired work is superior to uninspired work, and he finds that when he is working with inspiration his work progresses more rapidly. Wendy Palmer allows insight to flow through her and described the experience as an excited bodily feeling. Norma McLain Stoop expressed feeling excitement in her body when she writes. When she is very excited, she feels goose bumps, like electricity, running down her arms.

As a whole, the respondents reported experiencing serendipity and synchronicity as a part of their creative processes. Several respondents stressed encouraging synchronicity, and most emphasized the value of focusing awareness on it for the purpose of enhancing creative thinking. Paul Torrance thinks serendipity is important to creativity and people need to learn to recognize and use it when it occurs.

Patricia Sun values the process of allowing new ways of perceiving. She finds creativity follows a shift from the norm in consciousness or perception. She said she cannot will creativity; however, there are certain things she can do to facilitate its occurrence. She said the most important thing she does is care deeply. When she cares, she experiences an internal letting go that allows her intuitive mind to function more fully.

Arthur Young practices moving beyond linear thinking for the purpose of encouraging synchronicity. He insisted on the need to listen to the inner voice. One way in which he moves beyond linear thinking is by making decisions by flipping a coin. He stressed the importance of not letting information become more important than the flow of creativity. When considered within the currently popular theory of brain hemisphere functions, the descriptions of these exceptional respondents leads me to conclude that they are capable of a more integrated brain function, meaning that they coordinate their right and left brain hemispheres. Practices like meditation and decision making by coin flipping probably facilitate movement from a primarily linear mode of thinking to a combination of linear and spatial thinking.

For Arthur, building the Bell helicopter was not as difficult as learning to work within the corporate structure. He discovered that to build the helicopter, he had to learn how to cope with the organization and persuade people with seniority to learn something new. For him, coping with the organization was an ordeal. It was during this time that he began practicing yoga to deal with the stress. The yoga led him to Zen philosophy and ESP, which, in turn, led him to his greatest creative experiences.

Tom's response to my question, "Can you decide to do something creative and go do it?" exemplifies most of the respondents' ideas about their ability to will creativity.

> Oh yeah, I do that constantly. But I cannot decide that today I'm going to do first-rate work. Or better work than I did yesterday. I don't have a whole lot of control over that. I just sit there and work hard and do my best and sometimes it's better than others.

Tom described the creative moment as a happy moment that sometimes is filled with elation and joy. His reply to my question about how he brings on creativity is more personal.

> In my case, never letting myself know too far ahead what I'm going to do. Always keeping an

element of surprise there....When I begin a book, I haven't the slightest idea how it's going to end or even where it's going to be in the middle....Creative writing is like taking a shower in a motel. You have to fiddle with the faucets a lot to get just the right temperature and flow of water, and you're there luxuriating in it, and it's feeling really good, and everything is perfect; then somebody flushes the toilet in the next unit, and the whole thing is thrown off.

Although Tom sometimes conceptualizes a work complete, like Carl Rogers, he usually begins and works toward completion. Carl reported that he did not do much to prepare for writing. He was cautious about becoming too willful when beginning a new project and said he was more successful with projects that developed obliquely. He described the creative moment as an easy flow accompanied by a feeling of excitement.

Paul Torrance said that when the creative moment occurs, the work seems to put itself together. He sees the difficulty in willing creativity, but listed behaviors that can facilitate it. Paul thinks that to be creative, it is helpful to be absorbed in the project, to be willing to experiment with different approaches, and to be aware of creativity when it occurs.

Rowena Reed and Niels Diffrient, both industrial designers, experience creativity as exciting. When producing especially creative work, both feel physically stimulated. Niels described a relaxed responsiveness during the creative process. He said that sometimes ideas come to him easily, and other times he has to struggle for days. Niels also thinks some of his best works are the result of accidental events, in which he has faith. Most of the respondents immerse themselves in their subject matter to facilitate their creativity. While

404

working, Niels experiences himself wholistically, as if his body is his mind. Like Tom, when he begins a project, he has a sense of what it will be, but he does not know its final form completely. He allows the project to evolve. During highly creative times, he feels a rightness to the assembly of objects. He said that sometimes when he is working on a project, he lives in ongoing agony. It is interesting to note that the word agony comes from the Greek word meaning contest or victory. Niels's agony is, evidently, a suffering aspect necessary to the achievement of his current creativity. The pattern of creative surges followed by release, followed by building pressure and another surge of creativity was described by a number of respondents.

All of the respondents have formalities that aid their work by giving it structure. Tom surrounds his work with excitement, George with playfulness. Those respondents who tend to be compulsive formalize their complusions, thereby getting them out of the way, allowing entry into the creative process. When I asked Niels if there is anything he does to facilitate his creativity, he said that he makes order in his environment, that he even cleans his fingernails before he begins his work. He also said he works best when he can work without interruption, so he sometimes arranges to work when he can be alone in his studio. Frank Hogan does his professional writing after writing letters and reading the newspaper, clipping articles of interest. Like a number of respondents, Frank works on a several of projects at once.

Frank's letter writing serves another important function. It gets him into the writing frame of mind, helping his thoughts flow through his fingers to the typewriter keys. Frank also stops writing each day before he has exhausted his ideas, so that on the following day he has momentum to begin his work. Like Rowena, Norma, and Tom, Frank fears that too thorough an examination of his creative process might inhibit it.

George Leonard described some especially interesting things he does to encourage his creative process. Working with one other person, he uses brainstorming and other techniques to facilitate creativity and sometimes stages a production in the presence of an audience. The audience enhances the excitement and fun surrounding the act, which in turn enhances George's creativity.

George thinks there is more creativity going on than most of us realize. Like Frank, he believes that every human being is born creative. George stressed the need for fun in creativity, and he described his feelings during the creative process as euphoric. During these times he attains an altered state of consciousness that probably entails cooperation between his right and left brain hemispheres. Several respondents, including Wendy Palmer, Patricia Sun, and Frank Hogan, reported that the altered states they achieve facilitate their creative processes. The brainstorming sessions seem to provide George with the kind of drama Tom Robbins enjoys, although how Tom and George achieve drama is significantly different. Both George and Arthur stressed changing the context of one's normal life to facilitate the creative process by allowing for various thinking modalities.

This study confirms the findings that incubation is a necessary stage in the creative process (Helmholtz, 1896). It also supports the theory that certain factors are creativogenic (Arieti, 1976). Barron's (1968) description of the role of the unconscious in the creative process is upheld. He observed that although creative ideas sometimes arrive formulated from the unconscious to the conscious mind, usually they arrive fragmented, and effort is required to transform them into art. This research affirms Arieti's (1976) similar ideas about the functions of the primary and secondary processes. He proposed that it is ego strength that allows the creative person to enter the world of the primary process and return again, bringing with them imagery for expression. The secondary process then provides criticism and refinement through conscious effort.

406

6. a. How do creative people characterize themselves as human beings? b. How do they see themselves as similar to and different from other highly creative individuals and people in general. c. Do these people see themselves as risk takers, rebels, and nonconformists?

The answer to this question is related to the answer to the second research question: What personality characteristics enable creative people to persist with their endeavors? To respond to this question, I have addressed each of the three question segments separately.

a. How do creative people characterize themselves as human beings?

The respondents in this research characterize themselves in a variety of ways. When I asked him to characterize himself, Niels Diffrient used an interesting metaphor. He said that he had gone through life like a piece of fly paper, picking up whatever stuck. Niels said he never made any real choices about his life. He told me he uses what he calls the sawing off the limb approach to decision making. In this metaphor, Niels explained that he climbs out on a limb that he is sawing off the tree, and thereby he is forced to act to avoid disaster. Niels also described himself as conservative, low-key, able to endure, intelligent but not an intellectual, and he said he is not a self-lover. He said his work is flamboyant in concept, but not in execution.

Norma McLain Stoop's description of herself was quite different than Niels's. She stressed choices as important to her. She thinks the act of choosing is more important than the choice itself. Norma said she likes herself and feels self-satisfied. She described herself as extremely disciplined, outgoing, and as more intelligent than creative. Norma likes people and struck me as being concerned about other peoples' opinions of her.

Carl Rogers used an interesting metaphor to illustrate his approach to life. As a boy, his favorite stories were stories about trappers and explorers on the American frontier. He liked reading about the way these men could walk through the forest so softly that they could not be heard. Because they could move undetected, they were able to accomplish their tasks. Carl described himself as like these men because he walked softly through life, thereby achieving his task. He also described himself as a man with a whim of steel. Carl said he was equally creative and intelligent, persistent, determined, highly disciplined, sensitive, gentle, intense, and moderately adventurous. He characterized himself as a loner and preferred the company of women to that of men. He reported feeling satisfied with himself and his life.

Getting Arthur Young to talk about himself was difficult. He did not seem to want to talk about himself personally, although he was quite willing to share his ideas and theories. He suggested that he mostly avoids introspection and described himself as inquiring into the nature of existence. I was surprised that he did not see himself as introspective, because of his work with the evolution of his own consciousness and the personal nature of his book, <u>The Bell Notes</u>.

Rowena Reed was also reluctant to talk about herself, wanting to discuss ideas. She described herself as outgoing, thorough, particular, conventional, and equally intelligent and creative. She said she dislikes boring people, is satisfied with herself, and thinks her good disposition may have interfered with her creative output.

Although other people sometimes portray Paul Torrance as a workaholic, he does not classify himself as one. For Paul, work is recreation. He is persistent and dedicated to a vision. Paul told me he is more creative than intelligent.

Curiosity, courage, and kindness were the 3 qualities Patricia Sun chose as her best assets. She characterized herself as a problem solver and said other people have characterized her as strong, thoughtful, and determined. She said she is fascinated by people.

When I asked George Leonard how he characterizes himself, he responded that he has a Don Quixote aspect. "I mean I can see myself as a ridiculous knight on a mule, tilting windmills....My whole life could be a caricature....Actually, I guess we are all tilting windmills." He continued to say that although he is less pompous than he used to be, he still has an aloof quality. He described himself as playful, creative, and disciplined.

Tom Robbins characterized himself as a Hermes type. He is a private person who doesn't enjoy groups, and when he finds himself in a group of boring people, he creates mischief. When I asked him to account for his originality, Tom responded, "As a child I decided I either wanted to be French or eccentric, and I could never pronounce French." Tom said he avoids too much introspection, although I experienced him as an introspective person. He thinks he is more creative than intelligent.

This research demonstrates that creative people have some personality characteristics that are idiosyncratic and that they, as a group, generally share some characteristics. Some of these are: persistence, discipline, determination, endurance, and intelligence. Creative people are somewhat satisfied with themselves and their lives. They are problem solvers and question finders. They are motivated and attach value and meaning to their behavior. First searching for questions, and then for the answers, sustains their creative output.

b. How do creative people see themselves as different from other highly creative people and people in general?

One way I expected the respondents to see themselves as different from less creative people was by being more courageous. Some of the responses I received surprised me. Patricia Sun expressed an idea held by many of the coresearchers about courage. She said her life looks more courageous than it feels. She thinks courage is sometimes the result of innocence and naivete. Arthur Young's perspective was similar. When I said to Arthur that when he was testing his helicopter, he was risking his life, he responded, "I didn't think of it that way. I always thought I'd break the helicopter or something." Some responses were more predictable. Tom, Paul, and Frank described themselves as more courageous than most people, and Rowena Reed thinks that to be creative, one must be courageous.

How the respondents saw themselves as different from other highly creative people fell into one of two categories. First they see themselves as individuals and therefore as different from all other people. The other is in the type of work they do, be it write poetry, design funiture, teach, write novels, or practice psychotherapy. Arthur, like a number of respondents, said he does not see himself as exceptional.

One difference between more and less creative people is that creative people are willing to receive creative insight from a variety of sources and they are willing to work hard, persist, and follow through on that insight. Less creative people are less open to receiving insight and often fail to act on it when it does occur. For example, when Frank Hogan received guidance through a dream from what he described as a spiritual realm, he accepted this guidance as legitimate and worked hard to translate it into the substance of a play. Less creative people may not have such dreams, or if they do have them, might be inclined to consider them only dreams and of no significance to their lives.

All the respondents represented themselves as risk takers. Tom Robbins said that all artists must take risks. Tom also described himself as an outlaw, a term I found helpful throughout the interviews. Most of the respondents described themselves as rebels and nonconformists. Wendy Palmer said she is highly antiauthoritarian and identified with outlawism. A number of the respondents described themselves as antiauthoritarian, saying that authority is detrimental to creativity. All of the respondents who commented on authority described its effects on creativity as hampering.

Some of the respondents distinguished who they are from what they do, like Paul Torrance, who said he is a conformist, but takes risks. Patricia Sun did not describe herself as an outlaw or rebel, although she spoke of her individualism and her ability to transcend social laws. She uses existing rules when they work for her and makes new ones when they do not.

Industrial designers Niels Diffrient and Rowena Reed see themselves as conservative and law abiding, but also as risk takers and rebels. Frank Hogan described himself as a risk taker, rebel, and outlaw. The strong sense of individualism, the success, and the sense of general self-satisfaction combined with the desire to strive for greater accomplishment and growth apparent in all of the respondents, lends support to the theory that more creative people are likely to be more self-actualizing than less creative people.

Recommendations For Future Research

My naivete and innocence were probably my most potent researcher qualities in that these traits enabled me to enter the worlds of the respondents, open to perceiving their creative experiences. These same characteristics were also weaknesses. They do, however, help lay the groundwork for future research because questions remain unanswered that a more sophisticated researcher might have asked.

This volume contains numerous observations of patterns and themes that surfaced and offers tentative theories as explanation. Future research can corroborate their validity. Are the findings from these respondents true for creative people in general? Are my explanations accurate or arbitrary? The leap that occurs here, from pattern to theory, is one of generalizability. The following hypotheses and questions are examples of possible explanations for patterns offered in this work, which could be confirmed or negated by future research.

1. Creativity is fostered in childhood if the child faces and successfully copes with, and overcomes, some perceived hardship. This early success against adversity plants the seed that grows the belief that the child has the strength and creative potential to succeed in life. It is important to remain aware that this hardship or adversity occurs naturally, it is not imposed.

2. An educational system that embraces self-development, self-discovery, and the intrinsic wisdom of the inner voice rather than the assimilation of facts and socialization of behavior would encourage creative development. Nontraditional education, including experiences such as travel, enhances creative development.

3. Time spent in solitude facilitates the developing creativity of children. Time infirmed may foster creativity in children.

4. Creative people attach value and meaning to behavior.

5. Creative people are question askers. Finding questions is more important to creative people than finding answers.

6. A society or culture that encourages people to trust their internal processes, such as intuition, would be more creativogenic than our society, which trusts facts. Similarly, a society that encourages people to know and trust their bodily feelings and bodily wisdom would be more creative than one that discourages the full experience of feeling phenomena.

7. Creative people work because of an internal drive to do so. Creativity rewards and perpetuates itself.

8. Creative people are creative because they have learned to use self-discipline balanced with play.

9. Although having a mentor is conducive to moderate success in creative fields, highly successful people are more likely not to have had mentors.

10. Creative people are more rebellious and antiauthoritarian, take more risks, and are less likely to conform than less creative people.

11. Creative people have highly developed critical faculties. Because they are self-critical, they generally experience outside criticism as detrimental to their work.

12. Serendipity and synchronicity are vital elements of the creative process and can be encouraged by focusing awareness on them, by expecting them to function in life, and by moving beyond causal thinking by altering habitual behavioral and decision-making patterns.

13. Creative people are capable of a more integrated brain function, meaning that they use both their right and left

brain hemispheres more fully than less creative people. Combining linear and spatial thinking modes increases the likelihood of the occurrence of creativity.

14. Creative insights often occur during periods of rest, when the will or conscious mind is disengaged. Willingness and expectation allow for creative insights. Hard work, vision, and determination carry insight through to manifestation.

15. The ability to achieve altered states of consciousness enhances the quality and quantity of creative insights.

16. Creative people, in aggregate, demonstrate persistence, discipline, determination, endurance, and intelligence.

17. At some point early in their lives creative people turn inward because of some perceived adversity, and later as adults, they translate that internal experience into creativity projecting it outwardly in the form of a creative project.

18. Relationships with other people affect creativity. This effect is sometimes helpful and sometimes hurtful to creativity. One determining factor is the life phase during which the relationship occurs. Relationships with other creative people are helpful early in a career. Solitude is helpful later. In what other ways do relationships affect creativity?

19. Creative people evidently are capable of entering the world of their unconscious minds or primary processes, experiencing themselves in a manner different than they do during normal consciousness, and then returning, bringing with them material which they translate into some creative project (Arieti,1976). Because the unconscious is seemingly so vast,

at our level of evolution it is effectively limitless. Is creativity increased in some proportion related to the amount of the unconscious that is accessed or accessible?

20. This group of respondents qualified as a group of volunteers, and the group was different from creative people in general because of this factor. In what ways were the results of this study biased because of volunteerism?

21. The culture in which people live affects their creative productions. Everyone who participated in this research was living and working in the United States. To what extent are the findings of this research a result of our culture and in what ways might the findings about creative people's personalities and creative processes differ had the data been gathered and analyzed in another culture such as in the Soviet Union?

22. The respondents in this study were all poly-creative. People who are mono-creative would differ. How would the findings be different if the respondents had been creative in only one area?

23. Generally speaking, results are affected by design. In what ways were the results of this research biased by the design of the study?

Support for all of the preceding hypotheses and questions was presented in this volume. Future research is needed to answer the questions and to substantiate or refute the hypotheses offered. It is my hope that other interested researchers with different biases than mine will undertake the task.

Philosophical Implications

To see a world in a grain of sand,
And a heaven in a wild flower,
Hold infinity in the palm of your hand,
And eternity in an hour.

William Blake

The subject of this search was creativity. To advance this search, creatives were selected to respond to questions about the dynamics in their lives relating to their creative projects. The data gathered allow the researcher to assume a perspective, which provides the opportunity for comment on the aggregate of the responses.

The data reveal that creatives can effectively formulate their ideas, and then implement these ideas to completion in synchronization with some inner timing. Fulfillment is experienced in the leap from imagination into actualization. A problem is solved, be it a problem in literature or design, poetry or martial art, psychic or academic.

In response to life's routine and mundane matters, creatives access their imagination, pursue inspiration, and harmonize themselves with a personal felt experience (Gendlin, 1962), thereby fully engaging themselves creatively. What is their technique for arriving at a point at which they can undertake a creative project wholesomely? Discipline is the first dynamic that comes to mind when reflecting on the data.

The way in which discipline most clearly facilitates creative thinking is that all of the respondents are able to immerse themselves in their subject matter and direct their focused attention on their project, working within the expectation that they will experience creativity. The ingredients of expected creativity and focused attention produce an interactive psychic state that allows creative movement to occur. A number of felt experiences of lesser importance to the creative process often occur simultaneously, increasing the likelihood and quality of the creative outcome or product. Some of these are question asking, determination, flexibility, endurance, thoroughness, persistence, curiosity, hard work, and humor.

Movement from inspiration or insight, through the formalization of an idea, to the outcome or creative product also requires a deep belief in the likelihood of a successful end result. That deeply experienced belief is sometimes an expectation of personal abilities or fate, and sometimes it is a closely held value in the intrinsic rightness of the concept. Norma McLain Stoop exemplifies the former and Carl Rogers the latter. Norma experiences herself as talented, competent, and capable of achievement in whatever field she might choose, be it dancing, writing, singing, or photography. Carl experienced the rightness of his theory so strongly that his focus and dedication could have been, through the energy of his deeply held belief, sufficient to promote success. What links the creative accomplishments of all the respondents is that a deeply felt belief combined with genuineness can power the thoughts and actions of individuals, enabling manifestation of a product, be it theory, art form, or object, into the culture or marketplace.

It may be that a part of what is being addressed here is intentionality. How then does intentionality fit into this process of allowing insight and the carrying of insight through the necessary stages to manifestation? It seems the only legitimate measure of intention is outcome. Certainly if outcome is the measure, then as a group the respondents are intentional about creative output.

Although creative thinking is being investigated here, it is the feeling aspect of creativity that empowers the act, providing the energy necessary to propel insight into manifestation. The felt experience of creativity is the satisfaction that keeps the creative individual rewarded and fulfilled and is the bait for continuing creative output. Each of the respondents reported creativity as a satisfying, fulfilling, or exciting phenomenon. All of the respondents work creatively because of the quality of life they experience as a result of their work. Creativity continuously fills itself, occurring in an ascending spiral. Once people taste their creativity, they are more likely to continue to strive to achieve more of the sweetness of that potential.

The point then is that to grow, creativity must have both a thinking and a feeling aspect. Rollo May (1969) wrote of the combination of wish and will, which operate in polarity, as the ingredients of intentionality. Will provides the necessary movement for the hard work involved in creativity and wish encompasses the propelling energy of belief, desire, and playfulness that allows the creative leap. Both wish and will, or thinking and feeling, are necessary and vital elements of the creative process.

Even with study, creativity continues to be elusive and esoteric. Many of the artists I encounter tell me too thorough an observation and analysis may inhibit the flow of creativity, may interfere with its magical rhythms. I do not think we need to fear chasing away the muses; however, it seems that try as we may to demystify the creative process, creativity insists on her mystery. Consider the discoveries of this study. For creativity to occur, the creator must become immersed in the subject, obtain an open, allowing psychic state, experience intense, directed focus, operate within the expectancy of creativity, experience a deeply felt belief that success can occur, and then with the fertile earth plowed and seeded, God might smile and the rains may fall. Even as elusive as creativity is, we should not despair. Though creativity resists analysis, we have learned ways to facilitate its coming, and as with most living things, if we attend to our creativity, it flourishes. The greater the hospitality we extend to our muses, the more often they will visit and the longer they will stay.

What does this all mean? The subscribers to stricter definitions of science might walk away and search elsewhere, perhaps in the theories of social reinforcement, or abandon the investigation altogether. The sales executive or business manager might call up the powers of positive thinking, attend Dale Carnegie seminars, and energetically use old football metaphors of momentum and game plans. The metaphysician would answer that we create our own reality.

I propose that creativity falls directly under Universal Law (Wilde, 1983) or the metaphysical law of manifestation, that our experiences occur because our purpose for them is to actualize our emotional, psychological, and spiritual inner states in the physical and behavioral world, the world we often refer to with the notion of reality. So this investigation has ultimately led us to the bottom of the mountain, to the starting place, the place of questioning our culturally held structuring of reality, perception, and experience. The place we now sit is the place the ancient mystics sat years ago, and it is the place the theoretical physicists sit today.

I am not suggesting we discard our beliefs, theories, or ways of perceiving. What I am suggesting is what Patricia Sun often suggests, that we step out of polarity consciousness, or the belief that if one thing is true its opposite must by definition be false, and into the openness of accepting that our ways of negotiating in this world may be useful and that different ways of negotiating can also be useful. In this way we would say "yes" to life.

419

In his popular and often read book, The Tao of Physics (1975), Capra explored the parallels of Eastern mysticism and modern physics. He pursued his theory that subatomic physics has explored ideas about the nature of reality strikingly similar to the concepts of Buddhism, Sufism, Hinduism, and Taoism. Simply stated, both physics and religion suggest that complex structures cannot be understood as an assemblage of entities; they must be experienced and understood directly, as moving, interrelated events. All aspects of the universe are interconnected; the only way to understand any event is by understanding some other seemingly unrelated event because each event is contained within every other, which is impossible. Therefore, causal explanations are erroneous. The necessary step to understanding is direct experience, and experience must begin in consciousness. Capra sees the recent findings of theoretical physics as the entry between mysticism and science, because when these theories are accepted, it becomes necessary to be open to the relationship between reality and consciousness.

What then is our consciousness of reality? Deeper understanding often can be discovered by investigating the origins of the words used to convey meaning, because words are our tools for giving structure and form to experience so that it can be communicated. Let us consider the phrase "consciousness of reality." The word connecting consciousness and reality is "of", which means "from or away from," thus "away from our consciousness", or formalized differently, we are saying that for us, reality arises from or is a projection of consciousness (Partridge, 1983). If reality is a projection of our consciousness, then it follows that reality is manufactured by consciousness, that reality is a product of consciousness.

When contemplated in reference to individual consciousness and collective consciousness [see Chapter 2], the percept of creating one's own reality becomes vital. If we can, for arguments sake, wed the esoteric notion of creating one's own reality by means of consciousness and our daily experience of living in a physical world with other conscious entities, we then can fathom the postulate of a continuously expanding universe. If reality is a conceptualization of consciousness, then every conscious being who has ever existed has created reality. We then are born into an already existing consciousness of reality and have the ability to co-create, alter, and originate additional reality. Those who arrive after us also can project themselves into the realm of reality. As co-creators of reality with all other consciousnesses, we become an interconnected component of a dynamic universe participating in ultimate creativity.

When the relationship between reality and consciousness is considered within the confines of this study, we arrive back at the concept of intentionality. The manner in which the respondents project their individual consciousness into reality that is different than the ways in which more ordinary creativity occurs is qualitative, and it is a direct result of their intentionality. The respondents have said "yes" to life in the forms of behavior and manifestation that are possible in our current evolutionary state.

One way in which the respondents have expressed intentionality about their creativity is by stepping out of the work force and the control of others. Each respondent aspired to be classless, severing ties to the bourgeoisie and the proletariat, therein becoming more united with their creative productions. Carl Rogers and Wendy Palmer are examples of individuals who have joined with their creativity. Wendy's martial art has become intrinsic to her being, transforming all aspects of her life. Anyone who knew Carl and his theory would have difficulty finding a clear separation; each was an expression of the other. All of the respondents' work permeates their lives to such an extent that the work itself becomes heuristic to the whole of their lives, positively affecting them psychologically, spiritually, behaviorally, and physically.

Consciousness embodies several forces, as does intentionality. Intentionality, as was implied earlier, is an interchange of energies. The energies of will and wish operate symbiotically, each one giving life to the intended creative project. The will of intentionality brings to bear the power to complete the hard work of creativity, but it also is the expression of that critical psychic state of willingness that allows for creative insight, inspiration, or synchronicity. The wish transports the feeling states essential to creative production, but also supplies a propelling energy which is generated by the personality visualizing the existence of the new entity in the future. The wish and the will unite, sparking the focused attention and expectation necessary for manifestation to occur.

The realms of consciousness and reality also must be in a dynamic state of energy exchange. Feeling, thought, and belief are three guises of consciousness-energy. These could be associated with body, mind, and spirit, the energy trinity necessary in any form of creativity. Including spirit calls to witness the divine aspect of creation; however, it is essential to this association of ideas that we not think of divinity only in terms of our cultural or religious limitations. A Taoistic conceptualization of God in all is more useful here, reconciling the creation of reality by human consciousness and religious doctrines pertaining to the creation of reality by God, and as was theorized by Capra, the joining of ancient mysticism and modern science.

Returning to our attempt to comprehend the creativity of the respondents, it may be helpful to think in terms of reflexive action. In one sense, to reflect is to bend light. When light is viewed as a metaphor for inspiration, it is easy to comprehend how it is that the person breathes in, or becomes inspired, and then bends or shapes the light into a creative expression. A secondary definition (Webster, 1983) for the word reflex is the process of reception, transmission, and reaction. When the definition is expanded to include action and communication, becoming reception, transmission, reaction, action, and communication, with reception being unconscious, transmission and reaction preconscious, and action and communication conscious phenomena, it could be mistaken for a definition of the creative process.

The attitude of creativity as reflexive fits well with the concept of creativity as intentional, although it brings about the necessity of distinguishing between intentionality and willfullness. Intentionality is movement toward creative action and it encompasses willingness and reflexiveness as it excludes willfullness. Webster defines willful as "obstinately and often perversely self-willed," and willing as "inclined or favorably disposed in mind, reay." In his interview, Carl Rogers spoke of this difference. Carl expressed deep concern about the possible failure of his peace project. He had made a decision to work toward world peace, making that effort the aim of the remainder of his life. He feared failure because the choice had been made willfully. He said his greatest successes had developed obliquely, never from willfull decisions. Carl seemed to be expressing the value of creativity's reflexive qualities of receiving, transmitting, and reacting within a framework of willingness.

Reflexiveness is also an aspect of consciousness.

In Scholasticism: Reflection is a property of spiritual or immaterial substances only. It is, therefore, a capacity of the human intellect which not only operates, but knows of its operating and may turn back on itself and its performances. A particular kind of reflexion is, in Thomism, the reflexio super phantasma, by which the intellect retraces its steps, until it reaches the universal; this is according to Aquinas, the way the intellect comes to know the particular which, because material, is otherwise inaccessible to an immaterial faculty. (Runes, 1962, p. 267)

Being a capacity of human intellect, reflexiveness exists only within human consciousness, and understanding is its purpose. Understanding is also the aim of eastern mysticism, and according to Capra, only can be gained through direct experience, which must originate in consciousness. According to Sartre (1960), understanding is a force so powerful that once reached, a person who gains new understanding must subsequently experience a life change.

Although some of the respondents found it difficult to verbally describe their felt creative experiences, all have an experiential understanding of their creativity and that understanding has resulted in dramatic changes in their lives. For Paul Torrance, work is recreation because it is in his creative experience that he is fulfilled. Patricia Sun finds that the more open she is to receiving and responding to inspiration, the more she grows able to receive and respond. Transforming inspiration has become the power point in her life. Likewise, Arthur Young's time allotted for his creative process is his most precious part of the day, and as a result of his creative work he is continually evolving. In these ways the respondents are saying "yes" to life.

Another aspect of reflexiveness is the reflecting nature of the creative personality. A definition for reflection (Webster, 1983) is "a thought, idea, or opinion formed or a remark made as a result of meditation," and to meditate is "to engage in contemplation or reflection, to focus one's thoughts on: reflect on or ponder over." The focusing of one's thoughts is fundamental to meditation and creativity. A number of the respondents commented on the significance of the effective force of keenly focused attention and energy in creative production. As with intentionality, focus embodies both feeling and thinking, and it perhaps is the key ingredient in creativity.

Certainly all of the respondents take pleasure in the ability to direct their focus into their creative projects.

Conclusion

Much like Sartre (1965) postulated about the study of emotion, it appears that the study of creativity is not, and cannot become, a study of facts. We continually return to the awareness that the study of creativity is a study of consciousness, because phenomenologically speaking, creativity is a consciousness. To the frustration of scientists and the elation of artists, creativity is not limited to our knowledge of creativity, but reaches far deeper than the accumulation of facts, enabling leaps into the previously unknowable.

The purpose of this work was to approach a phenomenology of creativity. Husserl (1969) devised the term "transcendental phenomenological idealism," through which he expressed the philosophy that the difference between objects of consciousness, or subjective reality, and objects-in-themselves, or objective reality, is essentially spurious, which is to say that from his philosophical perspective, consciousnesses and reality are inseparable. Accepting an absolute connection between our intrapsychic states and the realities we encounter empowers us to operate creatively upon the environment, designing a more generous world culture. If it is true that we are as creatively effective as has been suggested, it is within our grasps to miraculously redeem ourselves, reversing our course toward self-destruction by greed and ignorance, and moving instead toward a world of and for the living.

The book Higher Creativity (Harman & Rheingold, 1984) which is as much about miracles as creativity, suggests that we can create a more vital world culture. It is a book about the availability of miracles to everyone willing to tap their

425

unconscious creative power. Global change through individual consciousness is the ultimate goal of higher creativity. The authors propose that we can create a peaceful world without hunger and poverty. To achieve this new world, the first and most important step to be taken by each of us is simply to change our belief that it is out of our individual control to make such changes to the belief that individuals can effect change in the world. The most important ingredient in putting higher creativity to work for us is the belief that it is possible.

This research certainly falls short of providing proof that we can, through our beliefs and consciousness, alter the fate of the world. It does, however, support the theory that the first step in any form of creativity is accepting the possibility of a breakthrough or leap. Perhaps we can combine our knowledge about creativity, our experience of creativity, and the expectation that creativity will occur, and use the combustion of those uniting forces to propel us toward a world that could exist, the world Patricia Sun calls "Heaven on Earth." I recall the last line in the film <u>Being There</u> (1979)....

"Life is a state of mind."

References

Agha, M.F. (1941). The mechanics of creativity. In P. Smith (Ed.), <u>Creativity: An examination of the creative process</u>. New York: Hastings House.

Anderson, H. H. (1959). Creativity as personality development. In H. H. Anderson (Ed.), <u>Creativity and its cultivation</u>. New York: Harper.

Ansbacher, H. L. & Ansbacher, R. R. (Eds.). (1956). <u>The individual psychology of Alfred Adler</u>. New York: Basic Books.

Arieti, S. (1976). <u>Creativity: The magic synthesis</u>. New York: Basic Books.

Arnheim, R. (1954). <u>Art and visual perception: A psychology of the creative eye</u>. Berkeley: University of California Press.

Barron, F. (1953). An ego-strength scale which predicts response to psychotherapy. <u>Journal of counseling psychology</u>. <u>17</u>, 327-333.

Barron. F. (1957). Originality in relation to personality and intellect. <u>Journal of personality</u>, <u>24</u>, 730-742.

Barron, F. (1963). The disposition toward originality. <u>Scientific creativity: its recognition and development</u>. New York: Wiley, 139-152.

Barron, F. (1968). <u>Creativity and personal freedom</u>. Princeton, New Jersey: D. Van Nostrand Company.

Bogdan, R. C. & Biklin, S. K. (1982). Qualitative research for education: An introduction to theory and methods. Boston: Allyn & Bacon.

Cannon, W. B. (1940). The role of chance in discovery. Scientific monthly, 5, 204-209.

Descartes, R. (1960). Discourse on method and meditations. New York: Bobbs-Merrill.

Durkheim, E.(1898). Representations individuelles et representations collectives. Rev. de metaphysique, 6. 274-302. Translated by Laurence J. Lafleur. (Original work published 1637)

Eccles, J. C. (1958). The physiology of imagination. Scientific American, 199, 135-146.

Ellis, H. (1904). A study of British genius. London: Hurst and Blackett.

Freud. S. (1908). The relation of the poet to day dreaming. In Collected papers. 4, Translated by Riviere. London: Hogarth Press.

Freud, S. (1951). Character and anal eroticism, Collected papers. (Vol. 2, p. 48). New York: Basic Books. (Original work published 1923)

Freud, S. (1960). The interpretation of dreams. New York: Basic Books. (Original work published 1901)

Fromm, E. (!957) The creative attitude. In H.H. Anderson (Ed.) Creativity and its cultivation. New York: Harper.

Galton, F. (1870). Hereditary genius: An inquiry into its laws and consequences. New York: Appleton.

Galton, F. (1911). Inquiries into human faculty and its development. New York: E. P. Dutton.

Gendlin, E. T. (1962). Experiencing and the creation of meaning. Toronto: Free Press of Glencoe.

Getzels, J. W. and Csikszentmihalyi, M. From problem solving to problem finding. In I. A. Taylor and J. W. Getzels (Eds.) Perspectives in creativity. Chicago: Aldine Publishing Company.

Getzels, J. W. and Jackson, P. W. (1962) Creativity and intelligence: Explorations with gifted students. New York: Wiley.

Glaser, B. G. & Strauss, A. L. (1967). The discovery of grounded theory: Strategies for qualitative research. New York: Aldine Publishing Company.

Goetz, J. P. & LeCompte, M. D., (1984). Ethnography and qualitative design in educational research. New York: Academic Press.

Goldstein, K. (1939). The organism: A holistic approach to biology: Derived from pathological data in man. New York: American Book.

Goodman, L. M. (1981) Death and the creative life: Conversations with eminent artists and scientists as they reflect on life and death. New York: Penquin Books.

Gordon, W. J. J. (1961). Synectics: The development of creative capacity. London: Collier-Macmillan.

Gough, H. G. (1957) Imagination-underdeveloped resource. Proceedings, first conference on research developments in personnel management, Los Angeles: University of California, Institute of Industrial Relations.

Gray, C. E. (1966). A measurement of creativity in western civilization. American anthropologist.68, 1384-1417.

Guilford, J. P. (1950). Creativity. American Psychologist. 5, 444-454.

Guilford, J. P. (1968). Intelligence, creativity, and their educational implications. San Diego: Robert K Knapp.

Gutman, H. The biosocial roots of creativity. In R. L. Mooney and T. A. Razik (Eds.), Explorations in creativity. New York: Harper and Row.

Hall, C. S. & Lindzey, G. (1978). Theories of personality. New York, John Wiley & Sons.

Hallman, R. J. (1963). The necessary and sufficient conditions of creativity. In J. C. Gowan, J. Khatena, & E.P. Torrance (Eds.), Creativity: Its educational implications (pp. 19-30). Toronto: Kendall/Hunt.

Harman, W. & Rheingold, J. P. (1984). Higher creativity. Los Angeles. Jeremy P. Tarcher.

Hathaway, S. R. & McKinley, J. C. (1943). Minnesota multiphasic personality inventory. Minneapolis, Minn: University of Minnesota Press.

Helmholtz, H. von. (1896). Vortrage und Reden, 5th auff. Brammschweig: Viewey und John.

Helson, R. (1965). Childhood interest clusters related to creativity in women. Journal of creative psychology, 29, 352-361.

Henle, M. (1963) Contemporary approaches to creative thinking. New York: Wiley.

Hersch, C. The cognitive functioning of the creative person: A developmental analysis. In M. Bloomberg (Ed.) Creativity: theory and research. New Haven, Conn: College and University Press.

Hirst, N. D. M. (1931) . Genius and creative talent. Cambridge: Sci-Art Publishers.

Husserl, E. (1969) Ideas: General introduction to pure phenomenology. Translated by W. R. Boyce Gibson. New York: Humanities Press. (Original work published in 1913)

Hutchinson, E. D. (1949) How to think creatively. New York: Abingdon-Cokesbury.

Jacobson, A. C. (1926). Genius: some reevaluations. New York: Greenberg.

Jung, C. G. (1923). Psychological types. New York: Hartcort, Brace.

Jung, C. G. (1948). Two essays on analytical psychology. Translated by H. G. and C.F. Baynes, New York: Dodd, Mead.

Jung, C. G. (1971). On the relation of analytical psychology to poetry: In J. Campbell (Ed.) The portable Jung. New York: Viking.

Kosinski, J. (1979). Being there (Film). United Artists.

Kundel, F. and Dickerson, R. E. (1947). How character develops. New York: Scribners.

Kretschmer, E. (1931). The psychology of men of genius. Cambridge, Mass. Science-Art Publishers.

LeCompte, M. D. & Goetz, J. P. (March, 1982) Sampling and selection issues in educational ethnography. Paper presented to the American Educational Association, New York.

Leonard, G. (1961). The transformation. Los Angeles, J. P. Tarcher.

Leonard, G. (1968). Education and ecstacy. New York, Delacorte.

Leonard, G. (1978). The silent pulse. New York, Dutton.

Leonard, G. (1984). The end of sex. New York, Bantam.

MacKinnon, D. IPAR's contribution to the conceptualization and study of creativity. In I. A. Taylor and J. W. Getzels (Eds.) Perspectives in creativity. Chicago: Aldine Publishing Company.

Maslow, A. H. (1968). Toward a psychology of being. New York: Van Nostrand Reinholt.

Maslow, A. H. (1972). A holistic approach to creativity. Climate for creativity. New York: Pergamer Press.

May, R. (1959). The nature of creativity. In H. H. Anderson (Ed.) Creativity and its cultivation. New York: Harper and Row.

May, R. (1980). _The courage to create_. New York: Bantam Books.

May, R. (1969). _Love and will_. New York: Dell.

Mednick, S. A. (1968). The remote associates test. _Journal of creative behavior, 2_. 213-214.

Mumford, L. (1970). _The myth of the machine: The pentagon of power_. New York: Harcourt Brace Jovanovich.

Myers, I. B. (1962). _Manual: The Myers-Briggs type indicator_. Princeton, New Jersey: Educational Testing Service.

Osborn, A. F. _Applied imagination: Principles and proceedings of creative problem solving_. New York: Scribner's.

Parnes, S. J. (1962). _Do you really understand brainstorming?_ In S. J. Parnes and H. F. Hardings (Eds.), _A source book for creative thinking_. New York: Scribner's.

Partridge, E. (1983). _Origins_. New York: Greenwich House.

Patton, M. (1980). _Qualitative evaluation methods_. Beverly Hills: Sage Publications.

Poincare, H. (1946). Mathematical creation. _The foundation of science_. Lancaster: The Science Press.

Prince, G. M. (1970). _The practice of creativity: A manual for dynamic group problem solving_. New York: Harper and Row.

Rank, O. (1932). _Art and artists_. Translated by C. F. Atkinson. New York: Knopf.

Rank, O. (1945). Will therapy and truth and reality. Translation by J. Taft. NewYork: Knopf.

Riessman, F. (1962). The culturally deprived child. New York: Harper and Row.

Robbins, T. (1971). Another roadside attraction. New York, Ballantine.

Robbins, T. (1976). Even cowgirls get the blues. Boston, Houghton Mifflin.

Robbins, T. (1980). Still life with woodpecker. New York, Bantam.

Robbins, T. (1984). Jitterbug perfume. New York, Bantam.

Rogers, C. R. (1954). ETC: A review of general semantics, 11, 219-260.

Rogers, C. R. (1980). A way of being. Columbus, Bell & Howell.

Rogers, C. R. (1983). Freedom to learn for the 80's. Boston, Houghton Mifflin.

Rogers, C. R. (1985). Toward a more human science of the person. Unpublished manuscript.

Rossman, J. (1931). The psychology of the inventor. Washington: Inventors Publishing.

Rothbart, H. A. (1972). Cybernetic creativity. New York: Speller.

Runes, D. D. (1965). Dictionary of philosophy. Totowa, New Jersy: Littlefield Adams.

Sartre, J. P. (1966). Being and nothingness. New York: Washington Square Press. Translated by Hazel Barnes. (Original work published 1943)

Sartre, J. P. (1960). Critique of dialectical reason. London: Verso/ NLB. Translated by Alan Sheridan-Smith. (Original work published 1960)

Sartre, J. P. (1965). Essays in existentialism. Secaucus, New Jersey: Citadel.

Schimek, J. W. (1954). Creative originality: Its evaluation by use of free-expression tests. Unpublished doctoral dissertation, University of California, Berkeley.

Sinott, E. W. (1959). The creativeness of life. In H.H. Anderson (Ed.), Creativity and its cultivation. New York: Harper and Row.

Stein, M. I. (1974). Stimulating creativity. Individual procedures. New York: Academic Press.

Stein, M. I. (1974). The teachings of the mystics. New York: Mentor Books.

Strong, E. K. Jr. (1943). The vocational interests of men and women. Stanford, California: Stanford University Press.

Taylor, C. W. (1964). Some knowns, needs, and leads. Creativity: Progress and Potential. New York: McGraw Hill.

Taylor, I. A. (1971). A transactional approach to creativity and its implications for education. Journal of creative behavior. 5. 190-198.

435

Taylor, I. A. (1972). A theory of transactualization. <u>Creative education foundation</u>, Buffalo, N.Y. <u>5</u>, 190-198.

Taylor, I. A. (1975). An emerging view of creative actions. In I. A. Taylor and J.W.Getzels (Eds.) <u>Perspectives in creativity</u>. Chicago: Aldine Publishing Company.

Taylor, I. A. (1975). A retrospective view of creativity investigation. In I. A. Taylor and J. W. Getzels (Eds.), <u>Perspectives in creativity</u>. Chicago: Aldine Publishing Company.

<u>The Holy Bible</u>. (1945). King James Version. Philadelphia, Universal Bible and Books.

<u>The Holy Bible</u>. (1977). La Habra, California, New American Standard Bible.

Torrance, E. P. Educational achievement of the highly intelligent and the highly creative: Eight partial replications of the Getzels-Jackson study. <u>Research memorandum</u> BER-60-18. Bureau of Educational Research, University of Minnesota.

Torrance, E. P. (1962). <u>Guiding creative talent</u>. Englewood Cliffs, N.J.: Princeton-Hall.

Torrance, E. P. (1983). <u>Mentor relationships: how they aid creative achievement, endure, change, and die</u>. Buffalo: Bearly Limited.

Vinacke, W. E. (1952). <u>The psychology of thinking.</u> New York: McGraw-Hill.

Wallas, G. (1962). <u>The art of thought</u>. New York: Harcourt, Brace.

Webster. (1983). <u>Webster's ninth new collegiate dictionary</u>. Springfield, Mass. Merriam-Webster.

Wertheimer, M. (1978). <u>Productive thinking</u>. New York, Harper.

Wilde, S. (1983). <u>Miracles</u>. Annapolis, Wisdom.

Young, A. M. (1958). <u>The bell notes, a journey from physics to metaphysics</u>. San Francisco, Robert Briggs.

Young, A. M. (1980). <u>Which way out? and other essays</u>. San Francisco, Robert Briggs.

Young, A. M. (1984). <u>The geometry of meaning</u>. San Francisco, Robert Briggs.

Young, A. M. (1984). <u>The reflexive universe</u>. San Francisco, Robert Briggs.

Zukav, G. (1979). <u>The dancing wu li masters</u>. New York, William Morrow.

APPENDIX

APPENDIX A

INTERVIEW GUIDE

1. What do you see as your most outstanding quality?

2. Describe your family life as you were growing up. Who lived in your house? What were these people like?

3. In what ways were you like other children? Different from other children?

4. How are you like and different from other adults?

5. Did your family think of you as creative? Do they now?

6. If I were to ask someone who knows you very well to describe you to me, what do you guess he or she would say?

7. Name a few people, living or dead, who you think of as being very creative. How are you like them?

8. How do you define creativity?

9. In what ways do you see creativity and intelligence as being alike? In what ways do you see intelligence and creativity as being different?

10. Do you see yourself as more creative or intelligent?

11. What differences do you see in genius, creativity, talent, and intelligence? How do you see them as fitting together?

12.   How do you account for your own originality?

13. Who or what in your life has facilitated your
self-expression?   Hampered it?

14.   How have you been perceived by your peers?

15. What in your opinion has been your most outstanding
accomplishment?   What was the genesis of that process?   Can
you recall for me what your life was like at that time?   What
were your thoughts and feelings?   How were others responding
to you?

16. How do you know when a project is finished?   When do you
quit?

17.   Describe the opposition you have met.

18.   What has motivated you to create?

19.   How do you define art?   Describe art's role in society.
What is the value of art for you?

20.   What is your fondest childhood memory?

21.   In what ways was your childhood unusual? Ordinary?

22.   When did you first begin to be paid for something you
consider an expression of yourself?   When did you first begin
leading a comfortable and secure life?   What is the role of
money in your work and life?   Did your feelings about your work
change when people began to pay you well?   Did you at one time
work for free?   How has that changed?

23.   Is creativity a willfull process?   Can you decide to do
something creative and do it?

24. How is your creativity brought on? In what ways do you prepare yourself to produce a creative work?

25. Did someone in your life guide or direct you in your growing creative output?

26. Describe a typical day of yours.

27. Do you ever see a product of yours having a life of its own?

28. If you could change anything about yourself, what would it be?

29. Have you in the past felt satisfied with yourself? Do you now?

30. How do you characterize yourself as a human being?

31. What about your creativity has been especially satisfying?

32. What do you see as the major benefits of your creative life? The costs?

33. How do you explain your success in our competitive world?

34. How do you conceptualize your creativity?

35. What sacrifices have you made in order to live your life style?

36. How do you account for your exceptionality?

37. Describe for me the way your body feels during times of heightened creativity.

38. What role do you think your unconscious plays in your creative process?

39. In what ways have you made use of adversity?

40. How might you explain the clustering of highly creative people throughout history?

41. Had you not been born, do you believe someone else would have performed your roles and provided society with your ideas, products, or services?

42. Do you think you have discovered something new or rediscovered something old?

43. In what ways has a desire for recognition affected you?

44. In what ways has a desire to be unique affected you?

45. Personal interpretations of others may be very different than what you intended to communicate. How do you deal with these personal interpretations?

46. How do you respond to criticism from people who themselves are not doing the kinds of creative work you do or address themselves to the kinds of issues to which you address yourself?

47. How do you deal with the "commercialism verses creativity" dilemma? In what ways are you affected by the demands of the marketplace?

48. How do you nourish yourself?

49. How have serendipity and synchronicity affected your life and work?

50. Have you ever experienced a sense of a "calling" or special reason for being?

51. How does the art, work, or thoughts of others affect you?

52. Has there been any special relationship that has affected your way of being?

53. Have you felt misunderstood? Has misunderstanding motivated you to create?

54. What has the role of inspiration been in your life and work?

55. In what ways have you been affected by the knowledge of your death?

56. Describe your experience of the creative moment.

57. Do you see the Divine as having a place in your life or work?

58. How are sex and creativity related?

59. Do you see yourself as a rebel? Risk taker? Outlaw?

60. In what extraordinary ways have you received guidance?

61. Have you needed more courage than most people?

62. Would you live your life to date the same way again? Has it been worth it?

63. What expectations do you have for the future?

DEFINITION OF TERMS

A number of terms appear throughout this book. Because there might be confusion about the usage of some of these terms, definitions for them are provided here. The meanings of these words extend beyond these definitions; however, even brief definitions may aid in clarity. The first four words are psychological terms and the definitions were extrapolated from text written by Hall and Lindzey (1978).

The conscious mind: The theoretical concept of the portion of our minds or psychological processes which are readily available to our awareness, whether these be of the inner or outer environment.

The unconscious: A term coined by Freud to represent the portion of our minds or psychological processes which are unavailable or difficult to access into our awareness. The vast region of the unconscious contains our repressed and suppressed memories, urges and drives, and it is influential in our thoughts, feelings, and behaviors.

The personal unconscious: A term coined by Jung which is similar to Freud's theoretical concept of the unconscious. In the personal unconscious we contain the aspects of Freud's unconscious and experiences that were simply forgotten.

The collective unconscious: A term also coined by Jung, the collective unconscious is the transpersonal aspect of our minds containing inherited memories which we receive in the form of archetypes. It is almost entirely detached from personal experience. Some of the respondents in this study used the term to mean an unconscious body of ideas and feelings that an individual has the potential of accessing.

The following notion is also a psychological term and was coined by Gendlin (1962).

Felt experience: In order to have meaning, any event or object must be felt. A felt experience is a prelogical "felt dimension of experience...that functions importantly in what we think, what we perceive, and how we behave" (Gendlin, 1962, p. 1.) Thinking without this felt demension is impossible. If this felt dimension is unconscious, it is therapeutic to bring it into awareness.

The following term, consciousness, is a philosophical concept. The definition for it is provided by translator Hazel E. Barnes in Satre's (1966) book, Being and Nothingness. Other terms necessary to understand consciousness are also quoted.

Consciousness: The transcending For-itself. "Consciousness is a being such that in its being, its being is in question in so far as this being implies a being other than itself." Like Husserl, Satre insists that consciousness is always consciousness of something. He sometimes distinguishes types of consciousness according to psychic objects; e.g., pain-consciousness, shame-consciousness. Two more basic distinctions are made:

(1) Unreflective consciousness (also called non-thetic consciousness or non-positional self-consciousness). This is the pre-reflective cogito. Here there is no knowledge but an implicit consciousness of being consciousness of an object.

(2) Reflective consciousness (also called thetic consciousness or positional self-consciousness). For this, see reflection.

Reflection: The attempt on the part of consciousness to become its own object. "Reflection is a type of being for which the For-itself *is* in order to be itself what it is".

There are two types.

(1) Pure reflection. The presence of the reflective consciousness to the consciousness reflected-on. This requires a Katharsis effected by consciousness on itself.

(2) Impure (accessory) reflection. The constitution of "psychic temporality," the For-itself contemplating of its psychic states.

Cogito: Sartre claims that the pre-reflective cogito is the pre-cognitive basis for the Cartesian cogito. There is also, he says, a sort of cogito concerning the existence of Others. While we can not abstractly prove the Other's existence, this cogito will disclose to me his "concrete, indubitable presence," just as my own "contingent but necessary existence" has been revealed to me.

Phenomenon: *Being* as it appears or is revealed. (Satre, 1966, pp. 801-806).

Following from the above definition of terms, creativity is to the respondents a *phenomenon*, and they might experience *creativity-consciousness* as a psychic object.

One final concept shall be defined here. It is a term with metaphysical, psychological, and spiritual implications which is used by several respondents throughout this volume.

<u>Becoming conscious</u>: The notion that we, as individual beings, can participate in the process of enlarging our personal and collective consciousnesses by integrating unconscious motivations and urges and our conscious minds, thereby enhancing our ability to make real choices. Becoming conscious also encompasses the process of realizing our higher-selves and behaving in a manner in line with the continued evolution of the species and of human consciousness.

APPENDIX C

DATA ANALYSIS PROCEDURE

The procedure of data analysis is as material to qualitative research as the gathering and presentation of the data. For that reason a brief description of this operation is included here.

In this study, data analysis first began after the completion of the fourth interview. At this stage, my process was primarily intuitive. I read each transcribed interview several times and discussed the ideas I had about possible categories with several people who were familiar with the project. Changes in the interview guide as a result of the analysis were minimal.

From this time forward, I read each of the interviews as soon as they were transcribed, and periodically I read all of the completed interviews to keep them fresh in my thinking. When it became evident that new categories were not emerging, I stopped contacting potential respondents and began a more formal analysis process.

My first step in this process was to read all 11 interviews twice. During the second reading I highlighted all of the quotations that seemed theoretically salient, especially interesting, or for any reason drew my attention. I then clipped these quotations and ordered them topically in files. These categories were: accomplishments, education, sacrifices, personality, relationships, a calling, opposition, courage, childhood, creative process, inspiration, synchronicity, sex, power, death, exceptionality, God, mentors, money, routine, art, criticism, self-care, finishing, the unconscious, risk taking, recognition, motivation, golden ages, intelligence and creativity, and future expectations.

Next, I began working with the quotations in each file. Some categories were eliminated, some were changed, and some were split into two or more new categories. The categories remained fluid throughout the analysis of the data. As I shuffled and re-shuffled the quotations within individual files, I also was developing a sense of the order in which I wanted to present the data, and I arranged the files in this order.

After ordering the files, I once again began working with quotations in individual files. I cleared a large area in my studio to make space, and put all the clipped quotations on the floor. I arranged and rearranged these clipped pieces of paper until I had achieved a flow from one to the next, taped them together in one large scroll, and entered the ordered quotations in my word processor, working until all of these quotations had been entered. I then made simple connecting statements between sections, and divided the data into tentative chapters.

The next process, describing the data, took several months. With the help of others, I elaborated on my connecting statements in an attempt to create flow and readability within the data chapters. The sentences grew into paragraphs. Once the data were described, I began drawing comparisons between respondents, followed by explanations. Each of these processes of description, elaboration, and theorizing were done cyclicly throughout the writing of chapters 4 through 8, and each was repeated several times. It seemed as if the chapters were slowly growing from within.

The final step in the data analysis was the writing of Chapter 9, the conclusions. First, I listed the research questions initiated in Chapter 1. Then I addressed each question individually, summarizing the findings and offering possible explanations. After answering the research questions, I generated a set of hypotheses and questions for future research, all of which were supported by the data. Finally, I presented some philosophical implications and concluded this book.